⌐ Cou
⌐D1 5LD

Powys

37218 00513715 8

Churchill's Secret Defence Army

To the memory of my friend Geoffrey Ernest Bradford 1926–2006.

Other books by Arthur Ward

Model World of Airfix (Bellew, 1984)

A Nation Alone (Osprey, 1989)

Resisting the Nazi Invader (Constable, 1997)

Airfix – Celebrating 50 years of the Greatest Kits in the World (HarperCollins, 1999)

Celebration of Flight (co-author with Roy Cross, Airlife, 2002)

Classic Kits (HarperCollins, 2004)

Buying and Selling Wartime Collectables (Crowood, 2007)

British Army Cap Badges of the Twentieth Century (Crowood, 2007)

TV & Film Toys and Ephemera (Crowood, 2007)

Classic Toys of the 1960s and 70s (Crowood, 2008)

The Boys' Book of Airfix (Ebury Press, 2009)

The Other Side Of Airfix, Sixty Years of Toys, Games & Crafts (Pen & Sword, 2013)

Churchill's Secret Defence Army

Resisting the Nazi Invader

Arthur Ward

Pen & Sword
MILITARY

First published as *Resisting the Nazi Invader* by Constable in 1997
This edition published in Great Britain in 2013 by
Pen & Sword Military
an imprint of
Pen & Sword Books Ltd
47 Church Street
Barnsley
South Yorkshire
S70 2AS

Copyright © Arthur Ward 2013

Hardback 978-1-84884-808-5

The right of Arthur Ward to be identified as author of this work has
been asserted by him in accordance with the Copyright, Designs and
Patents Act 1988.

A CIP catalogue record for this book is available from the British Library.

All rights reserved. No part of this book may be reproduced or
transmitted in any form or by any means, electronic or mechanical
including photocopying, recording or by any information storage and
retrieval system, without permission from the Publisher in writing.

Typeset in 11pt Palatino by
Mac Style, Beverley, E. Yorkshire

Printed and bound in India by Replika Press Pvt. Ltd.

Pen & Sword Books Ltd incorporates the Imprints of Pen & Sword
Aviation, Pen & Sword Family History, Pen & Sword Maritime, Pen &
Sword Military, Pen & Sword Discovery, Wharncliffe Local History,
Wharncliffe True Crime, Wharncliffe Transport, Pen & Sword Select, Pen
& Sword Military Classics, Leo Cooper, The Praetorian Press, Remember
When, Seaforth Publishing and Frontline Publishing.

For a complete list of Pen & Sword titles please contact
PEN & SWORD BOOKS LIMITED
47 Church Street, Barnsley, South Yorkshire, S70 2AS, England
E-mail: enquiries@pen-and-sword.co.uk
Website: www.pen-and-sword.co.uk

Contents

Acknowledgements

Countless individuals helped me during the preparation of this book and my sincerest thanks go out to them – especially to the many Auxunit veterans that I have remorselessly pestered.

Some individuals need to be singled out, however.

The late Geoffrey Bradford, one of that stalwart band of Auxunit veterans, really started the ball rolling when he contacted me shortly after my book *A Nation Alone* was published in 1990. He corrected my rather rash assertion that the inside story of Auxunits would probably never be told. On the assumption that most volunteers were middle aged during 1940s, I doubted whether any were still alive. He soon put me right and was then active in introducing me to the still flourishing network of Auxunit old comrades.

Richard Ingram has been equally unselfish with his help and advice. Probably the most expert student of militaria I have ever met, he has been invaluable in ensuring the authenticity in all the photographic reconstruction. Those that know him will realize he is also a popular model – appearing in many of my photo shoots! Richard also has extensive contacts amongst fellow enthusiasts and his networking has been a real boon to me.

Others have helped me with this second edition and two deserve special praise: Chris Pratt, from the British Resistance Organization (BRO) Museum in Parham, Suffolk, for his generous help providing images, and

Geoffrey Bradford during wartime.

Tom Sykes, of CART, who gave me an updated tour of Coleshill, including the surviving Operational Base there, and then later invited me to join him and fellow enthusiasts on a visit to The Garth, Peter Fleming's country house in Kent and the first training base for the British resistance patrols.

I have tried here to include everyone who helped first time around and with this second edition:

Bill Ashby, David Baker, Keith Badman, Charlie Ball, Luca Bisoni, Dick Body, Martin Brayley, Joan Bright Astley, Donald Brown, Sid Brown, Nick Cordell, Barbara Culleton, Jim Daly, Juli Dear, Jonathan Driver, Thomas 'Nitroglycerin' Triton, Harvey Edginton (National Trust), Brian Evelyn, Colonel Norman Field, Arthur Gabbittas, Sid Gaston, David Gillings, Lady A.E. Gubbins, Michael Gubbins, Gary Hancock, Dean Harvey, Jonathan Heyworth, Nikita Hooper (National Trust), Richard Hunt, The Earl of Iddesleigh, Bob Irwin, Elliot Jarrett, H.E. Jarvis, Dereck Johnson, Eric Johnson, Kent Battle of Britain Trust at Hawkinge, Michael Larkin, Mike Llewellyn, Keith Major, Paddy McGuire, Bob Millard, Emma Morley, Frank Penfold, Paul Phillips, Chris Pratt, Joe Revill, Nick Scott, Nick Slee, Tom Smith, Alexander Stilwell, Mick and Kath Sparkes, Bob Steadman, Darren Steed, Tom Sykes, Mark Taylor, Neil Thomas, Nora Trego, John Warwicker, Bill Webber, Syd Weller, David Wickens, Sir Peter Wilkinson and Colin Wright.

Preface to the Second Edition

Since I penned the first edition of this book in the mid-1990s and saw the tangible results of my efforts on the shelves of bookshops in 1997, the story of Auxiliary Units, the top-secret cadre of intelligence gatherers and saboteurs who faced the threat of a Nazi invasion of Britain in 1940, continues to attract attention.

Though the whistle was well and truly blown by author David Lampe with the 1968 publication of his seminal book *The Last Ditch*, and by further revelations in the 1990s from Auxunit veterans determined that their part in the war effort was recognized, it still amazes me that most people assume that the defence of the UK in 1940 was partly in the hands of fictional characters like those in the TV series *Dad's Army* rather than the real life heroes who had agreed to sacrifice all if 'the balloon went up'.

We now know that when Hitler surveyed his conquests in June 1940 he didn't really know what to do next.

After four years of bloody warfare in Flanders between 1914 and 1918, Germany's short-lived prize was Belgium and only a small part of north-eastern France. Yet from 10 May 1940, after only six weeks of fighting, Hitler's Third Reich had captured all of France as well as Belgium and Holland in their entirety. Norway and Denmark were occupied around the same time. Poland had fallen victim to a quick and violent campaign the previous year. The demilitarized Rhineland, Austria and Czechoslovakia had already been subsumed within the Reich without a shot.

Following the evacuation at Dunkirk all Hitler's successes seemed to be working to plan – a master plan for a master race. On the contrary, there was no real plan and although most observers assumed an invasion of Britain was Hitler's next objective he had no serious intentions of war with an empire of which even he was in awe.

I said Hitler had no plan, but he did have one rabid ambition – for living space, or *Lebensraum*, in the east. He believed Eastern Europe was occupied by inferior peoples, a race of serfs for his thousand-year Reich.

Soviet Russia, home of the hated Reds, with whom he had cynically reached accord just before the attack on Poland on 1 September 1939, and with whom he shared the spoils in recognition of their acquiescing to his onslaught, was his real target.

Occupation of Britain was never a serious consideration but events had conspired to offer the opportunist Hitler with a prize that he could, perhaps, grab. So, half-heartedly, preparations were made to continue the campaign against the British until, as Hitler expected, the new government of Winston Churchill agreed to peace terms. Only Hitler and a small clique of his lackeys knew that Stalin's Russia was the real goal.

To everyone else, including the British Government, an invasion attempt during the summer of 1940 appeared inevitable. Although the hastily erected barricades and pillboxes, freshly dug ditches and the emplacement of myriad anti-tank and anti-glider obstacles and, especially, the urgent creation of an under-armed and undertrained citizen army – the Home Guard – suggests Britain's anti-invasion defences were amateurish in the extreme, this was not actually the case.

In the face of a seemingly invisible Wehrmacht, Britain had a few surprises in store should the Nazi invader attempt landfall in 1940. This book considers one of them, the still little-known Auxiliary Units – a top-secret formation of stay-behind parties designed to gather intelligence and create havoc behind German lines in the event of a successful incursion.

We know that the Luftwaffe never secured air superiority from the RAF defenders – the major tactical prerequisite for achieving a secure amphibious assault. Aside from the courage and tenacity of the young pilots of Fighter Command, the main reason they failed, despite superior numbers, to wrest sovereignty of the English skies from the defenders was due to a top-secret defence – radar.

Auxiliary Units were another top-secret defence, though, unlike radar, they were never tested in battle. Despite this, their potential contribution and undoubted bravery must never be taken for granted.

Since the early 1930s, most military specialists had foreseen the potential of what became known as terror bombing. Former Prime Minister Stanley Baldwin even predicted that 'the bomber will always get through.' But few could have guessed the terror the Nazi regime would unleash upon the occupied territories.

Though they did little about it, the democracies knew that the Jews, the people Hitler classified as *Der Untermensch* (the subhuman), were suffering terrible oppression. However, in 1940 Jews were not being rounded up for extermination by Nazi special action groups or being murdered in concentration camps. But thousands of so-called intellectuals, political opponents, homosexuals, gypsies, Slavs and those simply unfortunate enough to be born disabled were being subjected to imprisonment, sterilization and euthanasia. The writing was on the wall.

Even though the full horror of Nazi brutality was not experienced in Britain, it in no way diminishes the perilous risks undertaken by those who chose to defend the nation in an emergency. If the Nazis did invade, they faced being added to the millions ultimately murdered in the holocaust.

Since writing the original edition of this book we have been able to build a better picture of the part Auxiliary Units might have played should *Unternehmen Seelöwe* (Operation Sea Lion), the Nazi plan for invasion of Great Britain, been given the go-ahead by the Führer.

I guess few people have done more to compile a comprehensive account of Auxiliary Units activities than John Warwicker. Despite penning *With Britain in Mortal Danger: Britain's Secret Army* and *Churchill's Underground Army*, two excellent volumes about Auxiliary Units, not to mention being a co-founder of the British Resistance Museum, John Warwicker told me he never really intended being an author.

'I did not think of writing any book,' he said. 'In fact, it was first done in desperation because there was so much information aggregating that simply couldn't be contained. Material was coming to the fore without any organization, systematic classification, archiving or an appreciation of subversive warfare.

'My background was that I was a career Special Branch officer at Scotland Yard; during the last six years of my service there I was based at Downing Street, in charge of the protection team for three prime ministers: Wilson, Callaghan and Thatcher,' John told me.

'During the time I was there, travelling the world with prime ministers and [being] close to them daily it was inevitable that I would meet some influential people. The man who became the most influential for me was Robin Butler. Back then he was the private secretary responsible for Treasury matters. He originally served with Harold Wilson and then overlapped with James Callaghan, the normal term being three years, by which time private secretaries are promoted and knighted. He came back as Second Principal Private Secretary to Mrs Thatcher. He left, but upon his return was promoted to Principal Private Secretary and Cabinet Secretary, the only non-elected member who regularly attends Cabinet. He then retired and became Lord Butler and one of the nation's great and good.

'However, in 1992, when I was mystified by the story of the Auxiliary Units as a whole and had made one or two local contacts, I discovered that they would not tell me anything,' John added.

'To one of them in particular, Herman Kindred, I said, "If I got authority from Whitehall would you tell me about Auxunits then?" He said that he might, so I wrote to Robin Butler reminding him of our association and of our travels together and he wrote back a formal letter.

'Even though it began "Dear John" and was signed "Yours, Robin", it was a formal letter nonetheless,' said John.

The letter said that after all this time there was no residual national security risk and that those John questioned were free to talk about their past activities in Auxiliary Units.

'He thanked me for seeking approval to make inquiries and told me that if I had any difficulties with the Official Secrets Act that I was to contact a man on a given number in Whitehall.

'So I had a note in writing and I've got it now,' said John. 'It served me in very good stead when I spoke to Herman Kindred again, showing him the note as he sat in my kitchen, and saying, "Well now, Herman, you can tell me all about it." He said, "No, I won't, but I tell you what I will do. If you would like to ring that man in Whitehall and he tells me it's OK, once I have spoken to him personally, then I will tell you." So I rang this guy, spoke to him and handed him over to Herman. The official said, "Look here, Mr Kindred, I've got 150,000 classified items that I'm trying to declassify and I can't even find mention of the British Resistance Organization, so leave it to Mr Warwicker to contact me if there's any doubt, but go ahead." And that's when the dam burst, and it all started from there.

'I've been in touch with that man since and he has been quite helpful. That's how it all started and that was before I had access to your book!'

John later discovered that because initially the erroneous title 'BRO' (British Resistance Organization) was used, as opposed to the correct designation, GHQ Auxiliary Units, records about this clandestine organization could not be found in Whitehall. The term BRO is frequently used today, I think principally because it conjures up a 007 stereotype beloved of so many 'secret war' enthusiasts. Actually, during my most active interviewing of Auxiliary Unit veterans in the mid-1990s, 'Scout Section' was the classification they used most frequently when they told me the general term used for their secret platoon.

The BRO Museum was opened at Parham, Suffolk, in August 1997. It was unveiled by Lieutenant Colonel J.W.S. Edmundson, one of the original eight intelligence officers appointed by Colonel Gubbins on 2 July 1940 to recruit suitable volunteers for his proposed stay-behind teams. Lord Edmund Ironside is patron of the museum at Parham. He is the son of Field Marshal Ironside, who was appointed Chief of the Imperial General Staff (CIGS) on the outbreak of war and was Commander in Chief of Britain's Home Forces until 19 July 1940.

THE COUNTRYMAN'S
DIARY - - - 1939

HIGHWORTH'S FERTILISERS

DO THEIR STUFF UNSEEN
UNTIL YOU SEE

RESULTS !

With the Compliments of
HIGHWORTH & CO.

**YOU WILL FIND THE NAME HIGHWORTH
WHEREVER QUICK RESULTS
ARE REQUIRED**

John says that all involved did a good job but that its inauguration left 'a load of information and archives', which encouraged him to begin making audio records, 'which I did in quite a big way, scouring the country to find survivors, which resulted in us being left with an inordinate amount of information. I could see little chance of us getting it co-

The Countryman's Diary 1939, front cover.

ordinated in any way so I offered to write a book for the museum at Parham's benefit, with the proceeds going to them.'

We also have the BRO Museum to thank for the discovery and publication of *Auxiliary Units History and Achievement 1940-44*, written in October 1944 by Major Nigel Oxenden MC as an official history and long thought lost or buried in the Civil Service archives.

I believe the publication of Major Oxenden's account of Auxiliary Units is particularly significant for two reasons. Firstly, it records that it wasn't until 1943 that the three administrative battalions, 201st for Scotland and the north, 202nd for Wales and central England, and the 203rd, located below a line between the Thames and the Severn and covering south-east England, the most likely invasion site, were formalized.

Oxenden's opening words give a pretty good idea of the haste with which Auxiliary Units were formed and, especially, of the dire emergency in which the military authorities found themselves following Dunkirk:

The Auxiliary Units came into being at a time when invasion was imminent and the available arms in the country practically nil. The Home Guard numbers passed the million mark almost as soon as recruiting opened, but they were almost without arms or training ammunition.

It's understandable that operational niceties such as the precise nomenclature of units were not considered a priority with invasion imminent. Consequently, until 1943, when in uniform volunteers wore standard Home Guard regional titles on their shoulders. This sometimes caused problems when they were operating away from their local area or had been noticeably absent from regular HG duties.

The second significant thing about *Auxiliary Units History and Achievement 1940-44* is what it doesn't mention – namely, anything about the Special Duties Section, that 1,000-strong band of reconnaissance gatherers, largely recruited from the civilian population, many of them women, who passed on messages they received via nearly 200 hidden radio transmitters, communicating them either to Intelligence Officers or leaving them in 'dead letter drops' for the leaders of Operational Patrols. Recruited from the great and good by British Intelligence before the war, Special Duties personnel would likely have played a more valuable tactical role than previously realized if German troops had indeed achieved a foothold in Britain.

The BRO Museum at Parham is the best place to see surviving examples of actual weapons and equipment issued to Auxiliers during their wartime service. It is also the repository of many original documents bequeathed by the friends and relatives of departed Auxunit veterans.

Following the opening of the BRO Museum, 'many Auxunits from the operational side came out from underneath their stones and wanted to dispose of ammunition, firearms, explosives, papers, *The Countryman's Diary* etc.; all those artefacts that were so valuable just poured into the museum,' John Warwicker recalled, 'but again, with very little chance of them getting properly archived, which confirmed my decision to collate it all in a book.'

I wondered if John thought Auxiliary Units would have given a good account of themselves if invasion had actually happened.

'I have to say that I'm very sceptical about it now. I think they all meant well. They were all picked for their qualities: sturdiness, reliability, patriotism, ability to learn dirty tricks etc. I think Coleshill did a good job, in a very short time, of training them and then passing the training down the line, but I don't think any of them … in fact, I don't think *anybody* at the time, realized the ruthlessness of the German forces and their counter-espionage forces in particular. I don't think anybody realized just what problems there would have been with the relatives of these people if they were caught and with hostage-taking in the locality if Auxunits had gone into action. I don't think anybody had the slightest idea of how serious this kind of warfare was, and when what was happening in France began to filter back via SOE [Special Operations Executive] it put the wind up those back home. In fact, in 1942 Auxunits *were* put into uniform, clearly an inadequate stratagem for clandestine warfare, but no doubt it was felt it would give the men at least a measure of prisoner of war status if they were caught. However, I don't think it would have given them one moment of sanctity myself.

'In answer to your question,' he added, 'I think they would have been of very modest value at all and they wouldn't have had *any* value in intelligence-gathering matters because they didn't have any communications. Not only were they unaware of the need for an intelligence service, they were unable even to communicate details about what they did get, and I've certainly worked on the assumption that once they were underground and once the enemy had taken over above, in the area in which they were operating, they would have been out of touch absolutely and fighting on their own initiative.

'If they realized this, I think this is where the bravery of the men possibly comes in most,' John added.

'They would have had no contact with Army officers, they would have been making decisions as civilians on matters of life and death, they got different instructions from different Intelligence Officers (IOs), and so it was terribly confusing. What you find happening in Devon is completely unknown in Essex and vice versa. They were working on completely different concepts. If the Germans had taken their area, Auxiliers would either have had to fight until they died, which would probably have been sooner rather than later, or wait for a counter-attack because they had no means of contacting any British units. They didn't even know where these units were going to be or even where the front line was, for God's sake!'

I must say that while I was revising this text I was reading John Hughes-Wilson's *Military Intelligence Blunders* (Robinson Publishing, 1999), and I couldn't help thinking how 'blind' the men in the operational Auxiliary Units really would have been. This excellent and very readable book tells the stories behind some disastrous military mistakes, mostly caused by faulty information and bad interpretation. It seems clear to me that cut-off from GHQ and without the means to even speak to adjacent Auxunits, even if they knew where they were, those hardy subterranean volunteers would have been really isolated.

John Warwicker also stressed the importance of the bilateral structure of Auxiliary Units in the field.

'I regard the Special Duties Section as far more important than the Operational Section of Auxiliary Units. The Operational Section was really only about pinpricks, but the Special Duties Section was a much more secret and significant organization,' he said.

'Please don't underestimate the significance of the Special Duties Section, because that's what the Auxiliary Units were all about. The Operational Section is notable in terms of the security and secrecy surrounding them, only because they are associated with the Special Duties Section (SDS). It's all about SDS and the pre-war establishment by Colonel Grand and others of the Section D Home Defence organization in March of 1938. That was stood down in July 1940, after Dunkirk, and then re-established, with many of the original members retrained as intelligence gatherers as the Special Duties Section and administratively put together with the Auxiliary Units, but frankly, they had very little in common. One was entirely intelligence and the other essentially operational.'

John also told me that he thought that 18 October 1942, the date of Hitler's Directive No. 16, the infamous Commando Order, was very significant. This order decreed that all commandos and parachutists should be shot out of hand, even if they were in uniform – a command that could only be bad news for Auxiliers:

> In future, all terror and sabotage troops of the British and their accomplices who do not act like soldiers, but rather like bandits, will be treated as such by the German troops and will be ruthlessly eliminated in battle, wherever they appear.

'It was issued just after there had been a clear breach of international law by the British on the island of Sark,' he said.

During the night of 3-4 October 1942, ten men of the Small Scale Raiding Force landed on the German-occupied Sark to gather intelligence and capture prisoners. Though they did return with one prisoner, they had captured five, allegedly painfully tying their hands behind their backs. One prisoner tried to call out for help and was shot dead, but as the raiding party returned to their boat the others struggled for freedom; three of them were killed, one of the Germans being stabbed to death.

'I'm pretty sure the British action was significant in causing Hitler to write the *Commando Directive*, the result of which was an escalation in atrocities against men in uniform behind the lines,' said John.

Such barbarity was particularly evident in 1944, following D-Day, especially during Operation Bulbasket, when, following an attempt to cut the Paris to Bordeaux railway line to prevent the infamous SS Das Reich Panzer Division threatening the Allied bridgehead, thirty-six members of 1st Special Air Service were captured and executed.

'The raid on Sark infuriated Hitler so much that assassinations, executions and breaches of international understanding became lawful, indeed mandatory, under Hitler. This clearly altered the whole course of subversive warfare.'

I said I thought that all the talk of special weapons and irregular warfare training has been completely exaggerated, belying the Auxunits' true purpose – gathering intelligence and planning covert raids of sabotage and disruption after dark.

'Completely, by me amongst others,' John laughed. 'It's what you do when you write a book, isn't it? If it's not significant you don't mention it. However, as a result, the whole story has now developed into a series of dramatic "poster headlines" and clichés about life expectancy being only two weeks after Auxiliers were activated and about so-called suicide missions. All these sorts of things have been perpetuated by the press and then, inevitably, they become part of your lectures because people understand these kinds of slogans. But it doesn't really do the memory of the Auxunits much good.'

I told John I was particularly interested in 7 September 1940, the date when the Cromwell alert was issued and also when the German tactics shifted with the beginning of the Blitz. GHQ wasn't sure what this switch signified but wondered if it might presage invasion. There are even stories of HGs firing at civilians who didn't halt when challenged.

'Cromwell was absolutely totally chaotic,' he answered. 'It wasn't systematically notified; it was bits and pieces here and rumour there – misunderstanding all round, and a lot of people in the Home Guard thought it meant the enemy had landed and it signified a stand-to. Church bells were rung and in King's Lynn the Royal Engineers [RE] even started to blow up the dock gates because they thought the enemy had landed! Of course, it signified nothing more than the most likely date of the autumn of 1940 when the state of the tides, the phase of the moon, made it the most likely date for an invasion.

'But we all know now that a seaborne invasion by the Germans, while they were actively re-engineering canal boats so they could be used as amphibious assault vessels, was totally unfeasible. The myriad vessels were, in fact, totally unsuitable for a channel crossing.'

John listed the obstacles German soldiers would have encountered long before they waded ashore in England.

'The Royal Navy was still in operation, the RAF was still in operation, and it would have been nothing less than a massacre. Hitler never got to the stage of actually authorizing an invasion – he only authorized the preparations for it. A lot of Auxiliers got behind the false story invasion was thought imminent. There's still rumour down here in Suffolk and Essex that we set the sea on fire around here as 30,000 Germans landed and perished! It was rubbish, absolute rubbish. Technical rubbish and not at all feasible, but many still believe it. Some Auxiliers, especially the younger ones, tended to get behind what they had read in the press and make it their own story.'

I took the opportunity of talking to John to ask him a question about something that has long intrigued me. Did he know who supplied author David Lampe, a retired USAF officer, with the presumably still classified information he revealed in his seminal 1968 book, *The Last Ditch*?

The Romney Marsh area had three Auxiliary Unit patrols (Mushroom, Truffle and Toadstool), each with their own Operational Base built by Corben's of Maidstone for about £300 apiece. Because of the exceptionally high water table, they were built of concrete and lined with bitumen. The Coleshill Auxiliary Research Team organized a field trip to Toadstool OB, which the landowner had pumped dry especially for the event. The tidemark in the top picture provides an idea of how much water had to be removed before inspection could commence. Below, the author negotiates the tricky descent through a concealed entrance hatch and down a slimy steel ladder into the cavernous pit below.

John Warwicker addressing the not inconsiderable crowd at the unveiling of the replica OB at the museum of the British Resistance Organization at Parham Airfield.

Bob Millard in 1940 – a seventeen-year-old 'teenage terrorist'.

Bob Millard and the late Geoffrey Bradford attending the unveiling of a replica Operational Base at the museum of the British Resistance Organization at Parham Airfield in July 2004.

'I am in no doubt whatsoever it came from Colonel Bill Major, who had by then gone to MI5, working for them in Africa for many years, I understand,' was John's instant answer.

'I've no doubt he was the one who had the records and, of course, he was the one who altered the Auxiliary Units so much when he took over at the end of 1940, changing many of the concepts and disciplines that Gubbins had imposed, establishing the group system and so and on and so forth. I've no doubt that he was the man who gave the information to David Lampe. He must, for example, have kept a list of the group commanders because these were published by David Lampe. He must have kept these after the war because there were very few official records indeed and very few have emerged since.

'After scouring the Public Records Office, as it was [now the National Archive], I was very lucky to find the Government's security report filed at the end of 1940, after the re-establishment of the Special Duties Section. I believe the papers have now been removed. So I was very lucky to get them and the copies are now in the museum at Parham.'

John was at pains to tell me that the BRO Museum also contains audio CDs of all the interviews he did with those involved with Auxiliary Units and the other areas of Britain's military resistance organization during the Second World War. These are also in the Imperial War Museum, where they are available to the public.

The Coleshill Auxiliary Research Team (CART) was established in June 2009 by experienced marketing man Tom Sykes after he was informed about Coleshill and its wartime activities. Realizing that the history of Auxiliary Units was still being written, with new discoveries of forgotten Operational Bases (OBs) being made on a frequent basis and information about Operational Patrols still surfacing, Tom set up a website as it seemed the easiest way to collate the information he was unearthing. The CART website exhibits all the professional polish that the skills of its founder Tom bring to the project,

A pre-war photograph of Sir Peter Wilkinson when still a captain in the Royal Fusiliers.

Sir Peter Wilkinson at home in more recent times.

but it must be stressed that it is non-profit-making and survives entirely because of the efforts of volunteers.

I have Tom to thank for organizing two fascinating outings in the summer of 2011. The first was to the grounds of Coleshill House, where the National Trust is currently improving interpretation of surviving premises linked to Auxiliary Units, especially the unique 'model' OB used to train Auxiliers prior to them establishing similar subterranean hideouts. CART's Coleshill Information Officer, Bill Ashby, accompanied Tom and I as we toured the remnants of the Inigo Jones mansion and the administrative offices of the Auxiliary Units. The son of Lieutenant W. Ashby, an East Sussex Scout section officer, Bill is a veteran of the post-war Malayan Emergency.

My second trip with CART was even more revealing because it included a visit to The Garth, the legendary Kent home of Peter Fleming. We then visited an

Major-General Colin Gubbins. Lady Gubbins, his widow, told me, 'He was full of life and needed very little sleep.' Today he is best remembered for his military prowess and his superb management of SOE. But Lady Gubbins told me that he 'loved parties – to get him to leave one could take ages.' One of his maxims was, 'You should know something about everything and everything about something. And you ought to be able to play a musical instrument.'

Operational Base – Toadstool – hidden at the edge of a farmer's field in Romney Marsh. Because of the high water table and consequently damp conditions on the marsh, Toadstool and the two other OBs built in the vicinity were fabricated from concrete and protected from the ingress of water by a thick layer of bitumen. CART is to be applauded for their very worthwhile efforts.

There's no doubt that without the efforts of John Warwicker, CART's Tom Sykes, the 600 volunteers involved with The Defence of Britain Project (which ran from 1995 to 2002 under the auspices of the Council for British Archaeology, recording nearly 20,000 twentieth-century military sites, including a handful of Operational Bases, with a view to the future preservation of surviving structures, and, in a small way I hope, other authors like myself) the story of Auxiliary Units might not have received the recognition it deserves.

Sadly, but not surprisingly, given the passage of years, many of those redoubtable individuals I started speaking to nearly two decades ago are no longer with us. For me, at least, the most notable absence has to be that of Geoff Bradford, who died in 2006. If it hadn't been for Geoffrey writing to me following the publication in 1990 of my book *A Nation Alone*, a 50th anniversary commemoration of the Battle of Britain in which I touched upon the Aux Unit story, assuming that even then few who volunteered for such deadly clandestine warfare could still be alive, I would have been unlikely to have discovered the true story of what many dub the British Resistance Organization.

Geoffrey and I met many times and I grew to like him immensely. He also introduced me to a network of contacts, which grew by word of mouth until, like a very benign virus, a panoply of names and addresses multiplied before me.

One of the key witnesses I was fortunate enough to interrogate was Sir Peter Wilkinson. He died in 2000, aged eighty-six, following an incredibly eventful life in which he was awarded numerous decorations. Second only to Auxiliary Units' military chief, Colin Gubbins, with whom he later worked in the Special Operations Executive (SOE – Gubbins was 'M'; Wilkinson was 'MX'), Sir Peter told it like it was, obviously irritated by the myth of a secret society of ninja-like assassins that was becoming an accepted part of Aux Unit folklore. During the short period he and Gubbins governed Auxiliary Units (they left to form SOE in the autumn of 1940 as the chances of a Nazi invasion diminished), everything was organized with expedience – it was fantastic, but certainly no fantasy.

Sir Colin Gubbins died in 1976, but twenty years later I met his widow, Anna Elise, following an introduction by Gubbins' grandson, Michael, a friend of a friend. Anna Elise Gubbins (née Jensen) died in August 2007.

Many other bright lights that I had the honour to meet and interview and whose stories grace the pages of this book have also been extinguished in recent years and the memories of those few still with us have naturally faded.

However, despite the passage of years – and at the time of writing it is more than seventy since the heady days of the so-called 'invasion summer' of 1940 when an enemy landing seemed a real possibility, some surviving Aux Unit veterans are as sharp as a pin. And here I have to mention Bob Millward of the Bathampton Patrol near Bath, in England's West Country. Bob is an inspiration and his story alone deserves its own book. After a brief spell in the Home Guard, Bob joined Auxiliary Units, which proved a much more suitable outlet for his inventiveness and vitality. After Aux Units he joined the Fleet Air Arm and flew in torpedo bombers above the fjords of Norway and the warmer, though shark-invested, waters of the Pacific. He suffered freezing conditions after his crew ditched their Barracuda in the North Sea, and the anxiety of another dunking, this time in a Grumman TBF Avenger, as the Japanese fought to defend their home islands. While on board his aircraft carrier in between sorties he was also on the receiving end of more than one kamikaze attack. Bob's story enriches these updated pages.

I first met Bob, briefly, in 2004, at the unveiling of the replica Operational Base at the Parham Airfield Museum, which I attended on 4 July that year with the late Geoffrey Bradford. I have CART's Tom Sykes to thank for reacquainting me with Bob. Between September and October 2011, I enjoyed (and poor Bob *endured*) a series of fascinating telephone conversations with Bob, which I immediately transcribed, adding to them and my phone bill as recently as March 2012. I think Bob's important oral testimony is a valuable addition to this second edition.

Author David Lampe was the first to bring the story of Auxiliary Units out in the open with his book *The Last Ditch*, in 1968. Since then there has been a steady stream of books, magazine articles and newspaper features about Aux Units. TV producers have got in on the act, helped by the current vogue for docudrama that encourages the use of reconstructions – essential given that, not surprisingly, very few photos and certainly no cine footage exist of Auxiliary Units.

At the time of writing, a film version of *Resistance*, Owen Sheers' acclaimed 2007 novel, has just been released. *Resistance* features the absence of menfolk from a valley on the Welsh borders as they disappear in the middle of the night, going to ground, literally, in the face of a German invasion in 1944 (D-Day has failed) at the centre of a poetic story about the human spirit. Auxiliary Units are but a delicate trace in the novel and even less distinct in the film adaption, much to the consternation of those who went to see it expecting to see more about the BRO.

And there's more. One time when I was not engrossed in completing the revisions for this volume, but rather 'doing my day job' at big:group, a marketing communications agency in London, my old friend Nick Scott, the agency's CEO, just home from his house in Wells-next-the-Sea in Norfolk, gave me a copy of a weekend edition of the *Eastern Daily Press*. He'd noticed a review for a new play touring East Anglia and thought I'd be interested in it. I was. It was about Britain's secret wartime resistance and yet another example of the growing interest in the Auxiliary Units story. *Private Resistance*, an Eastern Angles theatre group presentation, considered how the British might have coped with a German invasion. Written by Ivan Cutting and directed by Naomi Jones, this new drama tells the story of the bonds created and destroyed by wartime.

All of the above serves to prove that the fascinating story of Auxiliary Units endures. Whilst too much, perhaps, has been written about their combat readiness and their dark arts, just because invasion never happened, the balloon didn't go up and Auxiliers never faced the ultimate test, their commitment should never be ignored.

Volunteers all faced the prospect of ending up in cold, damp underground bunkers, sitting silently as they waited, with no means of contacting the military authorities or other Auxiliary Patrols until they judged the time right to surface, after dark, emerging into a landscape potentially teaming with battle-hardened German soldiers. These men were unaware of the atrocities being committed in Poland or the round-ups of undesirables beginning in France and the Low Countries. They could and would have walked into a whirlwind from which few would have survived. Perhaps they would have thought twice about joining Auxiliary Units if they had known what the repercussions of their sabotage and covert intelligence missions were likely to have been.

But I doubt it. They were prepared to do their duty whatever the outcome. They were brave. This is their story.

Chapter 1

Britain Alone

We have no thought of aggression: our one wish is to live at peace with all peoples. But if this wish is to be fulfilled we must be up and doing. We must make ourselves strong so that our influence for peace be real, and we must make ourselves safe so that others cannot be tempted to thoughts of aggression against us.

National Service: A guide to the ways in which the people of this country may give service, HMSO, January 1939

After the Fall of France in June 1940, Britain stood alone against the Nazis. But faced with the Third Reich's apparently indomitable military machine, it seemed to be only a matter of time before Britain would become another victim of the revolutionary warfare the Germans had unleashed on the Continent.

The storm from which the fatal shafts of lightning would ultimately emanate had been gathering with the reoccupation of the Rhineland in 1936 and had grown more ominous with the annexation (*Anschluss*) of Austria in 1938. In both cases German audacity was met with Anglo-French prevarication. The victors of 1918 were so keen to avert another conflagration that even Germany's dismemberment of Czechoslovakia on the pretext of reuniting the predominantly German Sudetenlanders was countered with little more than appeasement in the form of the Munich Agreement of 29 September 1938. While British Prime Minister Neville Chamberlain proclaimed that this was 'peace in our time ... peace with honour', the Nazis quickly devoured what was left of Czechoslovakia, now all but defenceless after it had been forced to relinquish the Sudetenland. The potential for resistance of Czechoslovakia's thirty-five well-trained divisions was squandered. Hitler's daring didn't only win him territory – the world-beating Skoda arms factories significantly bolstered the Third Reich's military capacity. However, it was not until the Nazi *blitzkrieg* against Poland, beginning on 1 September 1939, that Europe was finally tipped into war. Britain and France, having given their guarantee to Poland, at last stood firm, though at the worst possible moment.

Britain had long expected war but, in contrast to 1914, it started quietly. No bunting or fanfares accompanied the soldiers of the British Expeditionary Force (BEF) who, like their fathers before them, sailed to France in preparation for a slugging match with the Boche. General Alan Brooke, who commanded the BEF's II Corps, said that, after Munich 'and only on the spur of the moment and to reassure the French' had the possibility of sending half of Britain's ground force to France in the event of war with Germany first been contemplated. Originally, five divisions was considered the minimum requirement to support the French but, in the event, the most the Ministry of Supply could initially arm and equip was two. This was to grow to four by mid-October and ten by the following March. American Senator

The Government calculated there would be nearly two million casualties from enemy air raids within the first two months of total war. The evacuation of children was made a priority. Within seven months of the 'Phoney War', however, half of those evacuated returned home. Many missed the 'comforting' sound of city anti-aircraft batteries – at least they showed that Britain was fighting back!

Edward Bora dubbed the period of stalemate that followed, the 'Phoney War'; in Germany they called it the *Sitzkrieg* – the sitting-down war. RAF Bomber Command dropped leaflets over Germany advising the populace that Hitler was leading them astray and that conflict with Britain and France would result in the same suffering and humiliation that defeat in the First World War had heaped on Germany. Just how credible this chastisement must have appeared to a people enjoying full employment, the world's first motorway system, the promise of a 'people's car' for all, a resurgence in the arts (however naïve), and income tax reductions for families, is best left to the imagination. Doubtless the fact that the RAF was forbidden from dropping bombs on German factories – because they were 'private property' – must have reinforced their feeling of self-righteousness.

In April 1940 the focus of attention was the strategically important seaway around Norway. While Chamberlain ordered the mining of Norwegian waters, thereby denying their use as conduits for the Nazi's Swedish iron ore supplies, Hitler unleashed a seaborne expeditionary force of 10,000 men, fully trained and equipped for Arctic warfare, and set about deciding the issue by occupying Norway and Denmark on 9 April. The shortcomings of Allied preparations were revealed when it was discovered that the Nazis, who had control of Norwegian airfields, could resupply their forces with ease and provide their troops with air cover. The hastily arranged Allied expeditionary force was forced to begin evacuation from key Norwegian locations as early as 2 May. One of the few consolations was that the King of Norway and his government had escaped to Britain, placing more than a million tons of shipping at Britain's disposal.

At this stage, the most significant defensive mantle in the Allied suit of armour, France's Maginot Line, remained untested. But the Germans had no intention of throwing their troops directly against it and, in any case, because its purpose was purely defensive, it neatly bottled up dozens of French divisions while allowing the Germans to deploy their own troops more frugally. Only nineteen German divisions faced fifty-nine French divisions along the entire Maginot Line front. As historian A.J.P. Taylor said, 'In this absurd way it benefited the Germans and weakened the French.' Churchill assumed that the existence of the fortress must have enabled the French High Command to keep a large mobile force in reserve. Later, during one of the many frantic conferences between Allied commanders, he asked the French when this reserve would be deployed. He was incredulous when he discovered that they didn't have a reserve.

The British Expeditionary Force, consisting of I, II and III Corps, was sandwiched between the French 1st and 7th Armies along the 'Dyle

Confidential

Mrs C. S. Bridges no 4

AIR RAID PRECAUTIONS
TRAINING PAMPHLET No. 3
(August, 1941)

ADVISING THE PUBLIC
IN THE EVENT OF
INVASION

(NOTES FOR THE GUIDANCE OF AIR RAID WARDENS)

Issued by the Ministry of Home Security

LONDON
HIS MAJESTY'S STATIONERY OFFICE
1941
Price 1d. net

**Copies will be sold only on written application to
H.M. Stationery Office, York House, Kingsway, W.C.2,
by a principal of a public utility company, or industrial
or commercial concern.**

This public information leaflet dealt with tricky issues such as whether or not it was the duty of the average citizen to fight back – 'Should I defend myself against the enemy? – reassuring home owners that Nazi invaders were unlikely to attack individual properties.

THE ENEMY

14. Should I defend myself against the enemy ?

The enemy is not likely to turn aside to attack separate houses. If small parties are going about threatening persons and property in an area not under enemy control and come your way, you have the right of every man and woman to do what you can to protect yourself, your family, and your home.

This advice applies to you both as a warden and as a citizen. If enemy troops should come your way they may try to take advantage of your position and local knowledge to obtain valuable information concerning your district. They may want to know the situation of local telephones, the local Report and Control Centre or Police Stations ; they may try to use the telephone at your Post or get you to send bogus instructions or information.

YOU SHOULD GIVE ALL THE HELP YOU CAN TO OUR TROOPS.

DO NOT TELL THE ENEMY ANYTHING.

DO NOT GIVE HIM ANYTHING.

DO NOT HELP HIM IN ANY WAY.

A.R.P. Training Pamphlet No. I, " Notes on the Detection and Reporting of Unexploded Bombs and Shells " (Price 3d. net, Post free 4d.). A.R.P. Training Pamphlet No. 2, " Objects Dropped from the Air " (at press).
Copies will be sold only on written application to H.M. Stationery Office, York House, Kingsway, W.C.2, by a Clerk to a local authority, a Chief Constable, or by a Principal of a public utility company, or industrial or commercial concern.

69884. Wt. 1727A. 750,000. 3/41 : S. P. & Co.   S.O. Code No. 34—9999

The reverse of the leaflet reinforced key messages, advising the public to stay quiet and not to tell the enemy anything, give him anything or 'help him in any way'. Scary stuff.

Line' in 'neutral' Belgium. King Leopold of the Belgians had not wanted to provoke German aggression by extending 'Maginot Line type' defences along the German/Belgian border. Because France was sympathetic to her smaller neighbour's plight and was equally reluctant to antagonize Hitler, she was unwilling to extend her own protective shell along the Franco-Belgian border. France preferred to wait until Belgian neutrality had been violated and then push forward with the BEF to plug the gap on her northern flank. She was confident that, as soon as the Anglo-French armies were combined with the thirty-five Belgian and Dutch divisions, they could hold the Dyle Line and also secure the Ardennes, most of which was adjacent to Belgian territory. This disposition was known as 'Plan D' and was drawn up by General Gamelin, the senior French military commander. According to this plan, Allied armies would march across the Franco-Belgian border and hold the river and canal line, which extended through Wavre to the French border. Later, Gamelin revised the plan so that the line could be extended northwards to the Dutch frontier. Allied commanders were confident that, although far smaller than the Anglo-French air forces, the Dutch Luftvaartafdeling and Belgian L'Aéronautique Belge could muster sufficient fighters to usefully pitch in against the Luftwaffe. Few commanders and politicians had foreseen the surgical destruction of these two supplementary forces that the Luftwaffe speedily accomplished on day one. Moreover, although there was overall support in the UK for Gamelin's plan, BEF soldiers had little more than 2-inch mortars and simple slit trenches for protection against a full-scale armoured assault. When the War Minister, Hore-Belisha, who was against a Continental commitment, criticized these arrangements, he was forced to resign. Despite the obvious weaknesses of the Plan D sector, however, the British General Staff were reluctant to criticize their French allies, who, it must be remembered, were providing ten times as many men as Britain to confront the Germans. Even the 'Hero of Verdun', Marshal Pétain, who had been called from retirement to serve his country, declared, 'This sector is not dangerous.'

Although the French Army numbered nearly 2 million men, with 600,000 of its soldiers under the age of twenty-five it was not a particularly vigorous fighting force. France had almost 3,000 tanks, some of which were the best available, whereas Germany had barely 2,500 vehicles, many of them PzKw I and IIs nearing obsolescence. The Germans also depended heavily on captured Czech vehicles, such as the state of the art 38 (t). The British 1st Armoured Division was sent to France after Operation *Fall Gelb* started and, together with the ten infantry divisions of the BEF, the Anglo-French and German armies had virtual parity in the field. The Allies had actually read accurate details of *Fall Gelb* the previous January when a Nazi General Staff Courier aircraft containing confidential battle plans made a forced landing in Belgium. But, because the Allies suspected a deception by the Germans, they continued to overestimate the size of the German Army.

The one area where the Germans were definitely superior, though, was in the air. The French Air Force (Armée de l'Air, ALA) had barely 800 fighter planes, only 584 of which were serviceable on 10 May. The small RAF Advanced Air Striking Force (AASF) of 500 aircraft – some, like the Defiant, Gladiator and Battle, almost obsolete as front-line day fighters – was no match for the 3,500 aircraft of Hermann Goering's Luftwaffe. It was always assumed that the RAF could quickly reinforce its Continental contingents from Britain but the Allied deficiency in tactical air power within the combat zone would be critical to the eventual outcome of the Battle of France.

Things went from bad to worse for the Allies with the abrupt end of the Phoney War. Wehrmacht panzers were moving towards the Belgian and Dutch frontiers. Crouching infantrymen shielded by the advancing armour, equipped with light assault weapons, followed closely. They were accompanied by specialist sappers lugging explosives. Further south more armour threaded its way across the French border as a thin haze of blue exhaust smoke rose beneath the canopy of the 'impregnable' Ardennes. Yet more German tanks progressed through the wooded slopes that led down to the Meuse River. Operation *Fall Gelb* had begun. It was 10 May 1940.

Throughout the Low Countries on the same morning, Fallschirmjägers – Luftwaffe paratroops – tumbled from their 'Auntie Jus', the Luftwaffe's reliable Junkers 52 tri-motor transport aircraft, its 'tin donkey'. Others landed in DFS 210 gliders, heading for the strategically important Albert Canal nearby. As soon as these soldiers had secured a landing ground they quickly set about attacking pre-selected targets. Soon German airborne troops from 'Assault Group Koch' were scrambling onto the smooth curved turrets of Eben-Emael in Belgium – the most advanced fortress in the world and, like the Ardennes forest, thought to be inviolable. Shaped charges – small man-portable mines that shot a jet of molten metal through the toughest armour – made short work of Eben-Emael's gun turrets long before they could be brought into action.

The German High Command had second-guessed Gamelin. Hardly had the Allied armies moved into their Plan D positions when the speed and impact of *blitzkrieg* forced them to retreat south again. British and French commanders were well aware of the risks of a German offensive through the Belgian gap in the Maginot Line but they never expected German panzers to be able to manoeuvre through the heavily-wooded Ardennes. This new form of warfare didn't depend on consolidation – 'digging in' – but instead allowed tank commanders to motor around obstacles, avoiding unnecessary action, while still keeping the final objective firmly in mind.

Whilst Allied attention was concentrated on the Franco-Belgian frontier, much further to the south, the key sector around France's hallowed Great War fortress of Sedan, the hinge between two great French armies (Huntziger's 2nd and Corap's 9th) suffered heavy panzer and dive-bomber attack. It was part of French folklore that if Sedan fell, France would fall.

In France, by 13 May, German amphibious assault troops had crossed the river Meuse. Their armoured divisions followed the next day. Rotterdam surrendered on 13 May, and became the second European city after Warsaw to suffer Luftwaffe terror bombing. To many this event was an evil portent of the invincibility of modern air fleets and vindication of Stanley Baldwin's theory that 'the bomber always gets through.' On 15 May, Dinant and Sedan were further probed by advance parties of Rommel's and Guderian's panzers. Soon the entire Allied line was split. It was clear that an unparalleled disaster was imminent. Yet, the same day, Churchill told the French, who were panicked by the speed of the German advance, 'All experience shows that the offensive will come to an end after a while … after five or six days they have to halt for supplies, and the opportunity for a counter-attack is presented.' But no serious counter-attack was possible and, despite some gallant fighting around Arras by the lightly-armoured Infantry Tank Mk 1s of the Royal Tank Regiment – which smashed through part of Rommel's 7th Panzer Division, momentarily catching the German High Command off guard – and some resistance from the French at Peronne and St Quentin, the German advance proved unstoppable. Directly the German flanking manoeuvre through Belgium had been completed, Hitler's panzers were free to slice clear through France. They proceeded to race for the Channel coast, which they reached on 20 May. A total collapse of the Allied line became inevitable.

Meanwhile, General Auchinleck had arrived in Norway to see if he could make a positive contribution to the Allies' other Continental debacle. Auchinleck was appointed GOC Designate in Norway on 5 May and he first went ashore on 11 May, the day after the start of the German *blitzkrieg* in France and the Low Countries. Auchinleck now considered the option of evacuating the entire British contingent. The sudden breakdown of Allied dispositions along the north-eastern sector of France on top of the calamitous Norwegian campaign, about which a furious national debate had raged for weeks, most recently in the House of Commons, virtually brought the British Government to

The respirator eye-pieces would have quickly fogged, making life very hard (and accurate shooting all but impossible) for this Vickers Medium Machine Gun crew.

Civilian respirator (gas mask) and specially designed spectacles with thin arms, which fitted under the mask but retained an air(gas)-tight seal.

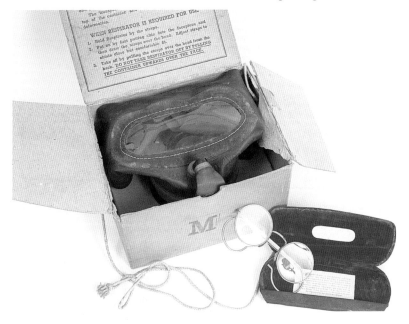

the point of collapse. It was clear that Prime Minister Neville Chamberlain would have to go. On the evening of 10 May, King George VI sent for Winston Churchill and asked him to become prime minister. Whilst there is no doubt that Churchill was the best man for the job at hand, it is ironic that it was a campaign instigated by Churchill while he was at the Admiralty that was to force Chamberlain's resignation.

In his memoirs Churchill recalled that the coalition government he assembled – largely to assuage opposition politicians who were hungry for the restructure of government machinery – was probably easier to form 'in the heat of battle than in quite times'. Clement Attlee, the Labour leader and Lord Privy Seal, was deputy leader of the coalition and, effectively, second in command to Churchill. As a fellow soldier in the previous war, Churchill was perfectly happy to work with him; the only differences in their mutual outlooks were 'about socialism'. Perhaps sympathetic to Chamberlain's plight and aware that the full extent of recent disaster was not entirely the incumbent prime minister's fault, Churchill offered the elder statesman the important position of Leadership of the House of Commons. Churchill also ordered that Chamberlain need not vacate his home at Number 10 for a month.

Some still feel that Chamberlain has been unfairly maligned, that he was Britain's 'arch appeaser'. According to Sir Peter Wilkinson, an Army officer within the Directorate of Military Intelligence in 1940, Chamberlain's appeasement was in fact a means of buying so-called time and avoiding an early war with Nazi Germany before Britain was properly prepared. Wilkinson says this was well understood within government circles at the time and had the active support of the chiefs of staff. Indeed, there was a very real risk that Germany would have won the Battle of Britain had there not been time to re-equip the RAF's squadrons with Spitfires. Sir Peter told me, 'I remember my father-in-law was in a shooting party with Neville Chamberlain during the winter of 1938-39. He asked the Prime Minister how things were going, because at the time things didn't seem to be going terribly well. Chamberlain said, "If only we can stop open hostilities from breaking out until we have got our aeroplanes coming off the line everything will be all right."'

In the face of the German juggernaut, saving the BEF had become a priority. On 20 May, Lord Gort, the BEF's commander-in-chief, informed the British Government that he was considering evacuation. That afternoon the Navy's Admiral Ramsey and representatives of the Shipping Ministry studied a document entitled 'The emergency evacuation across the Channel of very large forces'. Fortunately, most of the BEF was in one place – consolidated within the shrinking perimeter around Dunkirk, literally with its back to the sea. On 24 May, despite a furious aerial bombardment from Luftwaffe Stukas, it enjoyed a brief respite from the full force of Hitler's panzers. Concerned by overextended supply lines, keen to conserve his strength for the attack on Paris and unsure of Anglo-French intentions, the Führer issued his famous 'halt order', which went against the wishes of his army commander-in-chief, General Brauchitsch. Historians have since argued that in these forty-eight hours Germany lost the war. By 25 May, the valiant Belgian Army had surrendered and further fighting in Flanders was pointless. On 27 May, Gort gave the order for the total evacuation of his army. At Dover, Admiral Ramsey initiated Operation Dynamo and the saga of the 'little ships of Dunkirk' began.

In *The Nine Days Wonder*, published in 1941, John Masefield wrote:

> The enemy had proclaimed our complete encirclement and destruction; no doubt he had expected to achieve both aims. He did not do these things because he could not. He came up against inundations and defences which checked his tanks: against soldiers who defied him and drove him back against our Air Force. Against our Navy. He came up against the spirit of this Nation, which, when roused, will do great things. The Nation said to those men, in effect: 'Hold on: we will get you away.' They held on, and we got them away.

The reality of May 1940, however, was not quite as straightforward as the Poet Laureate suggested. Some saw the retreat from France as a very real defeat. Writing in his memoirs, Montgomery, then a general just back from France, was infuriated to see veterans of the evacuation sporting unofficial Dunkirk flashes and being feted as heroes. 'It was not understood that the British Army had suffered a crushing defeat at Dunkirk and that our island home was now in grave danger,' he wrote. 'There was no sense of urgency.' Montgomery was given command of the 3rd Division. From his headquarters at Steyning, on the South Downs near Brighton, he initiated one of his typically rigorous training programmes. His troops were in preparation for an immediate return trip across the English Channel to 'join up with the small British forces which were still fighting with the French Army.'

As the Dunkirk evacuation began, the future of the beleaguered garrison in Norway looked bleak. If it was to survive at all, it too had to be plucked from the jaws of the advancing German armies. This critical situation was further exacerbated by the fact that Britain's War Cabinet would sanction no reinforcements. When on 17 May the War Cabinet first seriously considered the possibility of a French collapse, even the new prime minister, Churchill, could see no other way out: 'One lived with the battle, upon which all thoughts were centred, and about which nothing could be done.' On 31 May, on one of his desperate last-minute trips to France during the final stages of her agony, Churchill told Premier Reynaud that Britain proposed to begin evacuating her forces from Norway on 2 June, and he offered to evacuate French troops directly to Britain. Two weeks later, Churchill, an ardent Francophile, actually proposed an official union between Britain and France. A massive Royal Navy bombardment of Narvik on 8 June did terrible damage to civilian areas of the port and heralded Britain's ignominious retreat from Scandinavia. The decision to leave the Norwegians to their fate was made all the more bitter because Britain's intention to retreat was kept secret from her ally. The last British troops left Norway on 7 June. The British did intend to carry on the fight in France, however. For a while Churchill's intention was to redeploy the BEF elsewhere, via ports such as Calais. As late as 2 June he asked Ismay to consider a scheme 'for a bridgehead and area of disembarkation in Brittany'. He ordered that the BEF in France 'must immediately be reconstituted' and said that, even if Paris fell, the French must be encouraged to continue to fight the Nazis with guerrilla warfare if necessary. But it very soon became clear that for the Allied democracies the Battle of France was lost.

Though not obvious to the stranded Tommies on the beaches below, the RAF had done its best to deny absolute air superiority above the French coast. During the nine days of the evacuation, the RAF lost 177 aircraft. Britain's soldiers often simply couldn't see the high-speed fighters when they shot down the cranked-wing dive-bombers, as they often did. Fighter Command's leader, Air Marshal Dowding, knew that it would be only his precious 500 Hurricanes and Spitfires that could hope to prevent a Nazi invasion. On 17 May he had already clashed with Churchill by refusing to allow any more fighter squadrons to be transferred to France. He showed the Prime Minister a graph that illustrated the fact that, if his squadrons continued to lose aircraft at their current rate (they were already a third below strength), then the Germans would have local air superiority above southern England if they chose to invade. No. 73 Squadron was the last RAF unit to leave France, arriving at Tangmere on 18 June. However, once back in England, RAF Fighter Command pilots were often bitterly taunted by BEF veterans and accused of being less evident than the enemy's Stukas in the skies above the French beaches.

At Dunkirk, every British tank within the contested perimeter was lost. Though Britain's fighting contribution to the war had started poorly, at least her soldiers, unlike the French ones, had returned to a land that was not occupied by the enemy. Critically, the withdrawal did bring most of Britain's Regulars back home. The Luftwaffe bombardment that systematically destroyed Dunkirk sent a pall of thick smoke high above the French town, paradoxically protecting the beleaguered Allied troops by helping to obscure their evacuation from enemy reconnaissance. The 'miracle' of Dunkirk surprised and encouraged everyone – not least Churchill. Soon after the evacuation had commenced the Prime Minister confided in his 'Shadow', Detective-Inspector Thompson, 'I thought we should be lucky if we got away safely 20,000, but now, thank God, 90,000 are already back in England, and we hope for many more to come.' On 4 June, the last troops, 26,175 Frenchmen, came ashore in England. At 2.33 pm on the same day, after consultation with the French, the Admiralty officially called off the operation.

On the evening of 4 June, in a carefully worded address that he knew would be analyzed by the United States (and he was desperate for President Roosevelt's support) Churchill told the Commons, 'Wars are not won by evacuations.' He went on to point out that Dunkirk was, in fact, a military disaster and that invasion was a very real possibility. But he said that at least the RAF was intact and he expected it to be vital during the coming weeks. Still, during the nine days since Vice-Admiral Ramsey initiated Operation Dynamo on the evening of 26 May, 385,000 soldiers, 100,000 of them French, were plucked to safety

One of the three Solent forts in wartime trim. Built to defend Spithead and the access to Portsmouth Harbour, Spitbank, Horse Sand Fort and no-man's-land, forts were the outmost defences of the home of the fleet.

With the Home Guard by Captain Simon Fine, typical of the books devoured by an anxious public during the invasion crisis of 1940.

Careless Talk Costs Lives by 'Fougasse', the pen name of artist Cyril Kenneth Bird.

by Royal Navy vessels, coasters, cross-channel ferries and the myriad 'little ships' harvested from the Medway, the Kent coast, the Solent and from the canals of The Netherlands. American magazine *Time* said that Dunkirk was a 'scene of carnage and valor more concentrated in time and space than anything modern history ever saw', and reminded its readers that it all took place 'on a patch of earth about the size of an average US county'. After the evacuation of the BEF from the beaches had finished on 3 June, the Wehrmacht had a free hand to finish off the remaining French forces and mopped up any further domestic resistance by taking the Maginot Line from behind. Paris fell on 14 June. Italy stabbed France in the back by declaring war against the Allies on 10 June and lamely joining in to attack from the south. Despite an advantage of six to one, however, Mussolini's troops took a severe drubbing at the hands of France's elite Alpine division. Finally, on 21 June, France had to suffer the humiliation of agreeing an armistice with Germany in the same railway carriage in the forest at Compiègne in which the victorious Allies had taken the surrender from the Kaiser's armies in 1918. Hitler then ordered the coach to be blown up. Now the final prize, Britain, stood before Hitler's all-conquering armies.

In an interview with the German fighter ace Adolf Galland I was told about a private encounter the famous pilot had with Hitler that tends to confirm the oft-held notion that Hitler never really wanted war with Britain. 'The war against England is completely against my interests,' Hitler told Galland. The fighter leader had sought an audience with his Führer to explain that London was such an easy target, the Luftwaffe simply couldn't miss. Hitler, irritated at what he considered Galland's overeagerness, continued, 'The English population are equal to us, they are related to us. I hate this war against England.'

'I immediately shut up, of course!' said Galland. Regardless of any benevolence, Hitler was certainly not prepared to risk a setback at this stage and was only willing to give his Luftwaffe a free hand above the Dunkirk beaches. In his memoirs after the war, Albrecht Kesselring, commander of Luftflotte 2 during the Battle of Britain, confirmed Hitler's reluctance to press home the attack against Britain. He said that even though Hitler had not 'reckoned with a blitz victory over the Western powers, [the] utter neglect of the invasion idea' still dumbfounded most of Kesselring's peers in the armed forces. 'In my view he seriously cherished the belief that England would grasp his hand with its offer of peace,' he added.

Britain's remaining home defence armoury was in a parlous state: the RAF had lost 386 Hurricanes and sixty-seven Spitfires since *Fall Gelb* had begun – 100 fighters and eighty pilots during the Dunkirk evacuation alone. This made a combined total of nearly 1,000 aircraft destroyed – half of which were fighters – since the Norwegian campaign started. In France the British Army suffered nearly 70,000 men killed, wounded and captured. It lost 64,000 vehicles (more than 300 of these were tanks), 90,000 rifles, 8,000 Bren guns, 76,000 tons of ammunition and almost 2,500 guns (including 400 Boys rifles, the entire British arsenal of anti-tank weapons). To this day, no one is sure who gave the order for so many weapons to be abandoned and for the heavy artillery to be spiked. France, however, suffered heaviest: 90,000 of her soldiers were killed. In barely six weeks the German invasion had netted Hitler most of Europe and cost Germany 29,640 men.

The British Fleet was committed to maintaining trade and communications with the Empire. In the Atlantic it was furiously engaged in keeping Britain's vital sea lanes open. In the Eastern Mediterranean the Royal Navy's vessels guarded British interests in Gibraltar, Malta, Egypt and the Suez Canal. With twelve battleships, eight aircraft carriers, fifty cruisers, ninety-four destroyers and thirty-eight submarines, the Royal Navy was proportionately the world's largest fleet. But it was spread far and wide and could do little within the narrow waters of the continental shelf of Europe, which would have been strewn with enemy mines and teeming with U-boats if the Nazis invaded.

Although Britain was now alone to fight Hitler there was a palpable sense of relief that she now had only herself to worry about. At RAF Fighter Command, Hugh Dowding reportedly commented, 'Thank God we are alone.' Churchill also felt a sense of relief. He thought Hitler had made a fatal mistake by not dragging out the land battle by pausing on the Somme after Dunkirk, thereby forcing the British to redeploy the BEF in strength elsewhere and to be sucked into a war of attrition on land that would ultimately finish off its army. Instead, by forcing the BEF back to the sea, it left no alternative but its entire evacuation. In Volume II of his account *The Second World War, Their Finest Hour*, Churchill reveals the enthusiasm with which he faced up to the responsibility of leading a nation alone against the unchecked might of Nazi Germany. 'The Prime Minister expects all His Majesty's servants in high places to set an example of steadiness and resolution,' he told the House on 4 July 1940. Churchill never once revealed even a hint of doubt that Britain would prevail and he really believed the invasion threat would melt away. On 23 July 1940, in a minute to Secretary of State for War Anthony Eden, Churchill was even then thinking ahead about ways of counter-invading Nazi-occupied France. 'As soon as the invasion danger recedes or is resolved, and Sir Roger Keyes' paperwork is done, we will consult together and set the staffs to work upon detailed preparations. After these medium raids have had their chance there will be no objection to stirring up the French coast

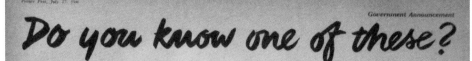

This full-page press ad issued by the Ministry of Information was designed to deter civilians from indulging in idle gossip and inadvertently revealing information that might be useful to an enemy. Published in *Picture Post* in July 1941, it illustrates just how a top secret organization like Auxiliary Units could stay secret. Even if people suspected that someone they knew was involved in hush-hush work, it was never discussed.

One wonders whether the journalist and photographer who set up this classic 'Britain can take it' photograph bought the unfortunate family a 'real' breakfast following the session.

by minor forays.' In *The Fringes of Power*, Churchill's Private Secretary, John Colville, recalls:

> Winston is inclined to think that Hitler's plans have had to be changed: Hitler could not have foreseen the collapse of France and must have planned his strategy of invasion on the assumption that the French armies would be holding out on the Somme, or at least the Seine, and that the BEF would either be assisting them or else would have been wiped out. The situation is now very different … it will still be difficult for the [German] escorting ships to penetrate the straits of Dover … the whole of the BEF is now back in this country to defend it.

Indeed, the British had even pulled back troops from the Channel Islands, which were effectively demilitarized. On 12 June, the British Government had decided that the islands were of no strategic value and, by 20 June, the last British troops had left. Unfortunately, but perhaps not surprisingly, the Germans were not told that the islands were effectively undefended. On 28 June, two days before the German Naval Assault Group cleared the way for Infantry Division 216's occupation of the Channel Islands, forty-four islanders were killed by Luftwaffe bombs as they unloaded the tomato harvest from civilian lorries. The Germans thought they were military vehicles. King George VI privately told the Bailiffs of Jersey and Guernsey that, though he deeply regretted it, 'for strategic reasons' the Army had been withdrawn. On 2 July, Churchill wrote to Ismay:

> If it is true that a few hundred German troops have been landed on Jersey and Guernsey by troop carriers, plans should be studied to land secretly by night on the islands and kill or capture the invaders. This is exactly one of the exploits for which the Commandos would be suited.

As Chief of the Imperial General Staff (CIGS) General Hastings 'Pug' Ismay was Winston Churchill's chief military assistant and the senior staff officer in the British Army.

In common with other island states, Britain had long considered the threat of an attack by seaborne raiders. In 1908, in the wake of the 'Dreadnought Race', an Invasion Inquiry was set up by the Committee of Imperial Defence. The recommendations it made were, naturally enough, designed to thwart a seaborne assault. The defence of the realm had traditionally been guaranteed by the Royal Navy and Britain's professional, well-trained army. When, on 25 July 1909, Louis Blériot landed his monoplane on a meadow at Dover Castle, everything changed. Britannia's island fortress was shown to lack a roof.

As early as 1911, only a day into his new job at the Admiralty (he was First Sea Lord), Churchill, also a member of the Committee of Imperial Defence, drew up a charter for defence against aerial attack that recommended the destruction of enemy aircraft and airships at their bases; the creation of an interceptor force of British aircraft based on the east coast; the concentration of AA (anti-aircraft) defences around military targets; a civilian 'blackout'; and the formation of a London air defence squadron based at Hendon. In September 1914 he had accurately prophesied that 'aerial attack upon England must be a feature of the near future.' On 17 August 1917, following public consternation about German air raids, a government committee, chaired by the redoubtable former Boer leader, Lieutenant General J.C. Smuts, published its results. These led directly to the establishment of the new Air Ministry and the implementation of many of the ideas previously espoused by Churchill. Principal among these was Brigadier General Ashmore's London Air Defence organization, and the report also led to the introduction of barrage balloons. Most significant of all was the establishment on 3 January 1918 of the RAF. The aeroplane was fast becoming king.

The development of military aviation during the early part of the First World War brought with it the nightmare of invasion from the air. The spectre became a reality when German Zeppelins first appeared in the skies above London. The British didn't awake from the nightmare until late in 1916, when, over Hertfordshire, the first Zeppelin was shot down. That air power severely undermined Britain's traditional reliance on naval and coastal fortifications, and made nonsense of the natural protection afforded by distance and geographical isolation, was a shattering discovery. It spawned a mass of pulp fiction to whet the appetites of a salacious and curious public.

War Over England, written by retired Air Commodore L.E.O. Charlton in the mid-1930s, was a novel that skilfully blended scientific fact with fantasy and warned of impending terror from the skies. But its publisher argued a serious case and said the book was a 'reminder and a warning of air raids over England, not written just to make our flesh creep, but much more to make our minds aware of a danger before it is too late.' In a review headed 'A FEW MORE THINGS TO COME' one magazine journalist said of the novel, 'If 270 tons of bombs fell in England between 1914 and 1918, killing 1,414 people, how many tons will fall in one night of nineteen hundred and x and how many people will they kill?'

As Germany rearmed during the 1930s many British observers bemoaned the fact that Britain had lost its early lead in military aviation. Some were highly placed, like Lord Rothermere, who, in November 1933, in an article in his paper, the *Daily Mail*, warned, 'We need 5,000 warplanes! Not since the Dutch fleet burnt British shipping in the Medway 250 years ago has this country been so inadequately protected against the possibility of foreign attack as it is today.' Two years later, he again argued, 'The safety of this country, and indeed its independence since the development of the air arm, rests above all on security against air attacks, to which Great Britain is more exposed than any other country in Europe.' In 1936, the Treasury grudgingly granted £185 million to home defence and rearmament was stepped up, including the further development of the new monoplane Spitfire and Hurricane fighters. However, in June 1940, only thirty-two Home Defence fighter squadrons were ready – fifty-two was considered the minimum requirement.

Alexander Korda's 1936 production of *Things to Come* convinced the cinema-going public that science, allied with air power, promised an aerial onslaught against which there was no protection. The film uncannily predicted war in 1940 and showed air raids on a city that had more than a passing resemblance to London. In *Aerial Wonders Of Our Time – War In The Air*, published in 1939, a spread of stills from the film showing the streets of 'Everytown' strewn with dying civilians, wrecked buses and upturned cars, captioned 'Apprehension and then inferno', left the reader in little doubt as to the terror that could be inflicted by an enemy air fleet. In the 1935 book *The Shape of Things to Come*, which had inspired the film, H.G. Wells foresaw a chemical and biological threat from the air from 'rare sub-radiant gases known as Pabst's Kinetogens, which affect the genes.' *Things to Come* also included such aerial weapons as 'Permanent Death Gas' and 'Green Cross Gas' and saw the public falling victim to 'Sterilizing Inhalation'. In the document 'Hate Eugenics', Wells wrote that there 'was a great clamour about the world for the extensive application of this new find [Kinetogens] to apply it from the air to Palestine, Arabia, Ireland, the whole of China and the African Continent.' It is worthy of note that, in 1932, Prime Minister Stanley Baldwin famously predicted 'The bomber will always get through, the only defence is offence, which means you have to kill more women and children more quickly than the enemy if you want to save yourselves.'

On 1 September 1939, Britain was first plunged into the darkness of a national blackout, in an effort to test Britain's ARP systems two days before the declaration of war. The Government pessimistically calculated that for every ton of enemy explosives dropped on British towns and cities there would be fifty casualties. This was based partly on the bitter memories of the power of high explosives between 1914-18 (the authorities had apparently forgotten that First World War shells had often fallen on densely packed trenches, not blacked-out cities) and partly because, like so many, the Government was caught up in the mood of hysteria that swept the country. In *War on Great Cities*, published in 1937, author Frank Morrison warned, 'The unrestricted use of lethal gas or bacteria upon the scale predicted by the experts implies a stampede of the threatened populations beyond all precedent.' The Government, perhaps sharing Morrison's view, opened the first gas mask factories the same year!

As early as July 1939, as the storm clouds gathered and war with Germany seemed inevitable, the Lord Privy Seal's office had distributed a series of Civil Defence leaflets. These were, of course, all issued in the hope that a European war might be confined to the Continental mainland. The cover of 'Public Information Leaflet No. 1 was emblazoned with the words 'SOME THINGS YOU SHOULD KNOW IF WAR SHOULD COME. READ THIS AND KEEP IT CAREFULLY. YOU MAY NEED IT.' It continued, 'All who have work to do, whether manual, clerical or professional, should regard it as their duty to remain at their posts, and do their part in carrying on the life of the nation.' Now, with France gone and the Nazis snapping at Britannia's heels, Leaflet No. 3, 'EVACUATION. WHY AND HOW?', which warned against 'anything like panic', took on more relevance. But it too was relaxed, stressing that the evacuation scheme was entirely voluntary and the key thing was that 'WORK MUST GO ON'.

Until the fall of France, the United Kingdom's anti-invasion contingency plan, the Julius Caesar Plan, drawn up by the then Commander-in-Chief Home Forces, General Sir Walter Kirke, was not given top priority. Julius Caesar assumed that the enemy would attempt to capture a port before they landed the bulk of their troops and equipment. Now, with the alarming rapidity of *blitzkrieg* and under the illusion that Hitler's forces were both numerically superior and equipped with revolutionary weapons, the United Kingdom was gripped by invasion frenzy. In mid-June, the Government distributed a leaflet entitled, 'If the Invader Comes'. It said:

> The Germans threaten to invade Great Britain. If they do so they will be driven out by our Navy, our Army and our Air Force. Yet the ordinary men and women of the civilian population will also have their part to play. Hitler's invasions of Poland, Holland and Belgium were greatly helped by the fact that the civilian population was taken by surprise. ... Do not believe rumours and do not spread them. When you receive an order, make quite sure that [it] is a true order and not a faked order.

One old woman told Mass Observation: 'I'm not worrying. I haven't even read it. I don't think they'll come because our boys are too good for them – and if they do come we'll get some sticks and beat them back.'

Issued by the Ministry of   Information on behalf of
the War Office and the Ministry of Home Security

STAY WHERE YOU ARE

IF this island is invaded by sea or air everyone who is not under orders must stay where he or she is. This is not simply advice : it is an order from the Government, and you must obey it just as soldiers obey their orders. Your order is " Stay Put ", but remember that this does not apply until invasion comes.

Why must I stay put ?

Because in France, Holland and Belgium, the Germans were helped by the people who took flight before them. Great crowds of refugees blocked all roads. The soldiers who could have defended them could not get at the enemy. The enemy used the refugees as a human shield. These refugees were got out on to the roads by rumour and false orders. Do not be caught out in this way. Do not take any notice of any story telling what the enemy has done or where he is. Do not take orders except from the Military, the Police, the Home Guard (L.D.V.) and the A.R.P. authorities or wardens.

What will happen to me if I don't stay put ?

If you do not stay put you will stand a very good chance of being killed. The enemy may machine-gun you from the air in order to increase panic, or you may run into enemy forces which have landed behind you. An official German message was captured in Belgium which ran :

" Watch for civilian refugees on the roads. Harass them as much as possible."

Our soldiers will be hurrying to drive back the invader and will not be able to stop and help you. On the contrary, they will

Convinced that roads choked with refugees fleeing from the advancing enemy conspired towards the Allied defeat on the Continent, the Government was determined that the British public would stay indoors in the event of invasion.

Issued by the Ministry of Information in co-operation with the War Office and the Ministry of Home Security.

If the
INVADER
comes

WHAT TO DO — AND HOW TO DO IT

THE Germans threaten to invade Great Britain. If they do so they will be driven out by our Navy, our Army and our Air Force. Yet the ordinary men and women of the civilian population will also have their part to play. Hitler's invasions of Poland, Holland and Belgium were greatly helped by the fact that the civilian population was taken by surprise. They did not know what to do when the moment came. *You must not be taken by surprise.* This leaflet tells you what general line you should take. More detailed instructions will be given you when the danger comes nearer. Meanwhile, read these instructions carefully and be prepared to carry them out.

I

When Holland and Belgium were invaded, the civilian population fled from their homes. They crowded on the roads, in cars, in carts, on bicycles and on foot, and so helped the enemy by preventing their own armies from advancing against the invaders. You must not allow that to happen here. Your first rule, therefore, is :—

(1) IF THE GERMANS COME, BY PARACHUTE, AEROPLANE OR SHIP, YOU MUST REMAIN WHERE YOU ARE. THE ORDER IS "STAY PUT".

If the Commander in Chief decides that the place where you live must be evacuated, he will tell you when and how to leave. Until you receive such orders you must remain where you are. If you run away, you will be exposed to far greater danger because you will be machine-gunned from the air as were civilians in Holland and Belgium, and you will also block the roads by which our own armies will advance to turn the Germans out.

II

There is another method which the Germans adopt in their invasion. They make use of the civilian population in order to create confusion and panic. They spread false rumours and issue false instructions. In order to prevent this, you should obey the second rule, which is as follows :—

(2) DO NOT BELIEVE RUMOURS AND DO NOT SPREAD THEM. WHEN YOU RECEIVE AN ORDER, MAKE QUITE SURE THAT IT IS A TRUE ORDER AND NOT A FAKED ORDER. MOST OF YOU KNOW YOUR POLICEMEN AND YOUR A.R.P. WARDENS BY SIGHT, YOU CAN TRUST THEM. IF YOU KEEP YOUR HEADS, YOU CAN ALSO TELL WHETHER A MILITARY OFFICER IS REALLY BRITISH OR ONLY PRETENDING TO BE SO. IF IN DOUBT ASK THE POLICE-MAN OR THE A.R.P. WARDEN. USE YOUR COMMON SENSE.

If the Invader Comes – a deadly serious public information leaflet bearing an amazingly relaxed title. The government found itself in such a serious potential emergency that no amount of rhetoric or hyperbole was required – just plain simple, matter of fact English.

Issued by the Ministry of Information in co-operation with the War Office
and the Ministry of Home Security

Beating the INVADER

A MESSAGE FROM THE PRIME MINISTER

IF invasion comes, everyone—young or old, men and women—will be eager to play their part worthily. By far the greater part of the country will not be immediately involved. Even along our coasts, the greater part will remain unaffected. But where the enemy lands, or tries to land, there will be most violent fighting. Not only will there be the battles when the enemy tries to come ashore, but afterwards there will fall upon his lodgments very heavy British counter-attacks, and all the time the lodgments will be under the heaviest attack by British bombers. The fewer civilians or non-combatants in these areas, the better—apart from essential workers who must remain. So if you are advised by the authorities to leave the place where you live, it is your duty to go elsewhere when you are told to leave. When the attack begins, it will be too late to go; and, unless you receive definite instructions to move, your duty then will be to stay where you are. You will have to get into the safest place you can find, and stay there until the battle is over. For all of you then the order and the duty will be: " STAND FIRM ".

This also applies to people inland if any considerable number of parachutists or air-borne troops are landed in their neighbourhood. Above all, they must not cumber the roads. Like their fellow-countrymen on the coasts, they must " STAND FIRM ". The Home Guard, supported by strong mobile columns wherever the enemy's numbers require it, will immediately come to grips with the invaders, and there is little doubt will soon destroy them.

Throughout the rest of the country where there is no fighting going on and no close cannon fire or rifle fire can be heard, everyone will govern his conduct by the second great order and duty, namely, " CARRY ON ". It may easily be some weeks before the invader has been totally destroyed, that is to say, killed or captured to the last man who has landed on our shores. Meanwhile, all work must be continued to the utmost, and no time lost.

The following notes have been prepared to tell everyone in rather more detail what to do, and they should be carefully studied. Each man and woman should think out a clear plan of personal action in accordance with the general scheme.

Winston S. Churchill

STAND FIRM

I. What do I do if fighting breaks out in my neighbourhood?

Keep indoors or in your shelter until the battle is over. If you can have a trench ready in your garden or field, so much the better. You may want to use it for protection if your house is damaged. But if you are at work, or if you have special orders, carry on as long as possible and only take cover when danger approaches. If you are on your way to work, finish your journey if you can.

If you see an enemy tank, or a few enemy soldiers, do not assume that the enemy are in control of the area. What you have seen may be a party sent on in advance, or stragglers from the main body who can easily be rounded up.

'It may easily be some weeks before the invader has been totally destroyed, that is to say, killed or captured to the last man who has landed on our shores. Stand Firm,' advised the Beating the Invader leaflet.

The ringing of church bells was prohibited on 13 June – except to raise the alarm if Luftwaffe paratroops started to descend from the sky. Everyone was encouraged to be on their guard against anything suspicious. They were ordered to refuse directions to anyone who was unable to produce official ID. Car owners were told to remove the rotor arm from their vehicles to disable them. If drivers didn't do this, policemen had the power to slash their tyres. From October 1939, citizens of all ages had to produce a National Registration Identity Card if challenged by a policeman.

State authority went into overdrive and key civil liberties were suspended. The Emergency Powers (Defence) Act, which was first introduced in 1939, was extended on 22 May 1940. This followed a debate by Churchill's new cabinet on the 18th that considered 'The Invasion of Great Britain and the possible co-operation of a 5th Column'. It was widely believed that German collaborators and saboteurs had greatly aided the Nazi advance through France. Even General Weygand had partly blamed his country's collapse on the streams of terrified refugees who blocked French roads, denying them to his troops. The British sympathized and many were infected with 'Fifth Column Fever'. The amended act enabled the Government to exercise 'complete control' over its citizens. People were compelled 'to place themselves, their services, and their property at the disposal of His Majesty'. Ernest Bevin, the new Minister of Labour, was given complete control of employment by the act, enabling in particular the increased conscription of women into the arms factories, most of which operated continuously. On 28 May, the Home Secretary, Sir John Anderson, recommended the introduction of press censorship. This was largely to shut down *Action*, the newspaper of Oswald Mosley's British Union of Fascists, and the Communist Party's *Daily Worker* (there was still a non-aggression treaty between Germany and the Soviet Union). His recommendations were ratified the next day and accordingly the Government gained control of all propaganda. Non-political organizations, including the Peace Pledge Union, were proscribed from distributing their pacifist flyers.

There was little cross-party opposition to the sudden – almost totalitarian – increase in state control. Indeed, in July, the Minister of Labour, Ernest Bevin, another Labour MP, was given the power, under regulation Reg. 58(AA), to prevent lock-outs, trade disputes and strikes. The fifteen Conservative, four Labour and one Liberal members of Churchill's cabinet represented the suspension of the unusual adversarial nature of British politics 'for the duration', though Parliament remained as free as ever to question the Government. In his autobiography the wartime Labour MP Emanuel Shinwell (in 1940 a rising Labour MP and from 1942 onwards chairman of the Labour

Ready for anything. This British infantryman stands poised to challenge an intruder outside a government building. Of interest is the fearsome 16-inch bayonet, which extends the soldier's reach to 6 feet. His gas cape is neatly rolled up on the top of his small pack.

Home Guards in the Edinburgh area organized a motor boat patrol for use on the canals and waterways in their district. In London the Upper Thames Patrol (UTP) even had their own smart brass badge to wear on their field service caps.

Home Guards advancing with vigour and brandishing Tommy guns (the 'Chicago Piano') fixed with the larger capacity fifty-round drum magazine. Because of the possibility of a misfire, soldiers were told not to force in an additional round. The box magazine held twenty rounds.

committee that created the 'Let us face the future' manifesto that helped his party win a landslide victory in 1945) said:

> The extreme danger in which Britain found herself after May 1940 and the general relief at the formation of a coalition government eased the clash of party politics both in the country and at Westminster, but the fact remains that for the duration of hostilities the administration was not only largely Tory but Tory in its policy.

Even the general election scheduled for 1940 was postponed by an amendment to the Septennial Act of 1716. PAYE and Purchase Tax, the forerunner of VAT, were both introduced in 1940.

As in the Great War, a Ministry of Information (MOI) was established when hostilities began. During the Second World War its bosses included Lord Macmillan, a former Scottish Lord Advocate, the BBC's John Reith, and journalist Brendan Bracken. Together with another ministry, the Political Warfare Executive (PWE), which took care of disseminating British propaganda abroad, these organizations were responsible for the production of hundreds of leaflets and posters during the war years. On 11 June, the then Minister for Information, Alfred Duff Cooper, had reported to the Home Policy Committee that the intelligence services were growing concerned about the widespread rumours of German landings and their effect on national morale. So regulation 39(BA) made it an offence to spread alarming rumours. A few civilians with loose tongues were duly reported for cynical speculation and some even went to prison. The Government also instituted the 'Silent Column', a patronizing propaganda campaign that featured within its ranks 'Miss Leaky Mouth' and 'Mr Secrecy Hush-Hush'.

One government scheme that did work, and protected city dwellers, particularly children, to boot, was evacuation. It was a well prepared plan. Britain had long been divided into 'Evacuation', 'Neutral' and 'Reception' areas in preparation for the evacuation of children. Like the blackout, this commenced immediately after the declaration of war. The Government, fearing an immediate and devastating aerial bombardment, had made billeting provision for 5,000,000 evacuees. By the end of September 1939, nearly 3,500,000 citizens had taken advantage of this. But, just as the compulsory carrying of gas masks had become a chore, by the summer of 1940 the appeal of evacuation had paled and by April 1940, 700,000 evacuees had returned home.

However, there were also some forced evacuations. Late in May 1940, British fascists were rounded up, principally the British Union of Fascists' leader, Sir Oswald Mosley, and thirty-three of his supporters.

Some were erstwhile colleagues of the German sympathizer William Joyce, who, as 'Lord Haw-Haw', broadcast pro-Nazi radio propaganda to Britain from Berlin throughout the war. Those classed as 'aliens' were categorized A, B or C, depending on how long they had lived in Britain, their 'specialist military knowledge that could be used to hinder the war effort' and their loyalty to the crown. Most 'aliens', of course, were of German, Austrian or Italian descent. Some 60,000, ironically mostly Jews fleeing Nazi oppression on the Continent, were interned in detention camps on the Isle of Man. In May alone, some 3,000 'foreigners' were forcibly detained. Some were actually serving in His Majesty's armed forces. One Royal Artillery gunner was apprehended after his return from Dunkirk and an Army lieutenant was even arrested while on parade. In June 1940, the *Arandora Star* set sail for Canada with nearly 1,200 internees packed on board. It was torpedoed by a German U-boat off the coast of Ireland on 2 July at 6.00 am, and more than 600 internees were drowned. Public opinion quickly turned from 'intern the lot' to 'free them now' and by early August the Government began investigating release categories. Originally, Churchill had supported such detentions, but, due to their random and unfeeling nature, the total failure of Germany's spy network plans and the success of Britain's 'Double Cross' counter-espionage initiative, which 'turned' all active Nazi agents in Britain, they became so unnecessary that he eventually referred to the process as 'in the highest degree odious'.

Perhaps Churchill's most significant change to the running of government was in the way he forged close links with the armed services. As Minister of Defence as well as Prime Minister, Churchill was the CEO of the War Cabinet and the Chiefs of Staff Committee – a unique position of power that curiously paralleled Hitler's status as absolute war lord. Unlike the Führer, however, Churchill knew that any of his decisions could be tempered by the democratic veto of his parliamentary colleagues. He saw nothing wrong with one man wielding executive power. Indeed, at times of national crisis he thought it essential, especially 'when a man knows what orders should be given.' In one of his many memos to General Ismay, his representative on the Chiefs of Staff Committee, Churchill insisted that, even during these frenetic times, he would accept no responsibility for decisions he had allegedly given if there was no written record of them. Not surprisingly, considering Churchill's fertile imagination and active interest in all things to do with Britain's war effort, his staff had their work cut out recording everything. Churchill awoke at 8.00 am, read the various despatches that had been placed before him and immediately began to dictate a 'continuous flow of minutes and directives'. One, a minute to the Chiefs of Staff (COS)

Camouflaged pillbox. Today we are used to seeing these brick and concrete relics of Britain's last-ditch defence in 1940 in drab, grey monochrome. However, during wartime they were often painted and camouflaged, like the example shown here.

Some surviving pillboxes display evidence of more careful and leisurely construction than others. This particularly neatly pointed one covers the approaches to Redhill Aerodrome in Surrey.

Built in 1942, this concrete gun emplacement near Pulborough Station in West Sussex overlooked both the railway line and the arterial A29, both of which crossed the river Arun, which looped through the flat flood plain beyond. Though marshy, this terrain would have been easily crossed by panzers and might even have been subject to glider-borne attack. Little more than a concrete shield, the emplacement housed a French Hotchkiss anti-tank gun, a relic of the BEF's brief activity on the Continent when, because it lacked enough of its own weapons, it was issued with a number of Canons de 25, which became known as Anti-Tank Gun, 25mm Hotchkiss, Mark I in British service.

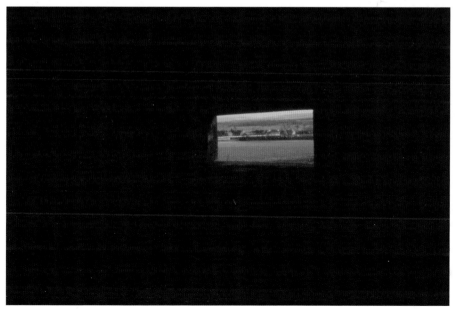

on 28 June, reminded them of the enemy 'trick of wearing British uniform'. He later said that in a total war it was quite impossible to draw a 'precise line between military and non-military problems'.

Churchill famously said, 'The only thing that ever really frightened me during the war was the U-boat peril.' He went on to explain that, even before the Luftwaffe started to lose the air war during the Battle of Britain, he was sure that a German invasion would fail. He, like others in Britain, had painful memories of Germany's U-47 torpedoing the battleship *Royal Oak* shortly after the war started. Churchill's warm relationship with President Roosevelt and the 'Lend-Lease' agreement, which enabled Britain to procure armaments from isolationist America on 'tick', were key confidence builders but a letter to Roosevelt in July 1940 confirmed Churchill's fears about the danger of unrestricted U-boat warfare. 'The Germans have the whole French coastline from which to launch U-boat and dive-bomber attacks upon our trade and food,' he wrote. In 1940, aircraft of sufficient duration to be able to patrol the mid-Atlantic didn't exist. Consequently, many British convoys were largely unprotected from enemy attack. Until countermeasures were devised, another maritime weapon employed by the Germans, the magnetic mine, further reduced the amount of usable imports to Britain. Food and materials became increasingly scarce. Foreseeing this, the Government had printed millions of ration books before hostilities commenced and food rationing was introduced in 1940. Clothing was rationed the following year. Citizens depended on having sufficient coupons in their ration books (the appropriate amount was torn out with each purchase) or had to resort to 'spivs' and the black market for unregulated supplies. Those in the country, who could grow their own vegetables, were more fortunate. 'Dig for Victory' quickly became the call to action of the age.

Early in 1940, Tom Harrisson's Mass Observation organization, which had been busily recording national demographics and social trends since the Depression, managed to receive partial funding from the Ministry of Information. In his memoirs, the Minister of Information, Duff Cooper, recalled:

> It was alleged that I had instituted a system of espionage which gave certain people the right to pry into the affairs of their neighbours. 'Down with Cooper's Snoopers' became a slogan of the popular press.

Despite this, Mass Observation's researchers made some interesting discoveries. In mid-May 1940, even before the evacuation of the BEF from France, 'there was much talk of the possibility of the landing of troops by parachute.' One observer overheard the following conversation between a group of 'artisan class' men and women:

They'd just sort of come down and shoot you before you knew where you were. They come down in open spaces … machine guns and everything. … They want us women a bit. …

Along the south-eastern coast of England – the invasion coast – things changed rapidly. Those that could afford to voluntarily move inland did so. The deserted detached houses of the stars and business families who had chosen a second home among the villas and mansions of Kent and Sussex were hastily requisitioned. 'All the posh people got into any transport they could and scarpered,' I was told by a woman from Angmering, West Sussex. 'The Army requisitioned the big houses and took them over to avoid encampments that could be seen by the enemy from the air. Lorries were parked beneath trees to conceal them,' she added.

Because of the state of emergency, people were often asked to do strange things in the name of national security. One elderly lady I have interviewed is still so concerned about what her neighbours might think about the potential impropriety of her actions during the wartime emergency that she has demanded that I use only her Christian name. Now a retired housewife in the Littlehampton area, in 1940, Emma, the daughter of a market gardener, lived at home with her parents. Keen to contribute to the war effort, she applied to join the ATS but was turned down because of a weak heart. 'When all the other village girls joined up I also tried but was turned down, so I had to be content to grow food by day and undertake either ARP or Red Cross duties at night. This was not enough, it seems, as a very mistaken person sent me white feathers in the post, denoting I was afraid to join up,' she told me.

Everything was relatively quiet in the Littlehampton area where Emma lived until 'the fear of being invaded became very real. Our lads had been driven back and were being landed in very bad shape; everyone feared the Germans would follow within days. It was about this time when I was asked by a soldier if he could talk to me … he was very pale and had a very modulated voice.' Emma then explained how, over a game of cards, she was recruited for some very secret and special duties. 'It seemed I had been investigated: they knew I had been turned down for the ATS because of my disability and now he was offering me another way to serve. He showed me the notes that had been made about me and my family. He said I would have to trust him as he would be the only one I would ever meet. He only ever told me his first name. I asked "Why me?" and all I got back was that I had been hand-picked because I could keep my mouth shut. I was a good-looker and I mixed well. Plus, I knew this part of the coast like the back of my hand. I was unmarried and had a quick wit.'

Pyramidal dragons' teeth tank traps littered the British countryside in 1940. Some survive, like these in St Leonard's Forest, near Horsham, Sussex.

Coastal artillery batteries possessed insufficient ammunition for any live-ammunition practice. This ex-First World War ship's gun is at Newhaven Fort, Sussex.

Classic Player's cigarette cards from the late 1930s.

Two days later, after letting Emma think things over, the stranger, a British officer dressed as a private but wearing concealed badges of rank, returned and she signed the Official Secrets Act. Emma was employed within the regulations of the Emergency Powers Act.

She was immediately given her first assignment. In what she calls 'my little job', Emma was asked to keep an eye on the movements, morale and actions of all those new to her area – especially the Canadian soldiers who were concentrated in the part of Sussex where she lived. British soldiers were under scrutiny too. Some, from regiments with proud histories, were unhappy about the relative inaction of coastal defence duties. 'My job was to try and get them to tell me things they shouldn't have,' Emma told me. 'I asked them "Where are you stationed? How many in your battery, your unit, your platoon?" If they talked, the photos with either a tick or a cross were put in our "dead letter box" in a tree. Those with a cross were moved far away from the coast. Then I was given others. Sometimes it meant going to dances and chatting up a soldier I'd never met. These could be bad soldiers. Those with a chip on their shoulders. Or those that just couldn't follow orders.' During one such dance a particularly amorous Canadian soldier attacked her but she fought him off. Having previously received some basic training in self-defence she managed to badly scratch the soldier's face. In fact, he did rape another local girl later that evening and it was only because of Emma's scratches that he was apprehended.

She only ever saw her 'control' once more, at the war's end, when he burned her papers in front of her and released her from her duties. 'He looked so ill and told me that he only had a few weeks as he had cancer. I never met anyone else. It was all done by "understanding", and if you "understood", you were a good operative.' As far as 'suspect' local residents were concerned, Emma told me, 'I was ordered to meet someone and tell them they were needed elsewhere. It

'Today was the first big test of the clothes rationing scheme when the big stores all over London are at full pressure serving shoppers and settling their coupon problems.' This press photo dates from 1 June 1941, the day that clothes rationing was introduced.

was the "official" reason for getting them out of the area. There were "sleepers" along the coast that were put here before the war.' It is because of this aspect of her wartime duties – which sometimes led to families being evicted and moved on without the right of appeal – that she is so secretive about her past. 'Nobody suspected anything – I could never be pinned down to regular hours because of my ARP and Red Cross work.' However, the animosity from neighbours who didn't think Emma was pulling her weight continued. 'They always resented the fact that I wasn't in the forces. The woman whose mother sent me the white feather is still alive,' was Emma's last word on the subject.

The response to Secretary of State for War Anthony Eden's 14 May appeal for volunteers to join the ranks of the newly formed Local Defence Volunteers (LDV) was phenomenal. The LDV's name was formally changed to 'Home Guard' on 23 July 1940, after Churchill first coined the phrase during a BBC broadcast. On 3 August, the Home Guard was given approval to adopt the county titles of local regiments. Police stations quickly ran out of application forms. The decision to do without fully detailed records of each applicant was an enlightened one that sped up the recruitment process. By July, a million and a half men had volunteered. Soon 'parashots', trained to pot enemy paratroops when at their most vulnerable – hanging suspended from their canopies – patrolled fields and golf courses. General Henry Pownall, previously Chief of Staff to Lord Gort in France, was the LDV's first Inspector General, a position Churchill regarded as a reward for his recent exemplary service. Gort, on the other hand, was rather unceremoniously packed off to be Governor of Malta. It is doubtful that Pownall saw his new appointment as an accolade, though, for on 20 June he noted in his diary:

This party [the LDV], already over half a million strong, was started some five weeks ago by an announcement in the House of Commons by Eden, without I gather enough time for previous thought by the War Office or GHQ Home Forces. ... The result, of course, is that it is a rare 'Dog's dinner' now.

By the end of June 1940, the force had swollen to 1,456,000 volunteers, and from August the (by now Home Guard) battalions were affiliated directly to the regiments of the counties in which the units were formed.

The LDV employed a variety of inventive and lethal weapons. These included the 'Fougasse', which was buried beneath sand bags at the side of the road. With the tug of a cord this lethal ambush weapon shot a jet of flaming petroleum jelly into the path of oncoming vehicles. The 'Sticky Bomb' was another. An ingenious idea of Churchill's, the Sticky

Bomb looked like a large toffee apple, but the mastic-type wrapping that covered the weapon enabled it to adhere to enemy tanks. Albright and Wilson (AW) phosphorus bombs were hand-thrown incendiaries that further supplemented the LDV armoury. AW bombs could easily be thrown at an advancing enemy patrol or vehicle. Because they were in short supply, LDV patrols seldom had the luxury of 'drill rounds' to practise with but patrols did try to rehearse bomb throwing if they could. To this day, smudgy black stains, high upon the walls adjoining the school classrooms or village halls within which the eager volunteers trained, are a legacy of the training that took place with these 'Molotov cocktails'. Whilst the LDV wasn't quite the 'dad's army' of popular fiction, its hastily collected armoury – a mixture of sporting and First World War vintage weapons and rifles from the US of varying calibre – did lend an air of muddle to a very determined citizens' army.

Despite the proliferation of propaganda on the Home Front that warned of German airborne landings, neither Germany nor Britain (unlike the Soviet Union) possessed trained, combat-ready paratroops and the British authorities never seriously expected an airborne assault. Surely if enough stout-hearted patriots blocked its path the invasion would falter? Readers of *Your Answer to Invasion* (the art of physical defence and attack practically explained and illustrated by James Hipkiss, Britain's Ju-Jitsu champion) were told, 'Should invasion come, the part which unarmed combat must play in the overthrow of the invader is rapidly being realized by the public,' and, 'Even if invasion never comes, the importance of unarmed combat is never likely again to die out.'

Government and voluntary schemes abounded. The public was encouraged to take part in National Savings schemes or join with their local communities and club together to buy a Spitfire. The government-sponsored scheme that encouraged individuals to save scrap metal was really only a morale booster as the grade of alloy that resulted from melting down pots and pans was not of sufficient quality to make the main spars of fighters that travelled at speeds of more than 300 mph. The public was told that 'carless words cost lives' and that 'tittle-tattle lost the battle'. By modern standards some wartime posters were distinctly sexist: 'Keep mum – she's not so

Emma in her wartime ARP uniform.

dumb', featuring an alluring blonde, and 'Be like dad, keep mum'. Some posters were unsuccessful and provoked criticism. One that emphasized class divisions – 'Your Courage, Your Cheerfulness, Will bring us victory' – was deemed by the man in the street to suggest that it would be the suffering of the common people that would enable 'us', the Establishment, to prosper. Very soon the Government was forced to encourage the nation that everyone was 'in it together' and that all should 'do their bit'.

At the war's outbreak the Government had distributed a booklet entitled *National Service: A guide to the ways in which the people of this country may give service*. It called upon men and women who were 'eager to fit themselves voluntarily for National Service' and 'wondering how they can be most useful' to 'find the answer in this guide.' It listed endless opportunities but chastened readers by saying, 'The call is to peace and not to war. We have no thought of aggression; our one wish is to live at peace with all peoples.' By 1940 Britain was divided into twelve Civil Defence regions that fitted within the national Air Raid Precautions (ARP) network, first formed in 1935. The ARP warden service worked closely with civilian, police, fire brigade and medical services, and each 'sector' of 500 inhabitants was entitled to a senior warden who was assisted by two junior ranks. Part-time jobs could be had in first aid and within decontamination squads – fear of gas attack was to the citizens of 1940s' Britain what all-out nuclear war was to those of the 1960s. Jobs in Rescue and Demolition units, the Police War Reserve, the Women's Land Army, the Territorial Army and the Civil Air Guard were among the myriad other voluntary employment opportunities available. The voluntary Auxiliary Fire Service (AFS) supplemented the regional county fire brigades at a time when there was no national fire service. The Women's Royal Volunteer Service (WRVS), Fire Watchers, Fire Guards, Heavy-Rescue personnel and Shelter Wardens all joined the ranks of citizens who were keen to 'do their bit'. Conscription, first introduced in 1939, had, by the summer of 1940, swelled the Regular Army alone to 1,650,000 and 36,100 women enrolled in the Auxiliary Territorial Service (ATS). The Observer Corps, a network of volunteers who scanned the skies looking for enemy aircraft, were the first civilian volunteers to be armed. Two rifles were issued to

AFS fireman.

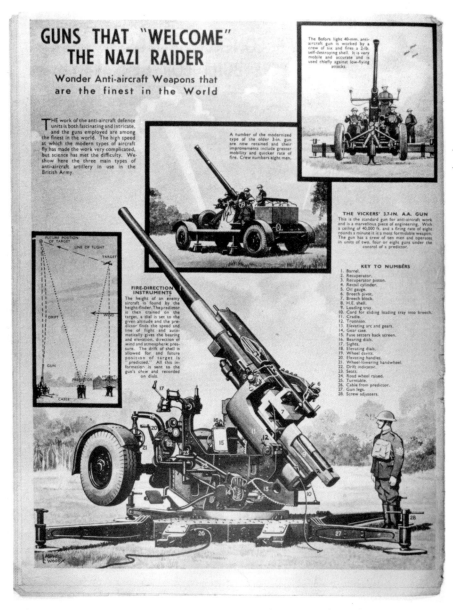

During the Blitz, Londoners slept more easily if they could hear the regular report of the large 3.7-inch anti-aircraft guns. In reality, the weapons hardly ever scored a direct hit against Nazi raiders.

A selection of home defence force armbands. In anticipation of thousands of victims after enemy bombing had begun, the Government went to great pains to ensure that regalia was available to denote 'official' helpers. As this Cornwall police messenger's armband clearly shows, 'Auxiliary' was a nondescript kind of word in common parlance in 1940.

units thought likely to be most at risk from an encounter with the invader. With their binoculars and trusty 'Micklethwaight Projector' (a Heath-Robinson contraption rigged together from parts of Meccano toy engineering sets and used to help plot the course of incoming enemy air raids), the Observer Corps consisted of some 27,900

Auxiliary Fire Service,
London, tunic emblem.

Typical Home Guard shoulder titles
for the 12th (London) Battalion.

Salvus breathing apparatus outfit – one of the proprietary brands that equipped Britain's still independent local authority fire brigades before they were unified into the National Fire Service after the Blitz.

personnel by June. On 15 May 1940, the following message was sent to all Observer Group centres and posts:

> As England is now within the range of hostile single-engined aircraft, single-engined aircraft from now on are not necessarily to be regarded as friendly.

So, if there was to be an invasion, how would it be launched and did Britain have the power to stop it? On 17 June, in response to a request by Churchill, the Chiefs of Staff Committee produced a report outlining Britain's chances of surviving a German invasion. Appropriately, the thirteenth paragraph read:

> Our conclusion is that, *prima facie*, Germany has most of the cards; but the real test is whether the morale of our fighting personnel and civil population will counterbalance the numerical and material advantages which Germany enjoys. We believe it will.

Sir Hastings Ismay, Churchill's representative on the Chiefs of Staff Committee, noted, 'The report contented Churchill, and the conclusion undoubtedly represented the views of the nation as a whole.'

Observer Corps volunteers scan the skies through binoculars, ready to compute range and altitude with the help of their Heath-Robinsonesque Micklethwaight Projector.

The following day, 18 June, after a frantic trip to Bordeaux to meet with the remnants of the French Government to prevent its still intact navy falling into Nazi hands, Churchill told the nation:

> What General Weygand called the Battle of France is over. I expect that the Battle of Britain is about to begin. … Let us therefore brace ourselves to our duties, and so bear ourselves that, if the British Empire and its Commonwealth last for a thousand years, men will say, 'This was their finest hour'.

Chapter 2

Britain's Guerrillas

I have been following with much interest the growth and development of the new guerrilla formations ... known as 'Auxiliary Units'. From what I hear these units are being organized with thoroughness and imagination and should, in the event of invasion, prove a useful addition to the regular forces.

Churchill to Eden, 25 September 1940

A s soon as it became apparent to Churchill that Hitler might launch an invasion of Britain after Dunkirk – 'that the man was going to try', as the premier put it – urgent thought had to be given to every aspect of home defence. Any effort that could reinforce the Spartan regular resources available was worthy of serious consideration. If a stay-behind resistance force, which would slow down advancing enemy troops and grant the Regular Army time to mount a counter-attack, was to be created, what form should it take? Were there any existing organizations or types of irregular warfare on which it could be based?

Although Britain was the first country in modern times to organize an underground resistance movement in advance of invasion and enemy occupation, the idea of irregular resistance was not new. Tacitus highlighted the difficulties that faced Julius Caesar's armies as they invaded England:

The troops, besides being ignorant of the locality, had their hands full; weighted with a mass of heavy armour, they had to jump from their ships, stand firm in the surf, and fight at the same time. But the enemy knew their ground; they could fire their weapons boldly from dry land. They watched the men disembark in small parties, moved down, attacked them as they straggled through the surf, and surrounded them with superior numbers while others opened fire on the exposed flanks of the isolated units.

The iconic image of the BEF infantryman stranded on the beaches of Dunkirk and with only his rifle to fend off marauding Luftwaffe Stuka dive-bombers was an enduring one.

More recently, the Boer Commandos taught the British the value of units that operated behind the enemy's front line and were able to melt into their surroundings after they had attacked. Indeed, in the dark days following Dunkirk, Lieutenant Colonel Dudley Clarke RE, a South African who had been weaned on the exploits of the Boer Commandos and was now on Sir John Dill's staff (CIGS immediately before Alan Brooke), had written a paper for Churchill and the War Cabinet in which he recommended the adoption of Boer tactics. T.E. Lawrence ('Lawrence of Arabia') also had a profound influence on British military strategists. From 1916, his command of King Faisal's Arab levies, the irregular supplement to General Allenby's troops during the campaign against the Turkish occupation of Arabia, culminated in the triumphal Allied entry to Damascus in 1918. Lawrence showed that properly led, lightly-armed troops fighting for a cause they passionately believed in were more than a match for an invader unfamiliar with the territory of the battlefield. In the *Seven Pillars of Wisdom*, Lawrence said that initially Faisal's 'only effective tactics against the enemy had been to chase in suddenly upon their rear by fast, mounted charges, and many camels had been killed or wounded or worn out in these expensive measures.' As Lawrence evolved new methods of irregular warfare he found that:

> The Arab's physical perfection let them lie relaxed to the stony ground like lizards, moulding themselves to its roughness in corpse-like abandon. ... The smaller the unit the better its performance ... three or four Arabs in their hills would stop a dozen Turks.

The activities of T.E. Lawrence were to have a profound influence on many of the British soldiers engaged in the formation of the Auxiliaries. Indeed, some had actually met him or knew many of the artists and writers that tended towards a similar view and understanding of the changing nature of warfare in the modern world.

Not surprisingly it was the oriental mind that first committed to paper such theorizing about balance and proportion. In around 500 BC, in his *Art of War*, the Chinese philosopher and military strategist Sun Tzu precisely summed up the principles of what would ultimately be known as irregular warfare. He wrote:

> Now all war is based in deception. Move when it is advantageous, and create changes in the situation by dispersal and concentration of forces.

By 1940, Sun Tzu's theories had found a new audience in Britain.

The Germans were not without their theorists either. Soldiers of the Oberkommando des Heeres (OKH) who stepped ashore or landed by parachute in Britain in 1940 would have no doubt been familiar with the writings of an illustrious predecessor of their own. He also argued that even when outnumbered the defender often had the advantage. In *On War*, written in 1832, Karl von Clausewitz, Marshal Blucher's Prussian adviser during the Napoleonic Wars, noted a warning to invading armies:

> Countless minor incidents – the kind you can never really foresee – combine to lower the general level of performance, so that one always falls far short of the intended goal.

His thoughts served as encouragement to outnumbered defenders, for he argued that they were capable of sowing mayhem and disillusionment among the larger armies of their opponents:

> So long as a unit fights cheerfully, with spirit and élan, great strength will rarely be needed, but once conditions become difficult … things no longer run like a well-oiled machine.

Events nearer to home also served to show the British how ineffective 'foreign' regular forces were when pitted against irregulars fighting for a cause in their own country. Sinn Fein's leader, Michael Collins, the 'Big Fellow', as he was known to his supporters, ran rings around the British Army in the south of Ireland from the Easter Uprising of 1916, when he was a member of the underground Irish Republican Brotherhood. Later, when he was director of intelligence within the IRA, his spy network proved to be far superior to that organized from London. His ruthless determination to end British sovereignty in Ireland eventually led to a treaty with Britain in 1921 and the establishment of the Irish Free State.

On 29 June, the Secretary of State for War, Anthony Eden, visited XII Corps, commanded by Lieutenant General Andrew Thorne, and was so alarmed by what he considered to be a reckless lack of heavy weaponry – 'no anti-tank regiment nor anti-tank gun in the whole of the Corps area' – that he reported the situation to Churchill. On 30 June, Thorne was ordered by Churchill to come to lunch at Chequers, where he pointed out the very vulnerable position XII Corps was in. Covering Kent, Sussex and parts of Hampshire and Surrey and responsible for the entire coastal strip from Greenwich to Hayling Island, XII Corps consisted of only one fully-trained division, the 3rd, which was due to be sent to Northern Ireland. Churchill said he was not confident British troops could adequately defend all the English beaches and pointed out that, 'A river line has never proved a real obstacle to an enemy.' Perhaps after surveying just exactly what weapons the British, Commonwealth and Continental troops (who had escaped from France with the BEF) could realistically bring to bear against the invader, Churchill's famous exhortation for all citizens to fight on the beaches if necessary, was not political rhetoric after all.

Although no detailed record of the lunch at Chequers was kept, in *The Fringes of Power*, Sir John Colville, Churchill's Private Secretary, who was present at the meeting, noted:

> Thorne thinks 80,000 men will be landed on the beaches between Thanet and Pevensy (which is Thorne's area); Winston is less pessimistic and thinks the Navy will have much to say to this. W. is not sanguine about our ability to hold the whole expanse of beaches and points out that a river line has never proved a real obstacle to an enemy. ... Thorne, who was military attaché in Berlin, is convinced that the Germans, acting according to their rule, will concentrate all their forces against one place, even if they make feints elsewhere.

Following the meeting, Churchill ordered that the 3rd Division should remain under Thorne's command, and the next day he instructed General Ismay (the Prime Minister's representative on the Chiefs of Staff Committee) to evaluate the practicality of 'drenching' the invasion beaches with mustard gas. The premier had told Thorne, 'I have no scruples, except not to do anything dishonourable.'

The lunch at Chequers was to have even more far-reaching effects, for it revived an idea that General Thorne had first considered years before – the formation of a 'stay-behind' guerrilla resistance force in Britain.

When Thorne had been British military attaché in Berlin in the mid-1930s, he had been impressed by the existence of a peasant militia that had, since the time of Frederick the Great, promised, as a condition of their tenancy, to muster when ordered in order to defend their landlord's estates. They were not expected to count for much in direct combat with a superior invader, but since they had intimate knowledge of their terrain, and had stockpiled secret arms caches, they were reckoned to present an obstacle out of all proportion to their strength.

After meeting Churchill, Thorne got in touch with General Ismay. He raised his idea for a covert resistance force based on the kind of thing he had witnessed in pre-war Germany and was told that a young officer who worked within military intelligence would come and see him to discuss matters further. The officer Ismay had in mind was none other than Peter Fleming, the traveller, author, special correspondent for *The Times* and brother of James Bond's creator, Ian Fleming.

Peter Fleming worked for MI(R) (Military Intelligence (Research)), a semi-secret department within the War Office. Back in May, John Colville had noted in his diary:

> Awoke thinking unaccountably of Peter Fleming's book *Flying Visit* and daydreaming of what would happen if we captured Goering during one of his alleged flights over London.

It is a nice coincidence that Fleming had written a novel about a Nazi invasion of Britain, an area in which he was later to become so intimately involved.

A former Regular Guards officer, Fleming was still on the Army reserve list. Well travelled, well educated and self-confident ex-soldiers of his calibre are always in short supply, but they are of special importance during times of mobilization. Following the success of his most recent work, *News from Tartary*, which documented Fleming's experiences on his 3,500-mile trek between Peking and Kashmir, where he saw the Red Armies 'making legendary night marches, sustaining defeat only in the columns of the press,' he was considered to be something of an expert on both China and unconventional warfare. Living rough wasn't a problem for him either: his acclaimed *Brazilian Adventure* testified to his exploits in the inhospitable surroundings of the Amazon Jungle.

In 1939, Fleming had written 'Notes on the Possibilities of British Military Action in China' for MI(R), into which he and others had been covertly recruited in 1938. MI(R) considered Fleming to be the best candidate to establish a British guerrilla unit, in particular one that would comprise men who could live off the land. So in a secluded farmhouse called The Garth, in Kent, Fleming set up the first regional training centre for a new, British, 'stay-behind' force. This, the first 'Auxiliary Unit', was known by the cover name 'XII Corps Observation Unit'.

In July 2011, I visited The Garth, Peter Fleming's brick and half-timber farmhouse at Bilting, a village between Canterbury and Ashford on the A28 road. John Warwicker recounts that Peter Fleming had a habit of tossing live fuses with detonators and, perhaps, even time pencils into the huge inglenook fireplace in the main hall. Certainly, even though the house was being extensively – and sympathetically, I might add – renovated by the current owners, this grand building, which sits on a grassy wooded hillside, seems to be redolent with the spirit of the early Auxiliers who gathered there.

Wartime home to Peter Fleming, the brother of James Bond creator Ian, The Garth, now known as Bilting Court and being heavily renovated by its current owners, was the scene of some of the earliest Auxiliary Unit activity. Fleming, then a captain in the Grenadier Guards, was tasked with building on General Thorne's XII Corps Observation Unit in Kent. He created something much bigger and, in partnership with Captain Mike Calvert of the Royal Engineers, some seconded regular soldiers and two Lovat Scout NCOs set about turning The Garth into a university for mayhem.

It would be useful to consider some of the background details of the intelligence world, including MI(R)'s involvement in irregular warfare, before we look at the Auxunits in sharper focus. It is also important to take into account the sense of paranoia that swept through Britain's High Command in June 1940, as things went equally badly wrong for the BEF in France. Britain's erroneous belief that a subversive Fifth Column in civilian clothes somehow conspired in the downfall of Poland, Norway, Denmark, the Low Countries and France is the final ingredient in this unfolding tale.

Peter Fleming's MI(R) was merely one of the many departments within Britain's intelligence community in 1940. British secret intelligence for both the Government and the military had long experience of covert operations. The Special Intelligence Service MI6, for example, had existed since 1909. Although, by 1940, the Security Service (MI5) and MI6 were numbered among other departments within the Directorate of Military Intelligence (DMI), in reality, MI5 reported to the Home Office and MI6 to the Foreign Office (FO). MI6 gathered intelligence that had a bearing on Britain's international relations and it included sections from the Army, Navy and Air Force. The Foreign Office paid MI6's bills and took political responsibility for it on condition that it passed on any political intelligence, employed its own staff and was physically distinct from the FO's own administration. The FO equally expected the DMI to keep out of politics! MI5, the Security Service, took care of domestic intelligence gathering – in fact, anything up to 5 miles from Britain's coast.

The DMI had expanded greatly since the outbreak of war in 1939. Previously it had been under the command of Lieutenant General Sir Henry Pownall, who was director of both 'operations' and 'intelligence' at the War Office (DMO & I). On the outbreak of war the directorate was split into two distinct parts, one for operations, and the other for intelligence. Pownall's fast ascending career continued on the up and up when he left the DMI to become Chief of Staff of the BEF in September 1939. Pownall's deputy, Major General F.G. Beaumont-Nesbitt, became the new Director of Military Intelligence. Between 1936 and 1938, he had been the British military attaché in Paris and so had wide experience of the intrigues within European politics. Upon his return to Britain in 1938 – the year of the Munich crisis, when many observers thought war with Germany would break out – Beaumont-Nesbitt put his important position within the intelligence community to good use. He was convinced, as were many, that war with Hitler was inevitable.

In her book *The Inner Circle*, Joan Bright Astley – that rare thing in the late 1930s, a female executive assistant within the British intelligence community – recalls Beaumont-Nesbitt combing the Army reserve lists for executives, writers, explorers, linguists and experts on foreign countries who might be put to good use within military intelligence should war come. 'He was determined to be ready with the right replacements,' she wrote, 'in his bearing a typical Guards officer, in his actions perspicacious.' It was from this initial selection that men of the resourcefulness of Peter Fleming and the Arctic explorer Martin Lindsay (about whom we will hear later) were recruited. After a series of informal discussions the recruits engaged in some after-hours training and were indoctrinated into the dark arts of military intelligence.

Department 'E.H.', Section D and MI(R) were the three departments that were most actively dedicated to methods of actually 'fighting' an enemy, both physically and by employing economic sanctions or propaganda (MI5 & MI6 were principally engaged in covert surveillance and intelligence gathering). After Hitler's *Anschluss* with Austria in 1938, the Government decided to encourage the Foreign

Office to set up a semi-secret department designed to subvert, via propaganda, the morale of the Third Reich's military machine. The new department, formed by Lord Hankey, employed Sir Campbell Stuart, a former editor of *The Times*, as its first chief. It was originally called C.S., after its boss. Soon it became known as Department EH, after its HQ, Electra House, on the Thames, within the City of London.

Major Laurence Grand RE had set up Section D of the Secret Intelligence Service (SIS) within the Foreign Office. This was a unit established to investigate unconventional ways to fight an enemy and was principally concerned with sabotage. (Grand had fought with Lawrence of Arabia and actually won the DFC when an airman in the RFC!) Grand's Section D was encouraged to determine the best ways of attacking a potential enemy 'by means other than the operation of military forces'. Section D helped to invent plastic explosives and made the best time fuses available. It liaised directly with yet another secret agency – General Staff (Research).

GS(R) was a section of the War Office set up in 1937 by the Deputy Chief of the Imperial General Staff, Sir Ronald Adam. After Munich GS(R) was asked to investigate fighting Germany by three methods: Royal Navy blockade; RAF bombing; and – until the Regular Army could be brought up to strength – well planned irregular or guerrilla warfare. Essentially, GS(R) was a kind of think tank that enabled bright young officers to spend a year investigating modern topics that had relevance to the new army. Reports were prepared for such diverse departments as the Army's Medical and Education Services. In 1938, Holland was appointed to study the techniques of guerrilla warfare that Britain might employ in the support of the many resistance movements that were bound to spring up in Eastern Europe should Hitler's expected quest for '*Lebensraum*' in Russia result in the Nazi occupation of the region. At that stage, such were official sensitivities about any suggestion of British militarism that no mention was ever made of a future Regular Army commitment to forthcoming European conflicts that did not directly threaten the defence of the realm. As Britain's Military Intelligence Directorate was expanded in the spring of 1939, GS(R) changed its name to 'Military Intelligence (Research)'. Interestingly, in November 1918, in the wake of the Russian Revolution, a different organization within the DMI called MI(R) already existed. But that MI(R) dealt with intelligence gathered from Eastern Europe (specifically Russia), Central Asia and the Far East.

In 1939, MI(R) was, like Section D, commanded by a Royal Engineer, Colonel J.F.C. Holland. Holland's MI(R) had been busy developing weapons that might be useful for guerrillas fighting behind enemy lines. MI(R) created many novel things, including the 'Blacker Bombard', a close-combat anti-tank mortar invented by an ex-Indian

Army gunner, L.V.S. Blacker, who had also experienced close combat with the Bolsheviks at Archangel. At the war's beginning, MI(R) mostly concerned itself with mines and anti-tank weapons. In 1939, an MI(R) notification said:

> If guerrilla warfare is co-ordinated and also related to main operations it should, in favourable circumstances, cause such a diversion of enemy strength as eventually to present decisive opportunities to the main forces.

MI(R)'s involvement with guerrilla warfare, and its special weapons development work, would create equipment that was ultimately to supplement the Home Guard's arsenal. Holland had also started up a variety of secret sections – one of them, MI9, the Escape Service, had developed magnetic escape compasses for shot-down pilots that were fashioned into trouser fly buttons for concealment. During the 1930s, Holland had made a study of Boer tactics and the methods used by guerrillas during the Spanish Civil War, Sino-Japanese conflict and Ireland's 'Troubles'.

MI(R) essentially undertook 'uniformed' activities and its personnel were nominally part of the British armed services and could expect the protection under law of a regular soldier. Section D was involved primarily in undercover endeavours – the 'sleuth' work of popular fiction. The Government would never acknowledge the activities of its spies and saboteurs and if they were caught they could expect no official protection. The fact that three distinct organizations – EH, Section D and MI(R) – were doing such similar work appears confusing now and in 1939 it seemed no less of a muddle. Indeed, as early as March 1939, the CIGS, Lord Gort, and the Foreign Secretary, Lord Halifax, and an unnamed official from the SIS first considered the integration of the three organizations into a single department, which, as we shall see, eventually became the famous Special Operations Executive. However, the outbreak of hostilities with Germany six months later temporarily relegated the subject to the back burner.

By 1940, Britain possessed a complete armoury of departments capable of adapting the machinery of state – in all its aspects – to counter the new kind of warfare that harnessed political and economic rather than purely military techniques. Furthermore, the idea of employing 'economic warfare' (reducing the enemy's morale) was given official credence on 3 September 1939, the day Britain declared war against Nazi Germany, with the formation of a government department: the Ministry of Economic Warfare (MEW).

One of the MI(R)'s personnel was Colin Gubbins. In the spring of 1939 he worked on *Guerrilla Field Service Regulations*, which Lord Gort had asked Holland's department to prepare that April. Gubbins wrote three booklets: *The Partisan Leader's Handbook*, *The Art of Guerrilla Warfare* and *How to Use High Explosives*. In July 1939, Gubbins was told that on mobilization he was to be the senior staff officer (GSO 1) to the British military mission in Poland and would be in overall control of the large MI(R) contingent there.

After the Soviet invasion of Finland in November 1939 there was widespread sympathy and admiration in Britain for the beleaguered Finns. France had even considered the possibility of a massive pincer movement against the Soviet Union using French forces that would be sent to Finland and those in Syria, commanded by General Weygand. This two-pronged assault would attack Baku on the Caspian in the south – seizing the Soviet oil fields there – and threaten Moscow in the north. The French argued that a decisive operation in the Caspian and Black Seas would sever Germany's petroleum supplies and paralyze the economy of its Soviet ally. French politics was sharply polarized between left and right – the far left forbidding war with the Soviets (the Second International had expressly forbidden French Communists from fighting Soviet Russia) and the far right clamouring for a war that they thought would end the 'communist menace' once and for all. Many in France considered Russia a more suitable enemy than Germany. However, the extravagant plan to assault Soviet forces was

The Defence Committee of Churchill's War Cabinet. Ismay and Dill are standing second and third from the right respectively in the back row.

shelved when it was realized that it risked bringing Germany and Russia even closer together. For the time being at least, Russia was not directly in Anglo-French sights.

The British War Cabinet had drawn up less ambitious plans to aid the Finns. Some MI(R) officers had observed how the white-clad Finnish troops had staged successful guerrilla operations against the Soviets. Colonel Holland was even given permission to send an MI(R) ski team to Finland. That country's successes, even though few in number and with troops that lacked most of the essential equipment for tackling modern armies, made a great impression on MI(R)'s observers. Finnish tactics were even carefully noted by the officers of the invading Soviet armies. One, Vyaschlev Oreshin, attached to the Red Army's propaganda brigade, wrote:

> The men have lain in the snow for three days and didn't dare lift their heads. ... The butchers are accustomed to fire carefully at our troops from the side of the road.

As soon as Finland surrendered on 12 March 1940, any thoughts of commencing a second front and picking a fight with another enemy disappeared. However, the skills of the Finnish Irregulars were not forgotten by the observers from MI(R).

On 11 April 1940, British troops commanded by General P.J. Macksey set sail for Norway and a combination of British, French, Polish and Norwegian forces attempted to eject the Germans from Narvik – Norway's only all-weather port. Despite successful action from the Royal Navy between 10-13 April, from an Allied point of view the operation went disastrously wrong.

Britain's Norwegian Expeditionary Force was supplemented by 'Independent Companies', fighters trained in a new kind of irregular warfare, an idea of MI(R)'s. In December 1939, Churchill, one of the few 'hawks' in Chamberlain's War Cabinet, declared to his colleagues, 'If land operations become necessary, it would be perfectly feasible to land British and French troops in Norway.' In March 1940, MI(R) was asked to evaluate plans for an amphibious raid on Norway and in April 1940, after the German invasion, Colonel Holland, who had already been studying the possibility of MI(R) involvement there, withdrew Gubbins (by now a Lieutenant Colonel) from Paris and asked him to select and prepare assault troops for amphibious raids in support of the Anglo-French expedition.

Inverailort, in Scotland's Western Highlands, was chosen as the training base for this new force, codenamed 'Scissorforce'. Each Independent Company comprised 270 other ranks and was led by twenty officers. Most of its personnel were recruited from the

Territorial Army. A single company employed experts from Army Signals and the Royal Engineers and was divided into three platoons that were each made up of three sections. Independent Companies were lightly armed but they did possess some Bren guns, mortars and one of the new Boys anti-tank rifles. Crucially, considering Gubbins' later activities, each Independent Company included a small nucleus of linguists who could encourage the local population to resist the German invasion. The first Independent Company – No. 1 – set sail on 1 May 1940 for its objective, Mo i Rana. 'Mo' was a strategically important town and harbour situated at the end of a typically rocky fjord south of Narvik, where Norway's waist tapers most and the Swedish border is closest. Gubbins' men were all trained in guerrilla warfare and the first five companies were to be reinforced by other Independent Companies that were then in training, the plan being for them to link up with the retreating Norwegian Army and threaten the German garrison.

Colonel Holland had sent some MI(R) officers to Norway prior to the German invasion. One of them, Peter Fleming, was later to be even more closely linked to Gubbins. At the Norwegian port of Namsos, Fleming came into contact with another 'personality' embroiled in the Norwegian campaign who knew Gubbins of old. He was the famous and strikingly charismatic General Adrian Carton de Wiart VC, who had been head of the British Military Mission in Poland. Gubbins had been de Wiart's senior staff officer in Warsaw during the German *blitzkrieg*. In his autobiography, *Happy Odyssey*, de Wiart recounts how he and Gubbins narrowly escaped Poland before Hitler's armies completely overran the country. After he had returned to Britain, de Wiart was again contacted by the War Office. 'It dawned on me the reason might be Norway, especially as I had never been there and knew nothing about it,' he recalled.

Carton de Wiart took up command of the Central Norwegian Expeditionary Force (codenamed 'Mauriceforce') on 14 April. He had assembled a unit that comprised British Territorials and French Chasseurs Alpins that were largely unfamiliar to him and he was told to organize a landing at the minor harbours of Namsos and Aalsund and then press on to Trondheim far to the south of Narvik. After his Sunderland flying boat was shot down on its approach to Namsos, de Wiart was taken on board a nearby British destroyer, where he met MI(R) Peter Fleming and Martin Lindsay (famous for his exploration of the Arctic). In his autobiography de Wiart recalled the two MI(R) officers:

Captain Martin Lindsay, explorer and traveller, picked up the bits where Peter Fleming left off. Whoever may have been responsible for sending them, I thank him now, for there and then I appropriated them and a better pair never existed. ... From being an adventurer and writer [Fleming] turned himself into general factotum number one. Peter Fleming managed to find us good billets in Namsos and a motor car with a driver.

Carton de Wiart made an equally strong impression with Fleming, who described the old warrior as having 'only one eye, only one arm, and – rather more surprisingly – only one Victoria Cross.'

Originally it was intended that de Wiart's Mauriceforce, by landing at Namsos, would co-operate in a pincer movement with another British unit, General Paget's 'Sickleforce', which landed far to the south at Andalsnesand. The two pincers were then supposed to outflank the German garrison at Trondheim in between. But, despite over-optimistic expectations from London, notably from Churchill, the attempt failed and de Wiart's men were withdrawn on 2 May 1940.

The Royal Navy's massive bombardment of Narvik on 3 June, which did terrible damage to her Norwegian allies, heralded Britain's retreat and the last British troops left Norway on 7 June. About the only consolation for the British from their operation in Norway was the fact that the German Navy (Kriegsmarine) was devastated. Three German cruisers and ten destroyers were eliminated from the Kriegsmarine's fleet. A further two cruisers and its precious battleship, *Scharnhorst*, were temporarily put out of action.

At this time Holland's idea of an organization that combined EH, Section D and MI(R) was revived and he and Beaumont-Nesbitt re-proposed their earlier scheme to Churchill. By now, however, their idea came into conflict with political necessity. Only the next month, the Special Operations Executive would be born. Control was to be taken away from the DMI, i.e. out of military hands, and given to politicians at the Ministry of Economic Warfare. Though he didn't then know it, Gubbins was to play a major part in SOE and his Independent Companies were to form the model for a new 'Special Forces' unit – Britain's Commandos.

With the Independent Companies the expertise of MI(R) had been finally put to the test and Major Gubbins had come to the fore. A Regular Gunner, born in 1896 in Japan, where his father was a diplomat, he had previously been on the staff of General Ironside (Britain's future Commander-in-Chief Home Forces) during the Archangel expedition of 1919. In 1919, Ironside, aged thirty-eight, was already a Brigadier General (Staff) and consequently closely involved with military intelligence. At Archangel Britain attempted to prevent the supplies it had sent to Tsarist White Russian forces from falling into the hands of the Bolsheviks, who had made a separate peace with

Germany. In 1921, in the Irish Free State, Gubbins was engaged against the IRA during the Irish Civil War. Both these experiences were to prove salutary for him. Before the war, Gubbins had been employed as an expert on irregular warfare. With Millis Jefferis – MI(R)'s explosives expert who had helped to develop Churchill's Sticky Bomb – he co-wrote *How to Use High Explosives*. All of the booklets were translated into foreign languages, including Czech, Danish, Dutch, French, Norwegian and even Chinese, but they were never published in England!

The contingency planning of the Director of Military Intelligence, Beaumont-Nesbitt, and the staff of MI(R) and Section D was soon put to good use on a new venture. Directly the Norwegian episode began to go wrong for the Allies, Whitehall began to seriously worry about the possibility of a dramatic reversal for the BEF in France and a subsequent German invasion of the United Kingdom. Although MI(R) was most suited to the study of guerrilla tactics, Laurence Grand's Section D was asked to investigate. However, his department simply succeeded in creating suspicion as they went about building 'secret' arms caches up and down the country. Complaints about Section D's actions had even reached General Ironside, who immediately decided that such activities must be co-ordinated by the military. So MI(R) was the ideal choice and Gubbins and Holland took over to sort it all out.

As soon as Gubbins had returned from Norway, Holland immediately decided to see if he and his staff could do better. After the successful deployment of his Independent Companies, Gubbins could have been justified in expecting a field command, perhaps a brigade. But his recent experiences and his earlier relationship with Ironside at Archangel in 1919 drew him like a magnet to more irregular activity and he approached his new task with gusto. Gubbins was chosen to establish in Britain a kind of warfare he had attempted to develop in Poland before being thwarted by the speed of the Nazis' *blitzkrieg* – the 'stay-behind' forces.

Gubbins was, perhaps, better qualified for this work than Grand for the following reasons: firstly he had the benefit of his MI(R) experience – he had written several authoritative handbooks about explosives and guerrilla activity and was considered an expert on unorthodox warfare. Secondly, because of the exemplary manner with which he led the Independent Companies in Norway, his qualities of leadership and his ability to motivate men who were expected to fight in the open and in extreme conditions were second to none. Thirdly, it was recognized that the new resistance organization was beyond the capabilities of Section D and MI(R) (the latter was stretched to the full as the demands of the real, as opposed to the Phoney, war created an ever-growing requirement for new and obscure guerrilla weapons and ingenious escape and evasion devices). The new organization would need the full resources of Britain's military and as such would come within the aegis of GHQ Home Forces commanded by General Edmund Ironside, under whom Gubbins had served during the British expedition to Archangel in 1919. Gubbins could not have been better qualified.

Intelligence suggested that, although the Germans might supplement their invasion attempt by the use of airborne forces, the main assault would be seaborne and might occur anywhere in the approximately 300 miles between the Norfolk and Hampshire coasts. Gubbins, however, felt that the entire British coastline stretching from southern Wales eastwards round to Scotland was vulnerable and he deployed Auxunit patrols throughout this region accordingly. He concentrated the best of his units in southern England on the seaward side of the GHQ Line. In this way Auxunits could be put to good use scouting and spotting areas the Nazis might use to expand a particular bridgehead as they began their inland push. Auxunit sabotage missions would have had the effect of slowing down this build-up, buying time for Ironside's GHQ reserve to reach peak efficiency, and be deployed directly against the most threatened area.

As Gubbins formed the Auxiliary Units he drew his own personnel around him, notably his chief of staff at MI(R), Peter Wilkinson. The name Auxiliary was chosen because it was thought a suitably nondescript term that was unlikely to arouse unnecessary attention. Gubbins ran the Auxiliaries – or Auxunits, as they were called by those in the know – from June through to November 1940, when he was given military command of Hugh Dalton's SOE, the organization chosen, in Churchill's words, to 'Set Europe ablaze!'. Gubbins joined SOE, after leaving the Auxiliary Units in October 1940, and in 1943 he became its executive director.

Joan Bright Astley, originally with Section D, remembered Gubbins as 'quiet mannered, quiet spoken, energetic, efficient and charming. A "still waters running deep" sort of man, he had just enough of the buccaneer in him to make lesser men underrate his gifts of leadership, courage and integrity. He was a man-at-arms, a campaigner; the fires banked up inside him as glowing as those round which his Celtic ancestors had gathered between forays for glen and brae.'

Interestingly, Dalton had met Gubbins over dinner at the Polish Embassy in Paris exactly a year previously. In *The Fateful Years*, Dalton recalls their first meeting. Gubbins was a 'most intelligent British soldier', he thought. 'He enjoyed life to the full, he never forgot a face or a name, and he had a gift for inspiring confidence in those working under him. He was a born leader of men.' When Dalton was later considering a military commander for SOE he said of Gubbins, 'I had a hard fight for his body against the Commander-in-Chief Home Forces (Alan Brooke).' However, with all his previous experience, Gubbins was clearly the only man who could manage an organization that Dalton said should be 'comparable to the Sinn Fein movement in Ireland, to the Chinese guerrillas now operating against Japan, to the Spanish Irregulars who played a notable part in Wellington's campaign or – one might as well admit it – to the organizations that the Nazis themselves have developed so remarkably in almost every country in the world.' It was the Spanish Irregulars, as Dalton called them, who gave us the word 'guerrilla' – meaning 'little war' in Spanish.

Sir Peter Wilkinson first worked with Gubbins in central Europe. He became Gubbins' personal military assistant and was later to be key to the formation of the Auxiliary Units: 'I was a captain just before the war; I was quite a senior officer. I had worked in MI3 (a) in the War Office in 1938 long before I joined MI(R); and sent off to Czechoslovakia [Prague] as a language officer during the Czech crisis. I was a first-class interpreter in Czech.' Of Gubbins, he says: 'He struck me as better dressed than most. He was a small wiry little Scotsman. His size gave him a tenacity of purpose that short people often have. He would have made a good scrum half. He was a man of great integrity though he was not much liked by his contemporaries for some reason; they thought him a little pushy and ambitious – which he was. ... Although he was distrusted in the Army this was absolutely groundless. He was an immensely humane character. He was the least personally ambitious man I have ever known. He was dedicated to his duty and was compelled by it to stay with SOE, thereby throwing away his Regular career. Gubbins simply straightened his back and soldiered on and got on with it.'

Within the Auxiliary Units Sir Peter Wilkinson and Bill Beyts were effectively jointly second in command to Gubbins. Beyts, late of the 6th Rajputana Rifles and one of the Indian Army officers in charge of training attached to the Independent Companies in Norway, continued to take care of the training of Auxunit personnel. On the other hand, Wilkinson, who had gained wide experience of intelligence work within the War Office and anyway was already a trained intelligence officer, looked after the organization of the new underground army. Wilkinson took care of the organization's ongoing strategic planning – what he calls 'the vision thing'.

Shortly before the war, in an attempt at co-ordination, Section D and MI(R) held classes in guerrilla warfare at the St Ermin's Hotel, Westminster. 'They were set up by MI(R) after consultation with Section D. At that time both departments were working closely together and sharing offices in Caxton Street,' Sir Peter Wilkinson told me. 'It was considered to be impossible to secure funds for a section of the War Office to specialize in what would have been almost illegal activities until the war actually broke out. So, as a result, MI(R) clubbed together, with the official approval of the CIGS, with Section D, which was a section of MI6. They had two or three courses during the summer of 1939; the first of which I attended was held in the Caxton Hall in Westminster. I suppose there were about fifty people present, of whom only about three or four were Regular serving officers. The rest were representatives of firms that were operating in Europe, particularly Eastern Europe, such as Shell, Courtaulds and the big accountancy firms. It was a very superficial course; they were just instructed in elementary demolitions and shown some of the devices that were then still in prototype form. They also had elementary radio communications explained to them, including the use, which was novel at that time, of the Ionosphere as a means of reflecting radio waves, so that you could send a message from Poland to London and it would jump Germany using high-frequency crystals.

'Both GS(R) (General Staff Research, as MI(R) was originally known) and Section D worked together in Caxton Street and were secretly funded from the Foreign Office.

'Just on the eve of the outbreak of war, in late August [1939],' Sir Peter continued, 'it was finally agreed to come out of the closet and MI(R) moved into the main War Office building and became formally and publicly acknowledged as a part of the General Staff, whereas Section D was to carry out unacknowledgeable activities, many of which they were to carry out in peacetime in Europe, and certainly making plans for sabotage and subversion in the event of the outbreak of war. MI(R), on the other hand, was essentially looking after paramilitary guerrilla operations but was not actually directly involved in sabotage or subversion as such, though obviously there were smudgy edges to both activities. Both MI(R) and Section D had their own workshops for making devices and the MI(R) ones were more obviously paramilitary – for derailing the trains and blowing holes in oil tankers, things like that. Section D had similar expertise but for more clandestine operations.'

The Auxunits were trained to blow things up in the UK so that they weren't actually destroyed and could be re-used. I asked Sir Peter if the things MI(R) and Section D were trained to do in Eastern Europe were of a similar nature. 'We did not really get as far as the niceties of that – all we did was try to train a few chaps to blow up a bloody bridge!'

By 1940 and the establishment of the Auxiliary Units under the control of GHQ Home Forces, Peter Wilkinson was entrusted with setting up the national organization that Colin Gubbins was to manage. 'First of all we had Peter Fleming, who was already in the woods between here [Charing] and Canterbury. It was decided that his organization was as good a model as any other.' Peter Wilkinson had known Peter Fleming long before the writer and adventurer was selected to set up the first covert resistance patrol in Kent. 'Peter Fleming and I shared an office in MI(R),' Sir Peter told me. 'He was eight or nine years older than me and one of my schoolboy heroes. I absolutely worshipped him. A very clever man. He turned me from being a very raw schoolboy into a civilized creature in about six months!'

Kent was considered the likeliest invasion area. The second most likely was East Anglia, and here Captain Andrew Croft (the holder of the Polar Medal for Arctic Exploration who had served with Gubbins in Norway) was invited to set up a similar organization. In Sussex, Captain John Gwynn, the owner of extensive land around Lewes and Arundel, was asked to do likewise. By the end of August 1940, the Auxiliary Unit organization stretched as far north as Brechin on Scotland's east coast, south to Land's End, and north of the Bristol Channel as far as Pembroke Dock.

To give some idea of the routine of the time, Sir Peter told me, 'My office day started at nine o'clock. I would have gone in and read the intelligence reports about the invasion barges massing at Boulogne, Calais and Nieuport, for example, and assessed what was happening. Most of my time was spent scrounging arms from anywhere, as there were so few about. Springfield rifles were the making of the Auxunits – the Army couldn't use them as they fired rimless .300 cartridges not .303, which was the standard British Army round.' Otherwise he was taken up with obtaining PHE (Plastic High Explosive), which the Auxunits had in advance of the Regular Army, pacifying a corps or divisional commander who had found an Auxunit operating on his patch, and rounding off the day with an explosives demonstration, before embarking on a night exercise in which he would teach skills such as setting up an ambush.

On one occasion, Auxunit patrols invaded the lawn of Montgomery's V Corps HQ at Steyning, Sussex, in July 1940. 'He was furious! We put time pencils into his lawn, which exploded during his morning meeting. He had no sense of humour whatsoever and he didn't enjoy that one little bit.'

Another soldier who was involved in the early days of Auxiliary Units was Colonel Norman Field, who took over from Peter Fleming. Colonel Field's story presents another valuable insight into the forgotten army that flourished so briefly during Britain's darkest hour.

'The Auxiliary Units would not have arrested invasion but they would have made life difficult for the invader. As far as I was concerned we didn't knit together with anybody, we were completely independent and we were to do just what we could do. It was left up

Colonel Norman Field, who took over from Auxunit pioneer Peter Fleming, seen in his garden, which overlooks the rolling countryside of Kent. This is where German troops would have broken out of their bridgehead and some of the bloodiest fighting would have taken place.

to us. It was not all that secure when it was formed. It couldn't be, because it had to be done with enormous speed and in a tremendous hurry. To train the number of people who had to be trained it was necessary to get them to come to some sort of central point and so there was a great deal of mixing of one lot with another lot, which, from a security aspect, was undesirable. But if it hadn't happened we would never have got them trained. There used to be a lot of getting together at Bilting, at The Garth, on Saturdays and Sundays when they all came in from the Sussex border to North Foreland.

'I got involved because I knew Peter Wilkinson. He was a subaltern in my regiment. On 1 September [1939], the day the Germans went into Poland, he was removed from us very quickly – he disappeared, and that was it. I went to war with my battalion as signals officer. I came back after being adjutant for some months during all the *blitzkrieg* in France, where I was mildly wounded on the evacuation beaches.'

While recuperating in Somerset after Dunkirk, Field was visited by Peter Wilkinson. 'We had a cup of tea and nattered for a while. As he was leaving I chanced my arm and asked if he thought there would be an opening within the area I assumed he was involved with and, if so, could he bear me in mind. I told him that I would like a chance of getting my own back in a way I hadn't been able to do so far. Especially on that beach. It was like being a sheep in a pen – you could do absolutely nothing about it. You couldn't use your wits, nothing.

'Being Peter Wilkinson and being a perfect diplomat he didn't bat an eyelid, he just took it in. He didn't comment on it at all. Well, "no harm done" I thought, even though nothing appeared to have registered. A week later I received a telegram telling me to go for an interview at Highworth, for what I didn't know but I guessed it had something to do with him.

'I went to Highworth and I was interviewed in the kitchen there by Gubbins. I didn't know who he was. I knew he was the head of the organization, but I didn't even know what that was. He was in civilian clothes and I thought he might be a civilian. He didn't grill me very much but told me roughly what was involved and asked me if I thought I could do it. I told him I thought so. I explained I was still a second lieutenant and medically classified as unfit for service. "Leave that to me!" he said. Within a week a special medical board in Taunton had upgraded me and I reported to Coleshill as a captain.'

Norman Field took over from Peter Fleming at The Garth during a single weekend. 'Peter Fleming was a very agreeable man,' he told me. 'He had a brilliant brain, was a quick thinker and a wit with a keen sense of humour.' Norman Field knew very little about the organization (XII Corps Observation Unit) that Fleming had built. His office was simply one room containing two barrack tables. One of them was his office desk, the other was a 'mess dining table' occupied, on his arrival, by a prostrate German pilot, recently shot down. There were two barrack chairs. That was all.

'Considering the time he had it was amazing what he had achieved,' Norman Field told me. 'He had to move very fast. He had to get his friends around him to give him a hand. His brother brought a platoon of the Lovat Scouts down. He had to requisition vehicles from here, there and everywhere, obtain explosives and, more importantly, go and see people in authority whose word he could trust to discuss recruiting leaders. He did all this, but there was very little record of anything. It was done in a hell of a rush. If, for example, after acquiring a suitable recruit, something like an obscure cellar existed in the area, material was just dumped there. The construction of a suitable base would follow. In one instance in Tenterden some material was left in a dried-up water course. Fine, unless it rained.'

General Thorne, the commander of XII Corps, in whose area Fleming's XII Corps Observation Unit operated, was an old friend of Fleming's. Thorne's air liaison officer, Squadron Leader Lawrence Irving (grandson of the great actor, Henry) was another of Fleming's friends. Irving suggested to Fleming that he needed a radio set and arranged to supply an RAF cipher expert and a radio operator. They had little idea who they were transmitting to, but assumed it was RAF Uxbridge! Fleming had simply told Field, 'We've got these people here arranged by Lawrence Irving. You needn't be bothered with them. They send their pay through. If you have any problem with them, get in touch with Lawrence.'

'In those days you didn't ask questions,' said Field. 'Everyone knew their place and you assumed that everyone who was in a place was there for a good reason. It didn't do to ask why.' To this day Colonel Field has no idea what the radio experts actually did. But given that Irving was in the confidence of the corps commander, General Thorne, he assumed their secret purpose was for the common good. 'I would never take a unit like that, with two extraneous people, now!'

Local British Army establishments were, after due warning, used as training targets. 'There was a divisional HQ nearby at Wye – barbed wire, sentries and all that. We gave notice of various nights when we might break in and place detonators. It was necessary to forewarn them to reduce the likelihood of us being shot. Even so there was still a risk of that.' When asked if it was easy to break into such establishments Colonel Field replied, 'Yes, if you have a perimeter of perhaps a quarter mile protected only by layers and layers of barbed wire and some thirty men acting as sentries who can't be in every place at once. So, where they are not and there is only barbed wire there it was not difficult to get through. The barbed wire was simply propped up with foot-long forked sticks so that you could crawl underneath. Not all the training took place at night. To help get the effect of night during daylight we had night goggles for those taking part. Those who were not involved were able to watch clearly to see what happened. It was quite an instructive technique.'

General Thorne was succeeded as commander of XII Corps by General Montgomery. The latter invited Captain Field to show him something of Auxunits. The story of what happened next was first told in David Lampe's book *The Last Ditch*. Some fifteen years later, it was exaggerated out of all proportion by the *Evening Standard* under the headlines 'Junior Officer Hoodwinks Monty'.

What actually happened was that they met near Lenham, where Field took Montgomery to a roadside spinney: 'He could not believe that, within 2 or 3 yards of him, were six men with loads of explosives. This did excite him a bit. He was obviously very impressed. He asked me if Winston had been down to see these places. I said no, he hadn't. He answered, "Well, I often see him. I would like to bring him to see this. He would be delighted," or something along those lines.'

Field then took him to the brink of Charing Hill, where they sat on a fake sheep trough. The bottom of the trough slid sideways to give access to an underground observation post, from which the outside world was viewed through rabbit holes in a steep bank. There was just sufficient space for two persons.

'In fact, Monty, who was sitting beside me, must have cottoned on as soon as he saw me fiddling with a nail that I was pulling out of a board to enable it to slide open. I lowered myself in and then he came down and had a look around.'

Charing Hill is in a position to view the convergence of two very major routes to London. It is the hub of a wheel: an ideal place for enemy dumps and depots to be set up.

Montgomery must have been impressed with Field as he invited him to his HQ prior to attending Staff College. This effectively ended his career in Auxunits.

Peter Fleming and Norman Field met up again in Kent in 1965. After their meeting, Field received a postcard from Fleming advising him to see the article by 'Strix', alias Fleming, in the next edition of *The Spectator*. Using the letter 'N' to identify Norman Field, Fleming wrote about their walk through the downland within which they had created and concealed their hasty anti-invasion measures.

On a day-to-day basis Gubbins ran the Auxunits from its HQ at No. 7 Whitehall. In the earliest days of Auxunits new recruits were trained in sabotage and guerrilla warfare techniques in the homes of intelligence officers but very soon a secret training establishment, Coleshill House near Swindon, became the national college for Auxiliaries. Coleshill was a grand Inigo Jones building near the town of Highworth in Wiltshire. In 1940 the fine Palladian manor house was the home of the Earl of Radnor's family, the Pleydell-Bouveries. Here recruits to the Auxunits learnt all the dark arts of guerrilla warfare.

Coleshill wasn't a James Bond-style secret agent training facility comprising small groups learning unarmed combat or stealthy killing on the lawns of a grand country house. According to Colonel Field it was, 'apart from an occasional explosion, all very quiet. I never went there on a course, only for the interview and a weekend's series of lectures for intelligence officers in a big hall room. Beddington-Behrens, who was in charge of the administration set-up there, gave some of them. They were simply designed to keep us informed about developments and to knit us together. In addition there were training courses for patrol members.'

Incidentally, Edward Beddington-Behrens did not only look after supplies at Coleshill. Apparently, he told his colleagues there that he was a highly paid company director in peacetime. They assumed that he made regular nightly journeys by car to London because he was intent on keeping an eye on his business activities there. In fact, he was helping ARP rescue teams in London's East End pull survivors from the debris of the Blitz!

Gubbins was in the unique position of being able to use General Ironside's name to unlock the doors of military bureaucracy, thus bypassing the usual Army red tape and procuring weapons directly from GHQ Home Forces stores. Churchill and General Ironside were kept informed about its progress by confidential weekly minutes. In 1966, within the HMSO's official *History of the Second World War*, M.R.D. Foot wrote of Gubbins:

> Through the months of worst disaster, through the fog of battle, through all the complexities of a large, confused, impromptu organization, he pursued steadily the course that he and Holland had dreamed of long ago in Dublin, and had worked out together months before the war.

Hitler's armies were barely 30 miles away across the English Channel. Now they had the tactical benefit of French air bases to operate from. It was widely believed that an invasion would follow shortly, either in July or August. Therefore, Auxiliary Unit recruits were mostly drawn from the ranks of the Home Guard, often men in reserved occupations who had joined up immediately they heard Eden's radio broadcast on 14 May calling for recruits to the Local Defence Volunteers, a clear indication that they were patriotic and prepared to 'do their bit'. Recruits were issued with Home Guard uniforms and told that they had joined one of the three battalions that had been established to provide cover for the entire nation. Patrol leaders were given the rank of sergeant and were selected by 'intelligence officers'. Contrary to popular belief, however, not all Auxunit recruits were gathered from the ranks of the Home Guard. A Special Forces organization such as this needed skilled and fit technicians, so many volunteers were drafted from the ranks of the Regular Army and told they were being sent to a special, secret scout reconnaissance unit that was being formed as an anti-invasion measure. Overall, in excess of 100 Army officers and some 600 other ranks spent time in the classrooms of Coleshill House. Some made repeated visits to the house, perhaps to learn a new technique or to enrol for a specialist explosives course. Throughout the life of the Auxiliary Units organization more than 5,000 recruits spent time studying at Coleshill.

In the early days some intelligence officers, like Peter Fleming, were recruited from the ranks of MI(R). They were not purely involved in recruiting and training but actually established and led volunteer units as well. Not surprisingly, farmers and landowners, who knew their local landscape intimately, were considered a premium. Often farmers were chosen as patrol leaders and asked to select recruits from their own labouring workforce to staff their patrols. Farmers were not only best placed to know the capabilities of their own workers; they were also able to select the best man for the job. Sometimes this would be the one who was the best mechanic. At a time when motor vehicles were still a novelty outside towns, it was often only farmers and their labourers who had the mechanical knowledge (garnered from the essential maintenance of tractors and power threshers) to maintain and, of more use to a resistance force, damage motor vehicles. Furthermore, at a time of extreme fuel rationing, farmers could be uniquely sure of extra coupons. Villagers would think nothing of tractors or farm lorries trundling back and forth, especially if they were driven by men familiar to them. This last point was important; the main advantage that a resistance force has is that it is defending its own territory. Householders were unlikely to spurn a late-night tap at the door from a face they recognized, and farm workers would be best able to negotiate the landscape at night from their secret hideouts buried deep in the countryside.

The patrols were generally formed of six-man teams. Their hides, or Operational Bases, a name chosen because, unlike 'hide-out', it suggested an *offensive*, rather than *defensive*, purpose, were obviously situated in the most inaccessible locations, or those that enemy troops would be unlikely or unprepared to investigate too closely. Suitable locations included excavations within muddy river banks or deep within inaccessible bramble-strewn woods. To this day, the original model – the pattern for the perfect OB – still exists in the grounds of Coleshill House, in a thicket a little distance from where Coleshill House once stood. It is complete in every detail: a vertical entrance shaft with a rebated blast wall at the bottom; kitchen area; Elsan cubicle; and space for six bunks (the remnants of which still survive) in the arched corrugated iron main chamber. The only major difference from OBs in the field is, where there would normally have been an entrance to the escape tunnel, there is a large walk-in entrance instead. This was presumably fashioned to allow plenty of room for students to observe the entire living chamber without having to resort to commando techniques every time they chose to enter it. This OB also benefits from the addition of substantial concrete reinforcements, a luxury that certainly wouldn't have been the norm in 1940 but was probably added as the invasion crisis passed but while Auxunits were still in existence. An interesting detail that still survives is the vertical chimney flue exit, which passed through a dummy tree trunk that had been cemented in place above the roof.

Although the main house at Coleshill was consumed by fire soon after the war, the stables block and outbuildings that once housed the

OB interior. Although few survive it isn't surprising that they are often mistaken for air raid shelters. Though exactly why they would have been built in the midst of deep woods seems to escape those that find them! Note the concrete breezeblock construction – a new building method in 1940 and one that was invaluable to the rapid construction of field works.

This photograph gives a good idea of the small size of the tubular concrete escape tunnels that were built into some OBs. Just how an armed Auxiliary burdened with code books and any reconnaissance material was supposed to exit in a hurry can be left to the reader's imagination.

Frank Baker's OB is preserved like a time capsule.

The remarkably preserved interior of Frank Baker's OB in Sussex. His son David remembers that his father, a farmer by profession, kept some of his Auxunit explosives to blow up unwanted tree roots immediately after the war!

David Baker, whose farmer father, Frank, became Mayor of Brighton, is seen sitting in the entrance of the Staplefield OB (built by a local detachment of Canadian troops), in which Frank Baker's unit (which included a farmer and a local milkman) awaited the expected German invasion. Apparently, after the war Frank Baker retained some of the service-issue gelignite he had been given as it was invaluable for the speedy removal of tree roots.

The emergency exit of Frank Baker's OB emerges in the muddy bank of a nearby stream.

The emergency exit to Bill Webber's OB on Firle Beacon.

Standing within the tomb-like interior of a surviving OB it is easy to imagine the sense of foreboding Auxunit personnel must have felt as they waited in anticipation of the signal 'the balloon's gone up!' and the command to go to ground.

Many of the surviving outbuildings at Coleshill are home to designers and craftsmen. The remainder are in a state of disrepair and house some of the iron fittings and decorative furnishings that were salvaged from the fire that destroyed the great house.

Auxiliary peering into the tubular escape exit at Tottington.

The emergency tunnel at Tottington. If the OB's security had been compromised Auxiliaries hoped there would still be time for them to escape to freedom in nearby woods.

The surviving handbasin at Tottington. Incredibly, a small brush survives.

administrative buildings survive as a kind of decaying time capsule, untouched (save for a collection of architectural relics salvaged from the main house) since the Auxunits moved out in 1944. Doors marked 'Camp Commandant' and 'R.E. Office' are the only surviving proof that the stables and workshops that are now home to tenant craftsmen and administered by the National Trust were once part of the busy encampment of Britain's secret army.

Secrecy was such that new recruits did not report directly to Coleshill House. Rather, after being instructed to report to 'GPO Highworth', Auxiliary Unit volunteers turned up at Coleshill House's local post office, which was only minutes from the grounds of the mansion. After being given the once-over by the postmistress, they awaited their unit transport to come down from Coleshill to collect them. They generally stayed at Coleshill for a long weekend of training. Unarmed combat was taught to them by W.E. Fairbairn, who, until 1940, was the commander of the famous Shanghai Police anti-riot squad, which he founded. He was expert in 'every known method of attack and defence'. He was also one half of the duo that invented the Fairbairn-Sykes fighting knife – the lethal dagger with which all Auxiliaries were equipped and which later became the unofficial emblem of the Commandos and SAS. In his book *All-In Fighting* (richly

Eric Johnson in his Kent garden. In the distance the sun gleams off the waters of Pevensey Bay – a likely area for German invasion.

illustrated with line drawings depicting unarmed Tommies tackling close-cropped and thuggish German *soldaten*) Fairbairn described throws, blows with the side of the hand, thumb holds and exotica such as the 'Sentry Hold', 'Japanese Strangle' and 'Drawing the Smatchet' (a fearsome-looking broad-bladed knife). He even recommended ways of attacking an opponent with a matchbox by swiftly jabbing it at your opponent's jaw – 'The odds of knocking your opponent unconscious by this method are at least two to one.' Fairbairn even argued that, 'Most lion tamers consider a small chair to be sufficient to keep a lion from attacking them. Should you be so fortunate as to have a chair handy when your opponent is attacking you with a knife, seize the chair … rush at him, jabbing one or more of the legs of the chair into his body.' Comical as some of this might sound, the pages of *All-In Fighting* are filled with bloodthirsty images and advice for recruits who would have had to employ these measures if they ever came to grips with the invader.

Auxunit veteran Eric Johnson was thirty-two in 1940. In a reserved occupation as a farmer (Boreham Farm in Sussex), he had enlisted in the LDV immediately following Anthony Eden's broadcast in May 1940. 'I've always been very active,' he told me (indeed, he stroked a winning team at Henley in 1934), 'and I wanted to do anything I could for the country. When I was approached about this [Auxunits] I felt that it was something that I could certainly do very well and combine it with my job. At that time we definitely thought there would be an invasion. Let's face it, during the retreat from Dunkirk every small boat from around here was out just trying to pick people up.'

Recruited by the local intelligence officer, Captain Gwynn (of 'raid on Montgomery's lawn' fame!), Eric Johnson joined Peter Wilcox's Ashburnham Patrol. Peter Wilcox was the manager of nearby Hooe Farm. After being shown the Official Secrets Act, Eric Johnson was led to understand that, 'If anything happened to us we would be absolutely on our own.' Eric Johnson and his colleagues in the Ashburnham Patrol were responsible for the coastal area that included Battle Abbey, the site of the most famous enemy invasion of Britain, the Battle of Hastings in 1066.

Eric remembers that Auxiliary unit personnel 'were all people with confidence who wouldn't get upset in an emergency and could cope with problems at critical moments. There was no pay whatsoever. Both Wilcox and I were in the regular HG, in different sections, from different villages. When we left the HG we simply said we had been seconded for other purposes … but we always felt there was a little bit of bitterness about it. Nobody knew exactly what we were doing.'

Eric Johnson had first met Colin Gubbins at Coleshill. 'He was quite an outstanding character. I was very impressed with him as a leader of men. When we got there for a long weekend course, he came along and had drinks with us. We had a bit of a drinking session that night before we started work and so he got to know us quite well. You felt that after only a few minutes you had known him for some time. He was a very good listener. I felt he summed each of us up very quickly. We were intensively trained the whole time in unarmed combat, explosives, field training and night training – under live fire. An ex-all-in wrestler taught us unarmed combat. As it was really Churchill's idea to set us up, we got plastic explosives before the Regular Army.'

When asked if there was ever any friction between the War Office and MI(R), Eric Johnson told me that Gubbins was in the fortunate position of being able to go direct to Churchill. In fact, Auxunits were under the direct control of Ironside's GHQ Home Forces. 'Gubbins backed us up to the nth degree,' he told me.

During their time at Coleshill each patrol was judged on its performance. 'While on competitive exercise at the end of our training at Coleshill we had to drop one man who was an initial member of our party because he was quite useless with both the rifle and revolver and he was totally unable to use grenades or bombs,' Eric Johnson told me. 'In fact, he damn nearly blew us all up; we were in a slit trench and we had to throw a Sticky Bomb at something and he only popped it just outside the trench – with the rest of us still inside! We all got out very, very smartly. We had to let him go, which was a shame as he was marvellous across country, as an observer and face-to-face – that sort of thing. Our patrol had a rifle and a Sten gun and we each had either a Colt or a Webley [pistol]. I had a Colt.'

Geoffrey Bradford, another Auxunit veteran, recalls his initiation to the secret army. His brother, Roy, who was adjutant of the Territorial Devonshire Regiment at that time, had been selected as an intelligence officer and put in charge of recruiting other Auxiliaries.

'After initially being stationed in Sussex (because of the invasion emergency) he was then posted back to Devon because there was a need for intelligence officers with local knowledge. By 1943, when I was over sixteen, I was recruited to Auxiliary Units through Roy's good offices. I was enlisted direct – not from the HG, for which I was too young. I was recruited into the Braunton Patrol based about 5 miles from Barnstaple in Spreacombe Woods close to RAF Chivenor. Apparently, we were vetted by the chief constable, who should then have arranged for the Special Branch to check us out. But as my father was a local businessman [he was a groceries wholesaler] I would have been OK. Our captain was the local timber merchant and he had a special petrol ration so he could pick us up in his vehicle. We didn't really mix with the regular Home Guard and tended to see ourselves as the 'elite'. But they must have wondered what we were up to.'

Home Guard battledress denims. When first formed, Auxiliary Unit personnel mustered in civvies. If they did have uniforms they were most likely to be of the battledress denim type, rather than the thicker serge that regular soldiers wore on duty. These practical and comfortable outfits were very successful – so popular, in fact, that they are now incredibly rare; most servicemen, volunteers and regulars held on to them and used them as utility items after the war. This example is in pristine and unissued condition.

Though they wore standard Devonshire Home Guard uniforms, each Auxunit member carried a side-arm, which was distinctly unofficial issue! As Geoffrey Bradford says, 'In my case it was a Smith & Wesson .38. We were issued with two kinds of ammunition: lead-headed bullets for practice and high-velocity nickel-jacketed ones for use on operations. We didn't have rifles, other than a single, silenced high-velocity one, which wasn't very popular because it had a telescopic sight that soon went out of adjustment. It was to be used for picking off sentries or guard dogs or even, the unspoken thing, collaborators. And given what happened in France, this was probably very likely. Our rifles were fitted with a "cup-discharger" for firing the Mills grenade, which had a three-second fuse. This wasn't popular because it fired a Balastite cartridge, which was similar to a blank cartridge and made a hell of a mess of the barrel, which meant a lot of extra cleaning. We each wore the Fairbairn fighting knife buttoned either on the right or left just above the knee. The scabbard had five leather buttonhole tags, which could engage any of the buttons on the battledress trousers. Weapons were not really for offence – they were for close-quarter defence. In no way were we supposed to engage in any sort of pitched battles! The idea was to ambush and get away quickly.

'We were also issued with "battledress denims" because a lot of our work was mucky, either crawling through woods or constructing OBs. We wore rubber boots, which were useful for two purposes. First, because of the rubber tongue, which sealed the boot (they were waterproof – essential for so much outdoor work in the woods, etc.) and second, because they were good for creeping around in quietly. We also had a brown or green webbing belt to support a leather pistol holder and either black or brown leather gaiters.'

Insignia was minimal, the cap badge being the standard cap badge of the county regiment, as was normal within HG units. Until October 1942, Auxunits wore only Home Guard shoulder titles and stripes for sergeants. They were not allowed to wear the county distinguishing letters or the battalion numerals of local Home Guard units as this was thought likely to encourage more rather than less questioning from the curios. Off-duty, members occasionally sported a small metal lapel badge bearing the numbers of the three Auxunit battalions: 201 (Scotland and the northern counties), 202 (the Midlands) and 203 (London and the southern counties). These numerals were in gold in a cross formation on top of the red and blue GHQ shield. Although clearly not available to the very first Auxunit volunteers, these mementoes are now amongst the rarest pieces of militaria.

'Coleshill mainly consisted of lectures, principally in unarmed combat based on W.E. Fairbairn's book *All-In Fighting*,' Geoffrey Bradford continued. 'We learnt detailed information about where to stick a knife in. The idea was that you used it from behind. It was a stabbing knife – the blade wasn't all that sharp. You wouldn't take anyone on from the front but hold them around the neck and in up through the ribs. It takes quite a time to die from a knife if you can't get it into the heart. You would have to stab them enough times and hang on there to see what happened. We also learned how to use the garrotte, which was better than the dagger for throat-cutting. Rubber truncheons and coshes – some were individually made, of pre-war origin – were also used. Cheese wires fitted to two simple toggles were popular. But I don't think we were turned into killing machines, like the US Marines, for example – we were much too gentlemanly. My brother Roy was even gentler than me. He was the last one you would have thought would have gone into the SAS.'

It should be pointed out that by the time Geoffrey Bradford was recruited into Auxunits, Roy was one of the first recruits to 1st SAS, who were then preparing for the 'second front' – the invasion of occupied Europe. Tragically, Roy would not survive the war. Along with an SAS sergeant, a REME fitter and a member of a local French Maquis detachment, he was ambushed in his Jeep far behind enemy lines some six weeks after D-Day. Doubtless it was because of Roy Bradford's rapid rise through Auxunits, and then in Britain's 'Regular' Special Forces, that Geoffrey Bradford, still too young to join even the Home Guard, was entrusted with his role as perhaps one of the youngest recruits to Britain's secret army. Geoffrey Bradford made an ideal recruit to an organization that, though staffed with enough confident 'wily old foxes', needed young and agile volunteers not solely because of the potential for offensive action but as stealthy couriers who could pass on messages to other Auxunit patrols should the balloon go up.

'During one exercise against the Army at RAF Chivenor, our patrol and several others went up the river Taw, landing at the airport. We laid small charges between the rows of parked aircraft and then retreated and made a false attack on the main gate. We then allowed ourselves to be captured. While we were being 'entertained' in the officers' mess and being commiserated with for our failed attack, all the charges went off! On another occasion during a night exercise at a large unoccupied country house, which had, I remember, a trout lake, I remember one of our sergeants chucking a hand grenade in. He stripped off and climbed into the lake to pick up the trout that had been stunned by the grenade. I can see him now, coming out of the lake naked with a couple of trout in his hands!'

I first met Bob Millard in July 2004 while attending the unveiling of a replica Operational Base at the museum of the British Resistance Organization at Parham Airfield with the late Geoffrey Bradford. The museum's OB was officially opened by Edmund, 2nd Baron Ironside, patron of the museum and the son of William Edmund Ironside, commander of Britain's home defence forces during in 1940.

At the time I knew little about Bob's wartime activities other than that he was a member of that select cadre of stay-behind resistors, the Auxiliary Units. Fortunately, I made up for my lack of knowledge, albeit it years later, when, in preparation for this second edition I was reintroduced to Bob by Tom Sykes, the tireless champion of the Coleshill Auxiliary Research Team (CART).

During the numerous telephone interviews and email exchanges I have had with Bob I have not only come to realize why he was recruited into Auxunits (continue reading and you will also see why), but have also developed admiration and gratitude that someone of, shall we say, such advanced years, is as bright as a button and capable of recalling events from so long ago in such precise detail.

Born in Bath on 1 January 1923, Bob originally wanted to join the Navy and go south-west to the Naval College at Dartmouth. Bob told me that his father wouldn't 'sign the papers' because he couldn't see a future, what with the cuts of the Geddes Axe. Consequently, Bob was in the West Country at the outbreak of the Second World War.

'In 1939, I was training to be a teacher and I was going to go to Exeter College, as it was then, and which trained craft teachers. I was supposed to go there in September but three or four weeks before I was due to start, they notified me that they had closed the course down. I found out it was because they were using the workshops to train munitions workers. Bath ran a student teachers scheme so I approached Bath education authority and subsequently went to Bath as a student teacher, where I studied until I was called up for National Service.'

A messenger with the Fire Service, Bob left Civil Defence in August 1940 to join the Bathampton Platoon of the Home Guard.

My apologies for interrupting the narrative here, but I do want to say something about the importance of messengers to civil defence during the Second World War. One reason why so many young men were employed in the ARP, the Home Guard and Auxiliary Units was for their abilities to get around quickly either on foot, or most probably on bicycle. We take communications for granted today but in 1940 there was no TV, little public radio, no mobile phones, no text messages, no emails and, for the vast majority, only public telephone boxes if they needed to call someone. As we know from the problems at Arnhem towards the war's end, even the British Army's own wireless radio net was woefully unpredictable. Messengers made sure information got through. At a time when a single Luftwaffe bomb was capable of severing the telephone network and when mobile radio communications were the province of Special Forces and Special Duties sections, there was no substitute for human couriers.

Bob didn't see much of the summer fighting overhead during the Battle of Britain because, being in Bath, he was far away from the activity in the south-east.

'We didn't know what was happening but as far as invasion was concerned, to us, in 1940, it wasn't "if", it was "when". We were fully anticipating it. It wasn't until October/November time when they started bombing Bristol that Jo (Bob's fiancée, whom he'd known since school days) and I used to go to the pictures and go to the fish and chip shop before we walked home. Before we turned into the street where she lived we could look right down the Avon Valley and you could see the flak and the searchlights above Bristol and we would say, "Bristol's copping it again." However, in Bath itself, initially we just had one or two stray bombs. I remember some Heinkels coming out of the cloud one afternoon but they were obviously on their way somewhere because they didn't drop any bombs, but it wasn't until 1942 that Bath had any real raids – the so-called Baedeker Blitz. But when the Sunday raid of the weekend's 'Bath Blitz' came we knew nothing about it because we had gone up to the OB to do some sorting out and, being underground, we didn't hear anything. But when we came out and started walking across Hampton Rocks we suddenly saw a Dornier coming across the top only 400 or 500 feet because Bath was a nearby target. When we got to the road we saw an ack-ack post set up by the Army with a Lewis gun on an AA mounting and the sergeant was swearing, saying, "Bloody planes came across here only 100 feet up and the gun jammed!" He was very upset.'

I was particularly interested to learn if Bob noticed a change to his routine on Saturday, 7 September. In the afternoon of that date the Luftwaffe suddenly changed its tactics and began to shift target from the RAF airfields to London. Fearing that this apparent escalation meant invasion was imminent, GHQ Home Forces issued their famous Cromwell alert, which was misinterpreted by many Home Guard units who assumed the invasion was actually taking place.

'The platoon was on duty that weekend anyway,' said Bob. 'We weren't told about the Cromwell alert; we just turned out a little earlier. My mate Tony Hunt [Anthony Bentley-Hunt] came round and said, "We've got to be off in about an hour's time." This was earlier than normal because we were due to fall-in at six o'clock but we went out just after tea time instead.

'They also put these knife-rest barbed wire supports across the road, which was different to usual. That wouldn't have stopped a tank, though, that's for sure! And we were also issued with a bandolier of ammunition as opposed to one or two rounds.'

Bob does remember one particular occurrence that took place that Saturday evening.

'It was a quiet night. There weren't many people coming up and down. There was one incident, however, when we saw four cyclists coming down the road from Bath at around half-past ten. I was on duty with Tony. The sergeant was there and immediately ordered us: "Stop those men!"

'So we said, "Halt! Who goes there?" and the front cyclist answered, "*Bandwagon!*" The sergeant said, "I'll *Bandwagon* you buggers," and he stuck a stake through the front wheel of the bloke's bike. It was chaos. Over the handlebars he went. They all ended up in a pile.

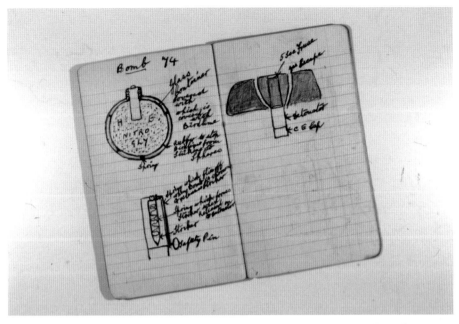

Hasty sketches made in a volunteer's notebook during a Home Guard training lecture.

Home Guards eagerly ambush a 'Nazi' convoy during a training exercise in October 1940. Note the ready supply of 'Molotov cocktail' incendiaries.

Bomben auf Engelland

Lied aus dem Film der Luftwaffe „Feuertaufe" von Hans Bertram
Worte: Wilhelm Stoeppler   Musik: Norbert Schultze

3.

So wurde die jüngste der Waffen im Feuer getauft und geweiht!
Vom Rhein bis zum Meer das fliegende Heer, so steh'n wir zum
Einsatz bereit!

Kehrreim:
Kamerad! Kamerad! Alle Mädels müssen warten!
Kamerad! Kamerad! Der Befehl ist da, wir starten!
Kamerad! Kamerad! Die Losung ist bekannt:
Ran an den Feind! Ran an den Feind! Bomben auf Engelland!
:/: Hört ihr die Motoren singen: Ran an den Feind!
Hört ihr's in den Ohren klingen: Ran an den Feind!
Bomben! Bomben! Bomben auf Engelland! :/:

A postcard featuring a Stuka and the words of Stoeppler and Schultst's hit *Bomben Auf Engelland*.

'They were really upset and the sergeant told them, "That will teach you to stop when I challenge you next time." If this incident had turned up on *Dad's Army* no one would have believed it.'

The cheeky cyclists were lucky; some unfortunates who didn't stop when challenged that Saturday were actually fired at. And, for the uninitiated, *Bandwagon* was a popular British comedy radio show that ran from 1938-40. Starring Arthur Askey, it was the first radio show to use catchphrases in a big way.

Bob's first experience of Auxiliary Units also occurred this weekend in September 1940, when the Bathampton Home Guard platoon was put on standby at its post on the Warminster Road because of the increased fear of imminent invasion.

'Late in the Saturday evening a small explosion occurred in the wood behind the post and a person in Home Guard uniform, who was talking to the officer in charge, remarked that the sentries were not much good as he had just blown up the post,' Bob told me. 'This was my first encounter with the timer pencil, a delayed action fuse with which I later became very familiar.'

Sometime later, Bob was approached by Anthony Bentley-Hunt, another member of his platoon, who asked him if he would like to join something more exciting than the Home Guard. Bob said yes and was immediately taken to meet one John Garnet Wyld, who lived nearby.

'I was questioned thoroughly about myself, my relatives and my geographical knowledge of the area and then told to come back in a week,' said Bob.

He was also interrogated about his knowledge of outdoor activities like camping – the ability to be able to live rough and off the land being an essential skill of the would-be Auxilier. Having a father in the RN and a mother who was a school teacher obviously helped.

'When I returned I was sworn to secrecy and told about the Auxiliary Units. Due to the clandestine nature of these units information was limited and very much on the "need to know" basis.'

J.G. Wyld turned out to be the patrol sergeant of the Auxiliary Unit patrol Bob would join. Unbeknownst to their colleagues in the Home Guard, Anthony Bentley-Hunt, J.W. Denning, J.M. ('Mick') Jones, and Bob comprised the newly formed and top-secret Bathampton Patrol of this clandestine force. They were later joined by A.C. Hannah, and G. James joined later still. J.G. Wyld was replaced as sergeant by J. Giles from Tadwick in mid-1941.

The Bathampton Patrol had its hideout in one of the disused underground stone quarries on Hampton Rocks. Although the adjacent area has changed following collapses, the original entrance can still be identified.

The entrance to the Operational Base was disguised by leaning a metal fence against the stone face. This was then covered with stones and earth to simulate a rockfall. A hole just large enough to squeeze through was left, and this was covered by a large stone that could be pushed outwards. Inside there were more stones that could be piled against this when the OB was occupied. Once inside the entrance there was a narrow opening to the right leading down a stone scree slope to a large cavern.

'We went up and built the OB – that sort of thing. Our OB was in the eighteenth-century stone mine and we sorted it out ourselves. We didn't have to do any digging or anything like that. Once we had slipped inside we had this fairly large stone cavern and it was a case of using the stone that was there to build up a blast wall and cover up one area so that if anyone looked in they wouldn't see the area we wanted. We got timber and we built our own bunks.

'It was never discovered. We used to leave "tell-tales", pieces of twigs and the like, by the entrance so that if anyone disturbed it they would have moved and we would know. As far as I know I've never heard of anyone locally who knew about it. Because there was a stone sort of slab we cut out a bit and fitted over the entrance and if anyone went there they wouldn't have seen a way in.

'We kept some heavy stuff – such as two or three boxes of hand grenades – in the OB. We didn't leave the detonators with them but we kept them there. But there was a quarry at the top of Bathwick Hill and Widcombe Hill that was disused and had its own stone-built explosives store and as that was disused we used it to keep some of the stuff in. Some of the stuff was kept at home.

'Tony Hunt had an attached garage at the side of his house and we kept some stuff at the back of that. We had access to a van so that we could quickly gather together anything we wanted and take it up to the OB if we were called out. But the majority of the stuff was in this old explosives store in the disused quarry. In April 1942 that was damaged because a bomb from the Bath Blitz dropped in the quarry. I was called out on the Sunday morning and went up there and met two people I didn't know and we had to unload the stuff from the explosive store into the van and we took it to Malcolm Shackle's farm (Captain Shackle).'

I wanted to know how self-sufficient the Bathampton Patrol was within its OB and wondered about the provision of water and the storage of supplies such as batteries and maps.

'Well, we had a stream within 100 yards running from a little brook that came out at Hampton Rocks,' Bob said. 'And we had the rations that the War Office had issued us with, which were supposed to last two or three weeks after we had been activated.'

HOUSE TO HOUSE FIGHTING.

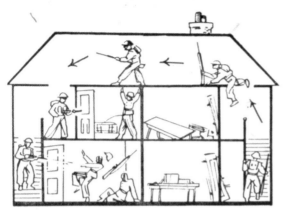

ASSAULT VIA LOFT, STAIRWAY AND ROOF FOR USE IN HOUSE TO HOUSE FIGHTING.

This form of attack has the valuable element of surprise as the enemy will never expect an attack to take place from above.

It is therefore suggested that all Home Guards should be well acquainted with the particular types of construction of houses in their own locality.

Home Guards were taught to clear the houses in a terraced street by scaling the end house, breaking into the loft space and flushing the enemy out into the street, where a waiting BAR team would shoot them dead. By moving from loft to loft along the whole street each house could be cleared with minimal risk.

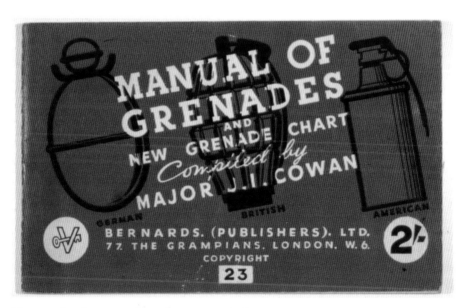

How to chuck a grenade at the enemy might seem simple and obvious, but if you didn't hit the dirt the moment you released the bomb then, like the opposition, you became a target for the fragmented casing as it exploded. Even this apparently basic weapon required some book learning.

Bob told me that rations would be supplemented by a 'little bit of extra food that we had collected from things that were off points, things that weren't rationed.'

The fact that there were a couple of warrens nearby meant that the very capable Bathampton Patrol were confident that they could supplement their diet with rabbits, which they would snare.

'We could cook in the OB. It was quite a big cavern and when we went up there at the weekend we tested it to see if any smoke or smell obviously escaped and none of it did.'

Bob told his mates in the regular Home Guard platoon he had just left that he had been drafted to set up a mobile anti-tank unit at the TA depot in Bath.

'They just accepted it,' he said. 'People didn't ask too many questions at that time. My family assumed I was still in the Home Guard. Don't forget, we were still in the Home Guard and I still had contact with the platoon in the pub and that sort of thing.'

Bob still managed to meet all his mates from the Home Guard on a Saturday night for a game of Solo Whist, where nobody questioned his absence from the regular platoon. While in Auxunits Bob wore the standard Home Guard uniform with shoulder titles sporting HG5 for Bath City and SOM (for Somerset), although Bob told me that his unit didn't really get proper uniforms and equipment until 1941.

The targets for this patrol were the railway junction at Bathampton, and Claverton Manor, if occupied by the Germans. Secondary areas for possible sabotage were the engine sheds at Green Park Station and Colerne Airfield.

Besides their hideout, the patrol had an arms/explosives dump in what had been the explosives store of a disused quarry on the edge of Claverton Down, near the top of Widcombe Hill. This store was damaged in the famous Luftwaffe raid on Bath on 26 April 1942, and its contents were then transferred to Manor Farm, Swainswick.

The original patrol sergeant, Jack Wyld, formed the patrol and located the hideout. He was a former quarryman and was familiar with the underground quarry workings in Bathampton Wood. Bob's patrol was busy from the start, meeting two evenings a week and at weekends, for training and construction work on the OB. The frequency of these meetings was reduced once the OB was equipped and ready for action should the balloon go up. Training took two main forms: familiarization with the local area and practice with explosives and sabotage devices. All training took place after nightfall. To get used to moving around at night and accurately arriving at pre-arranged destinations the patrol familiarized themselves with natural features such as barns and other farm buildings, the location of streams and ditches and even gaps in hedges, all of which were memorized so they could be quickly located without the aid of a torch in pitch-black darkness.

Apparently, the Bathampton Patrol unwittingly discovered two supposedly hidden OBs belonging to two rival Admiralty patrols.

'One was in the wood above the Warminster Road and the other in Prior Park!' said Bob.

In 1939, as part of the plan to decentralize certain offices from London, the Admiralty took over many large buildings in Bath, including the Domestic Science College and the hockey pitch and tennis courts, upon which it erected blocks of temporary huts. These acquisitions were not returned until late 1944, by which time the Admiralty had also established its own compliment of Auxiliary in the area.

It's not so surprising that the newly installed Admiralty establishment at Bath would have organized its own Auxunit patrols. For example, 1st Battalion, Devon Home Guard, in Exeter, comprised Admiralty Platoon, Fire Brigade Platoon, HH Prison Platoon and even the Express and Echo Platoons amongst other units similarly organized by local businesses and factories. There were five Admiralty patrols: No. 1 Kelston Park, Kelston, No. 2 Langidge, No. 3 Warminster Road, No. 4 Prior Park and No. 5 Newton Park, Newton St Loe. They were commanded by Captain Leonard Arthur Aves with Lieutenant Jeffery George Spearman and 2nd Lieutenants George Richard Hutchings and Ivor MacG Phillips as the other officers. (Lieutenant Spearman was later promoted to captain and Sergeant Frank Bradbury to 2nd lieutenant.)

Bob Millard's patrol actually encountered Bath Admiralty's No. 3 Patrol digging their OB. Amazingly, it wasn't until the Auxunit reunion at Coleshill in 1994 that Bob met up with the now late Jack Dennis (who actually spent most of his war with the Admiralty's No. 4 Patrol), one of those toiling, supposedly secretly, to create said OB located near the point where a stream descending from Hampton Rocks meets the bridle track from the Warminster Road to Claverton Manor.

'Water was supplied from the stream by a beer pump purchased from Bowlers in Bath. This was easy for this patrol to organize because they were mostly engineers,' said Bob.

In fact, most of those in the Admiralty patrols were highly skilled, ranging from marine engineers to submarine designers all prohibited from active service because of the importance of their reserved occupations to the war effort.

Interestingly, Bob was instrumental in helping Harry Banham, another member of the Admiralty's No. 4 Patrol, in receiving his defence medal in recognition of his work towards the defence of

Britain. Sadly, the passing of years claimed another Auxunit veteran when Harry died in January 2012, aged ninety-six.

Although explosives training was limited to prevent unwanted attention because of the resulting noise of plastic explosive (PE) and gelignite explosions, Bob's patrol needed to be conversant with the operation of the delay fuses (time pencils) and the assorted pull and pressure switches with which they were equipped in order to construct booby traps. Consequently, limited explosives training took place in the more remote areas of the woods lining the Limpley Stoke Valley and around the nearby stone mines under Combe Down. The patrol was also required to observe the movements of the military and to thoroughly explore the local railway to determine where demolition charges might be placed.

Knowing what we now know about how Nazi Germany waged war and behaved against insurgencies in occupied countries, I asked Bob if he thought Auxiliary Units would have made any difference.

'We weren't aware of the behaviour of German forces at the time but I'm quite sure having seen what happened that there would have been some rough reprisals,' said Bob. 'In 1940 and 1941 we simply weren't aware of what was happening in Europe.'

Because Bob and his fellow patrol members had a particular technical bent (Bob was training to be a crafts teacher and was pretty proficient at both wood and metalwork) the Bathampton Patrol was adept at manufacturing a variety of pieces of equipment that might be useful for nefarious activities.

'When I was in the Auxiliary Units I had the workshop facilities of the technical college at hand and that's where we made the punch knives and any components we needed for booby traps. Mike Jones, who was with us in Auxunits, was a student teacher, a craft teacher, with me. Tony Hunt and Gordon James were apprentice electricians. Gordon James's father ran an electrician's shop in Bath and Tony Hunt's father ran a radio shop there. So we had two trainee craft teachers and two blokes who had extensive electrical knowledge and access to useful bits and pieces for fuses and things like that. Our sergeant, Jack Wild, was a quarryman and he was a 'gen man' on explosives. So we were perhaps a bit different to the average Auxiliary Unit patrol. We were youngsters, enthusiastic and had certain useful skills.'

I said I thought that this contradicted the oft-told, but perhaps rather fanciful suggestion that members of Auxunits were primarily assassins and guerrilla fighters. Clearly success would depend on brain not brawn.

'We were different because we had a technical troop. We liked a beer and trying to think out new ways of making things like the pipe bomb we made. These many boozy think tanks were quite a lot of fun as we worked out how best to do something.'

I wondered what Bob felt about all the stuff written about what would have happened if Auxiliers had been captured and about the possibility of them committing suicide with cyanide pills, which were allegedly issued to some patrols. Did he ever think about what might have happened if he was captured, I asked.

'No. Because at seventeen and a half you are indestructible,' was Bob's abrupt and immediate answer. 'The chaps who climbed into Spitfires at the age of nineteen or twenty they didn't think "Am I going to be shot down today?" They thought, "Well, I'm better than the next bloke." We didn't get any cyanide tablets but I've heard that some were given pills; one to be used if you are injured and hurt, two to be taken in the event of severe pain, and three, that would finish you off. We didn't have anything like that. However, while at Coleshill we were told that the patrol mattered more than the individual and that if someone was seriously injured and you couldn't get them any help then they had to be shot. They would only be tortured and shot anyway.

'I keep hearing about our supposed two-week life expectancy but as I recall we weren't told "You are in this for ten days and that's it mate!" You were told that you had rations for a limited amount of time and that once you had gone past it you would have to live off the land, but I can't honestly recall being told that this was a suicide squad or anything like that. You were told that that was the job to do and you got on with it.'

I asked Bob if he could have delivered the *coup de grâce* to an injured colleague.

'That's a question I have been asked many times before. I simply don't know. Because we carried Mills bombs it was suggested that you used one of them to throw at the approaching Germans and used another to blow yourself up with. But fortunately it's something that never, ever happened in real life.'

Bob first went to Coleshill in February 1941 and again that September. While there he was 'shown how to set a charge on a railway line and use a rubber truncheon and knuckle dusters.' He didn't have one of the iconic Fairbairn-Sykes Fighting Knives when he first went to Coleshill, taking his own knife instead.

'Patrols from all over the country used to come to Coleshill, and when we went, we would arrived there on the Thursday evening and as soon as we had been shown our bunks and given a cup of tea, start training almost immediately. We worked through until Monday and left that evening.' Bob said that the training was very comprehensive and that lectures were held by officers from a variety of Army regiments. 'I don't know how many there were, I think four or five of them, and a number of Army personnel from the Lovat Scouts, who were a sort of commando unit,' he added.

'Training gave us more information on the use of explosives and explosive devices. We were shown TNT, gelignite and the plastic explosive we had been issued with. We were told how to estimate the size of charge that would be required for a certain job, shown the best place to place a charge to bring down a pylon or cut a railway line. We were also shown how to set up different types of booby traps, and techniques for disabling vehicles.

'Besides this sabotage training we were also given some training in personal defence. We were introduced to basic unarmed combat and shown how to use the garrotte and how to use the Fairbairn Knife that we had been issued with. I can always remember being told to strike upwards and keep your thumb on the blade in case the knife twists. Fortunately, one didn't have to do that sort of thing,' said Bob with relief.

Bob told me that members of his patrol would leave the tell-tale, which if disturbed in any way revealed if the OB had been compromised. 'In those days rabbits were plentiful and we would collect fresh droppings to scatter about to disguise any route taken,' he said.

'We operated on the assumption that we would get a few hours' notice of the need to assemble at the OB; a code phrase "the sun is rising" would be the signal. We all had personal knapsacks packed ready, a gallon of petrol and access to a small van, which was rarely used.'

Contrary to some of the fanciful stuff that has been written about them, Auxiliary Units weren't all that heavily armed. They weren't expected to engage in combat with German soldiers and, anyway, rifles would simply be too cumbersome inside the confines of an OB. Auxunits relied on stealth and subterfuge. Gunshot was a sure way to, literally, blow their cover. Despite this the Bathampton Patrol possessed a pretty comprehensive arsenal.

'As far as weapons were concerned we started with two .300 Ross rifles and, in early 1941, a Thompson sub-machine gun was issued together with a personal pistol and Fairbairn-Sykes fighting knife,' said Bob. 'I had a 5-inch barrel .38 calibre Smith and Wesson pistol. We also made "punch knives", which we carried in the slot intended for a cleaning rod on the webbing holster. I recall going a couple of times to a military firing range, possibly near Warminster, for range practice.'

I asked Bob how messages were passed should his Auxunit patrol need to assemble.

'Purely and simply through the sergeant. We met him regularly and he told us what we had to do and what we were going to do. Personally, I received nothing individually. My sergeant lived about ten minutes away from where I did and we used to meet in the local or occasionally we went round to his flat and he'd say, "Come round Friday evening about six and we will have a chat," and we went there.'

The 'need to know' basis of management and the individual isolation of patrols and their individual members from issues of wider tactical policy was naturally a guarantee of security but it is my belief, and that of many other commentators, that simply because they would have operated completely alone, perhaps without any instructions from a higher authority, their operational success was, perhaps, compromised from the very start.

'We didn't get any messages other than what the sergeant told us. We used to have a regular couple of meetings, two or three times a week. We either went to the pub to have a think tank or went to the OB to get it organized. If there was a change of plan or an emergency, like the time during the Bath Blitz when a bomb had landed near our explosives store and we had to empty it. I would get a telephone call from the sergeant and if my parents answered it he would just say he was calling from the Home Guard and wanted to speak to Bob. It was quite a normal call. On one occasion we were told to meet at the bike shelter in Henrietta Park to discuss the raid on Green Park Station and there were three chaps from some other patrol. I didn't know who they were or where they were from because we didn't talk about that sort of thing. We were just told that we had to do a raid on Saturday night at the railway sheds at Green Park. On that occasion we turned up in uniform to identify ourselves.'

Hitler had made it clear that individual *Francs-tireurs* – members of irregular military formations – could expect summary execution if caught opposing his armies. We also know that the Third Reich had few qualms about killing civilians if they were assumed to be protecting guerrilla fighters. Did the possibility of such treatment weigh heavily on his mind?

'We didn't occupy ourselves with the issue of reprisals,' Bob answered. 'We were told that we were there and had to sort out targets and get on with the job.'

These targets included the railway junction at Bathampton on the line that came up from Southampton and on to London, and the engine shed at Green Park railway station. There was a bridge across the Avon into a shed where there were engines. One notable target, and the site of one of his unit's greatest operational successes, was the airfield at Colerne, midway between Bath and Chippenham.

'We were trained to place explosives on the tail of parked aircraft, because if you blew that part off, the machine was useless. Usually there was a retractable tail wheel and you could stick ¼lb of plastic explosives in the wheel housing, which would take the tail off, and they'd have a job to fix it and have to use the plane for spares instead!'

The Bathampton Patrol's raid on RAF Colerne is also Bob's happiest memory of his time in Auxunits. 'That was a laugh,' he recalled. 'In late 1941 or early 1942 we were told that we had to do an attack on Colerne, a sabotage exercise against aircraft parked near the perimeter of the airfield. We were after the Mosquitoes. We were told that there would be other people attacking but we weren't told how many, where and when. We were also told where we had to go in. Our orders said we had to operate between sunset and six o'clock in the morning, when the exercise would stop.

'We set off at 4.00 am with the sergeant leading. We thought he knew the ground pretty well. He stopped us and signalled that he'd go on ahead. Then we heard a ruckus because he had been discovered by the RAF Regiment, who'd put in a sandbagged Lewis gun post that we hadn't found – they'd done it since our last reconnaissance of that place.

'There was a loud shout, "We've got one of them," and the sound of a noisy struggle from John, who was shouting and hollering and making a noise as they took him off.

'So the three of us had a quick consultation and we thought we could either call it off or go on. So we went on knowing that there was trouble ahead but when we spotted this sandbagged post we saw there was a Lewis gun installed but nobody there. So we took the Lewis gun. We had a couple of ten-minute time pencils, which we stuck in a potato and put them by the side of the post and carried on because we knew that there was a bridle path up to the road that crossed over to the airfield. So we went up into the top of that bridle path, looked down the road and saw the RAF Regiment standing in the road and a couple of trucks further down.

'Then we heard, "The bloody gun's gone!" which distracted the group on the road,' said Bob. Shortly afterwards, the time pencils went off.

'The ensuing confusion allowed us to roll across the road into the garden of what is now a well-known restaurant, The Vineyards, but unfortunately we had to leave our trophy behind. [The Vineyards stands on the site of the building, possibly a farmhouse, used by the RAF on the perimeter of RAF Colerne.]

'We left the gun in the hedge, rolled across the road because we knew there was a ditch under the fence around the airfield and that if we got into it we could get under the fence and into the airfield. So we went into the ditch and under the fence into the airfield. There was a farmhouse there and we lay still to see what would happen. Suddenly we saw a guard bring our sergeant round to the outhouse at the side of the farmhouse. Then someone went up to the door and banged on it. A voice shouted "Come!" and he went in. So we thought, "Well, there's only one chap in there and there are three of us – we'll get the sergeant out."

'When we started the exercise we arranged amongst ourselves the letter "X" in Morse as a recognition signal – dah dit dit dah. We had pencil torches so we could flash the signal but as we got to the door of the outhouse we banged on it, so the sergeant knew it was us and would assume it wouldn't be long before we burst in.

'So we put our shoulders to the door and burst in. There was this one RAF chap on the bunk with our sergeant lying on another, there being three or four bunks in the room. We said, "Well, you've had it mate!" to the RAF chap, to which our sergeant said, "Well done!" He also said, "We are lucky, because if you look under the bed there are two boxes of Mills bombs." So we helped ourselves to a couple of Mills bombs each and left one of our patrol there to keep an eye on the RAF bloke and then we went back out into the garden.

'We crawled around the garden, where there was a bean fence, which we lay under to watch. We saw someone come from down the road and knock on the door of one of the buildings and then heard a voice call, "Come!" Our sergeant immediately said, "Well, if he can do that, so can we." We crawled up to the door and the sergeant banged on it and the same voice uttered, "Come!"

'We charged into the office. We were lucky; there was Captain Hope-Hall, who was the captain in charge of the RAF regiment there, I suppose, an RAF staff sergeant, and another captain wearing a white armband, which showed he was an umpire for the exercise.

'We said to the umpire, "We've taken over this office." The umpire said to Captain Hope-Hall – I knew it was Captain Hope-Hall because his name was on his desk – "I think they have." If you've ever seen somebody purple with rage, Captain Hope-Hall was. He had a vein in his neck that was throbbing. What he said to his men the next day I wouldn't have liked to have heard!

'An RAF corporal came in and said, "I've come to collect the prisoners." And with that he was flat on the floor because we didn't mess about – we knocked him over! We said to the umpire, "I think we've got this bloke too." The corporal said, "No! I would have thrown a Mills bomb in," to which the umpire said, "If you had done, you would have killed everyone in here, including your captain." The umpire also pointed out that, anyway, he didn't have a grenade and had been fairly captured.

'He then asked us what we would do next. We said, "Well, we would put the office's communications out of action and go out the back way. By this time it was about half-past five and the exercise was due to finish at six, so we said we would place our remaining charges on the aircraft parked around the perimeter here. The umpire said, "Fair enough. Yes!" The exercise was over.

'It was a spectacular success. One thing about being part of the Auxiliary Units was that it taught you to think on your feet. We had never anticipated being in that situation – it was brand new to us – and you just had to think fast.'

I asked Bob if he knew of any repercussions following the raid.

'We didn't experience any repercussions but we heard indirectly that the RAF Regiment was confined to barracks for a fortnight and that if you were Home Guard in a pub in Colerne you had to duck if there was an RAF Regiment bloke in there at the same time!'

I wondered if Bob and his colleagues ever enjoyed opportunities to train with some of the explosives and weapons with which they were equipped.

'We had practice rounds, but the high velocity rounds we had were supposed to be for action only as they were probably more expensive. Most of the rounds we had were the ordinary lead-capped ones. The high velocity rounds had a longer range.'

Bob was adept at improvising a whole range of armaments.

'Explosive thuggery was the result of many boozy think tanks!' he smiled.

Auxiliary Units had to give thought to how established procedures, such as lighting fuses, could be effected in total darkness and possible in wind and rain.

'If you lit a Bickford fuse (the famous safety fuse patented by William Bickford in 1831 and first used in the West Country, and responsible for saving many miners' lives) you either did so with a striker cap crimped on to the end, which you would strike with a matchbox, but if you didn't have one you had to light it with a naked flame. If it's windy or wet a match doesn't work and a lighter produces a tell-tale flame. So, the match igniter would do the trick and if it was wet weather you would put it in a condom. So by cutting a notch in the fuse and putting a red-headed match in it we then made a tube from glass paper (on the inside) and if you dragged this over the red-headed match it would fire but couldn't be seen.'

Although every incendiary and explosive procedure was illustrated in the Bathampton Patrol's *Manual of Explosive Thuggery* and in theory would work if the instructions within were followed, there was really no substitute for trials with the actual objects.

'We would make one or two prototypes to see if they worked. I recall that in the 1940s you could buy black powder without any licenses or certificates. It was quite cheap – farmers often used it for blowing out tree trunks. We bought quite a lot of it. The regulations were much looser then than they are today. If I recall correctly, all you had to do was sign a register.

'If you take an ordinary torch bulb and rub it on some emery cloth or glass paper you can break a hole in it quite easily so air could get in, then when the circuit is connected the filament would fuse. We made a tube that fitted over the little round Bakelite lamp holder that we used to use in those days and we could buy black powder for either 3d or 6d an ounce, I can't remember. You didn't require a licence for it then as long as you signed a register. There was an ironmonger's into which we would go to buy gunpowder – gunpowder is very volatile. If you take a plastic holder and make a little tube that fits down on it and put the bulb in which the glass had been broken through and then fill it with black powder, as soon as you put a battery on it the black powder would flash. As long as you don't damage the filament it will work. The first one or two we tried was with a pair of pliers – squeezing the bulb gently and breaking the glass – but then we had the bright idea of rubbing it through with abrasive. And once there is a hole in it, without breaking the filament, it just burns out straight away. When you think that gunpowder was fired by the spark from a flint in a flintlock you can appreciate how volatile it is. It didn't need much to set it off.'

Bob also became proficient at mixing Vaseline and petrol in a tin to make what he called a 'useful incendiary', a kind of home-made napalm.

'We only wore uniform if we went on exercises. There was no point in wearing uniform. We wore it occasionally to keep the Home Guard cover up and if I went along on a Saturday night to play Solo I'd turn up in Home Guard uniform – just to be in the Home Guard.'

I asked Bob if he was ever scared.

'People keep asking me that. I don't think you would have been scared until the shot and shell started coming. You anticipated things – you weren't sure what was going to happen. It was *Boy's Own* stuff really. At that stage, 7 September 1940, I wasn't yet in the Auxunits. I was in the Home Guard. Previously I had been in the Civil Defence and when the Home Guard was declared I joined it. I found out that I joined on 5 May (Eden's broadcast was on 4 May). I knew that if there was going to be an invasion I was going to be part of it. I was a young man and if things happened, you couldn't avoid it. I wanted a rifle – so I joined and went down to get one!'

In event of invasion the plan was for the Bathampton Patrol members to retire to the OB and then begin prepared observations, attacking whatever targets presented themselves.

'We didn't need an OP (Observation Post, which some units established separately from their OBs) because we were in a wooded area and it was quite easy in the woods to stay in cover and get a good view of the valley.'

Bob confirmed that Auxiliers were certainly not do-or-die warriors imbued with a gung-ho spirit for mayhem and violence. They knew they would be fighting a trained and ruthless enemy, although perhaps they didn't know how ruthless, as it was apparent that they were eager to accept the King's shilling.

'We were told that if there was a danger of being discovered to abort the mission and try the next day. Caution was definitely part of the brief. You were told to avoid a head-on fire fight or anything like that. They said there are plenty of German soldiers; what they haven't got is petrol. That was more important than a dead German. If you killed one it was because he was in danger of discovering you and you had to get in there first.'

Because he was trained in unarmed combat and other nefarious techniques, I wondered if Bob could have killed someone in cold blood.

'I was taught how to. Like everyone else in the Army, I knew I was at war. That's all there was to it. One never gave it any real thought. At least I can't recall sitting down and thinking, "Oh dear. What shall I do if I see a German sentry?" I was told what to do. But we knew nothing of the kind of reprisals the Germans were capable of taking in occupied Europe. We didn't occupy ourselves with the issue of reprisals. We were told that we had to sort out particular targets and get on with the job.

'We got visits from people, probably from Coleshill, who looked at the ground around us and looked at maps and told us where to place explosives. At least two or three times we had a couple of mysterious chaps turn up and take a look at the OB to see where it was sighted in relation to places like railway lines and airfields.

'Our first sergeant, Jack Wilde, was a quarryman at Box Quarries and he was a "gen man" on explosives; he knew how to set up charges and link them, things like that.'

Bob thinks it was probably because of Jack that the Bathampton Patrol made its hideout in an old stone quarry.

'Our second sergeant was Johnnie Giles. He was a very quiet and unassuming sort of bloke. I think that by trade he was an insurance agent. He came from Jersey in the Channel Islands and had got out before the Germans occupied it to join an insurance office in Bath. He lived in the village of Padwick, which was quite near where Captain Malcolm Shackle, the intelligence officer who looked after our lot, lived and had his own patrol. Johnnie must have come to our patrol directly from the intelligence officer. I know he had definitely been to Coleshill.'

Bob remembers practising with the legendary Sticky Bomb on one of his visits to Coleshill. The Grenade, Hand, Anti-Tank No. 74, commonly known as the S.T. Grenade, was, like Auxiliary Units themselves, a product of Military Intelligence (Research), later known as 'Winston's Toyshop'. He used the Sticky Bomb against a variety of vehicles they kept at Coleshill for such purposes. But the only time these weapons ever really frightened him was after a Luftwaffe bomb damaged a stock of them in their secret ammo store in the quarry.

'With nitroglycerine leaking out the danger of a further explosion required what they call today a controlled explosion. In other words ... a very loud bang!

'The Sticky Bomb was pretty similar to a Mills bomb. The handle had a lever, like on a grenade, which you had to hold, and when you let it go it fired a fuse to a detonator and it was four seconds. If it stuck to your trousers you had a job getting your trousers off in time!

'In 1940, early 1941, I would think that it was an emergency situation. Obviously the possibility of invasion had been considered much earlier because there were "Army scout groups", stay-behinds, and, I believe, ammunition dumps scattered around the country shortly after war started. I think parallel with the establishment of the Auxiliary Units there was an awareness of the possibility of invasion and the appreciation that a guerrilla group needed to be set up, but as far as we were concerned in 1940, we got these couple of packs of explosives and the *Calendar 1937*, which dealt with basic explosives and incendiaries. It was issued as a kind of working handbook. We'd got a box of explosives, some of which was plastic, some dynamite – Nobel's 48, I think – and a couple of slabs of gun cotton, and we followed the instructions in the *Calendar 1937*, which told us basically how to use it all.'

I asked Bob if it was true Auxunits were given a mandate to deal with collaborators in the event of invasion.

'I've heard about that but we didn't have such information. However, the sergeant might have had a secret envelope, but that's guessing. I can't believe that. I certainly don't recall being told to target individual X or Y. I think somebody might have said something or made assumptions once upon a time and since then it has grown into a statement. I do remember one patrol saying that the local gamekeeper had come across them digging their OB and they thought they might have to take the gamekeeper out. But really that's hearsay and I wouldn't quote it as fact.'

Bob told me that one technique that was encouraged was for Auxiliers to have a handful of moss and dirt ready with which to gag

These remarkable images of the Sandford Patrol (Somerset) were taken on a camera that came free with coupons from the *Daily Mail* before the war. While clearing out her late husband's garden shed, Nora Trego came across a previously undiscovered assortment of photos and documents belonging to her spouse, a sergeant in Auxiliary Units. Author Donald Brown used them in his book *Somerset V. Hitler: Secret Operations in the Mendips, 1939-45*, and allowed me to use them here. 'A photographer friend re-processed the original 2-inch square prints,' he told me. 'What baffled us is how they lit them without flash or mains power. One picture shows a Tilley lamp, which would hardly have sufficed. My guess is that they extracted magnesium from something (Very flares, incendiary bombs, perhaps) and set it off as a flash.'

their opponents, stopping them from screaming out as they plunged the knife in. 'Anything that would stifle any cry was employed,' he added.

I wanted to know if Coleshill had a James Bond element to it.

'Not really. No,' said Bob. 'We went up and reported to Mabel Stranks, the Highworth postmistress, who said, 'Oh, you're one of that lot, are you? Hang around and somebody will come for you.' She went in the back and, I presume, phoned them. About fifteen minutes or so later, a 15cwt truck came along and took us to Coleshill. They couldn't have gone direct because Coleshill's only about ten minutes from Highworth and it took us about twenty minutes or so to get there so we must have gone via a bit of a roundabout route to confuse us as to where we were.

'When we got there we went into the stable yard and a chap in uniform came up to us and said "Hello. I'll show you your bunk." And we bunked in the stables on the first floor, bunks with tables down the middle. And then we came down for a cup of tea.

'The first chap we met was an officer who gave us a pep talk. It was very good and made you feel you were part of something. The next day we went on a general training course. The first visit was basic because not a lot had been issued.'

On his first visit to Coleshill Bob even had to bring his own knife, the FS Fighting Knife, then only issued to Commandos. However, he was shown how to silence a sentry with a garrotte, a truncheon or the aforementioned blade.

'We hadn't been issued with pull switches and time pencils then,' he said, 'but they demonstrated camouflage and showed that people could be hiding only 5 feet from you and yet you couldn't see them. It was very well organized – typical services training.'

I knew that Auxiliers were each equipped with Webley revolvers and wondered if they ever got much chance to practise with this weapon.

'Not a lot,' Bob answered. 'The first time we went to Coleshill we didn't have pistols. The second time we did and we were told to point and shoot, taking up the "A" stance using what the police now call the double tap. But, you see, a pistol was really a morale booster. It made you feel a bit "swaggery" if you had a pistol hanging around your belt. But if you think about it seriously, on operations it wasn't much use. If you were in a position where you had to fire your pistol you'd soon have the Wehrmacht on top of you! You can't fire a pistol when the German Army is sitting next door.

'Churchill had issued a memo saying, "These men should have pistols", and we started getting issued with a variety of them. I had a .38 Smith and Wesson … lovely pistol.'

I asked Bob if he handed it in at the end of the war but he told me that it was one of those things that was NSF, meaning 'not signed for'.

'I carried it until I retired from the Navy, taking out a firearms certificate after the war, and did a lot of pistol target shooting. It was a good weapon, very nice. I used to shoot it over a range of 25 yards and when my eyesight was good would score ninety-eight or ninety-nine (out of 100 shots). I actually became a qualified pistol instructor. In fact, my life has always centred on teaching. When I took up diving I became a national instructor of diving. I concentrated on shooting then and when I couldn't dive anymore and I found it very rewarding because you could soon spot if someone was any good and had talent. You'd help them become even better than yourself.

'The only rifles we had when we joined Auxunits were two P17s, which Tony and I brought with us when we left the Home Guard. Mind you, it wasn't much use because if you did fire it, as with the Webley, you'd get the whole German Army around your ears! You only used a firearm if you were in a desperate situation.'

Eventually, the Bathampton Patrol had another rifle, a Winchester 74.

'It wasn't silenced, it was "muffled",' said Bob. 'There were all sorts of other rifles issued in Auxunits. There was the BSA 12 and the bolt action Winchester 11A, but I reckon the Winchester 74 was the best of the lot. It had a tube magazine. All the other rifles were bolt action but this one had a tube magazine up the stock and all you had to do was pull the trigger and it went "Bang!" and reloaded itself. Unlike the bolt action weapons, with this one you could get three or four quick shots in. Because, if you were going to "drop" somebody with a .22, it had to be done within 100 yards or so. All this stuff about hitting someone at half a mile is a load of rubbish. You imagine that you are in a half-light and the adrenaline is flowing and there is a big hairy German with a helmet on standing in the distance, the only way you are going to kill a bloke with a .22 rifle is by getting a head-shot in. And you only get one chance. This was why the 74 was useful because you could shoot "bang, bang, bang, bang", and get four good shots in quite quickly.'

I wondered what the highlights of Bob's time with Auxiliary Units were.

'Meeting in the pub with the think tank to try to sort out devices, but the highlight of it all was the Colerne Raid and upsetting my future father-in-law by blowing up his railways station,' was his quick reply.

Bob told me that his then fiancée Jo's father was a journalist and a proud First World War veteran. It just happened that his HG platoon was on duty the night the Bathampton Patrol raided the Green Park engine shed they were guarding. Bob said, 'He was not very impressed by being confronted by a teenage terrorist intent on destroying the part of the railway he was protecting!'

Bob Millard left Auxiliary Units in 1942, but his war wasn't over yet. He joined the Fleet Air Arm as an observer in 1942. Bob's military career continued to be so eventful that I think some of it is worth recounting here.

Starting off flying in Swordfish biplanes, doing anti-submarine patrols, he eventually converted to the Barracuda, which, he said, 'flew like a brick.' During his career he endured two ditchings and survived a couple of kamikaze attacks. The first time he was forced to ditch was in the North Sea in a Barracuda and was due to engine failure. Fortunately, because 'a very sharp Wren' got a bearing on them, Bob and his crew were located. Despite this they were in a dinghy in the cold North Sea for many hours until a Walrus rescue aircraft arrived. Unfortunately, because of the swell, despite two attempts when the Walrus bounced the churning ocean, the amphibious aircraft was unable to land. The Walrus then flew around and flashed a message to the dinghy saying, 'You'll have to hang on, there's a destroyer coming.' Pretty soon, the destroyer *Reading* – an ex US WWI four-stacker purchased on Lend-Lease – arrived.

'We paddled alongside and they put a scrambling net down the side,' said Bob. 'Standing on the taffrail was a midshipman clad in duffle coat, hat, big thick gloves and all the rest of it. He threw a line and said, "Put a bowline around it and I'll give you a hand up." Well, having been in the sea that long my hands wouldn't work, it was a tough job. I could normally tie a bowline single-handed, but I was struggling. He said, "Come on, you amateur sailors! Can't you tie a bloody bowline?" I said, "Right, Mate. As soon as I get on board I'm going to throw you over." Eventually we made it.

'When on board they put us in a bath and filled it with cold water and very, very slowly warmed up the water so as to warm us up in turn. It was like warm tea with a lot of sugar in it!'

Flying from Ceylon in an Avenger III at 10,000 feet, Bob and his crew endured yet another engine failure. Bob's aircraft was practising dive-bombing on a destroyer that was towing a target.

'The engine stopped and when you've only got one engine …' said Bob, recalling the emergency.

Despite the Avenger's radial engine and large cowling that made the aircraft less than idea for ditching, the pilot prepared to do just that. Fortunately, the fact that the stricken Avenger was following a high-speed destroyer offered an opportunity that could make the exercise more likely to succeed.

'We called up the destroyer and asked it to make a big sweeping turn, which would flatten the sea out and give us a bit of flat water to land on.' Despite this, Bob was hospitalized for about ten weeks, losing the crew he was training with. Amazingly, when he was assigned a new crew he discovered that it was not only joining a pilot he had flown with previously but he also knew the wireless operator/gunner on the new crew.

Bob experienced the terror of kamikaze attack while in the Pacific with the aircraft carrier HMS *Formidable*.

'On 4 May 1945, a Kamikaze Zero landed in the middle of the deck. We had all the aircraft parked up and it blew a lot of them off the deck and did a lot of damage. And then, on the 9th, we had a twin-engined job come aboard. It blew a bloody great hole in the armoured flight deck. The Zero bent deck plates of 9-inch thick steel armour 6 feet down to the deck below!

'I remember that particularly, because it came on board at lunchtime, when I was down in the ward room having lunch. We had anti-flash gear on because we were at action stations. The steward came along and said, "There's corn beef hash or braised steak and a bloody great fire on the flight deck!" I lost a mate who was taxiing his aircraft across the deck when it landed and was very badly burned, dying five days later.

'It's funny how things happened. When we were at action stations the padre used to broadcast so that those down below would know what was going on. This was at about six o'clock in the evening. The ship was called to action stations but the aircrew and that being absolutely redundant were in the ward room having a drink. He said, "There are aircraft approaching. It looks like six torpedo bombers … one's down … they are coming in now on the port side." And everyone in the ward room moved away from the port side – not that it would have made the slightest bit of difference. But everyone shifted over to the other side regardless!

'I had a good war because I'm here to talk about it and a lot of people aren't. Like everything else, it was periods of boredom and periods of "What the hell am I doing here?" The camaraderie of the squadron was important and you all thought, "It's not going to happen to me."'

A private in Auxunits in 1940, Bob was demobbed from the Fleet Air Arm as a lieutenant in 1946. He told me he didn't stay in the FAA because his fiancée Jo wouldn't marry a sailor. Childhood sweethearts, Bob and Jo were married on 4 May 1946.

'After the war I received an educational training grant of £250, which was the equivalent of a teacher's salary. I went to Loughborough College for three years as a student. Then I taught at Bath Technical College from 1949 until 1953, and then I went back on the staff at Loughborough seeing the department through until it became

Loughborough University. In 1982, I retired as head of the department of design and technology.'

It was not until the first Auxiliary Unit reunion at Coleshill in 1994, which I had the privilege to attend, that Bob first discussed his time in Britain's clandestine defence force. Bob found out about it after reading an article announcing it in *Saga* magazine, which gave an address and telephone number.

'I didn't think anyone was interested before this. I don't think any of us who were in the patrol ever discussed it after the war and said, "Do you remember?" Anyway, after Auxunits we had all joined the services and gone our separate ways.

'Going back after fifty years was fascinating, especially walking into the stable yard where I thought, "I remember this. ..."'

He had gone back there once before but told me he had almost got 'chucked out for trespassing' until he explained that he had been there on special operations in 1940.

'Today we occasionally meet up and say, "Do you remember when we tried to blow that hut up?" Things like that.'

When I asked Bob if he felt recognition for Auxunits was a long time coming and if he felt he should have received the Defence Medal, he reminded me he got one automatically because he had served in the Royal Navy.

The spirit and honour of Auxiliary Units lives on in Bob's memory and in his deeds. He is actively involved with Tom Sykes' CART organization and even found time to help author Owen Sheers when he was researching his best-selling novel (and now a film) *Resistance*.

'I didn't spend a lot of time with Owen but we had several telephone calls.' However, like me, Bob Millard thought that the point at which in the novel a mislaid copy of *The Countryman's Diary* is found – a vital plot link – was perhaps a bit of artifice.

'We would have been shot if we had left something like that lying around!'

Initially, Auxunit personnel learnt the tricks of their trade by word of mouth and practical example. When they were first formed, the small number of trained intelligence officers handed down the wisdom assembled during the pre-war MI(R) and Section D years and that which could be gleaned from the various handbooks that Gubbins had worked on. However, as the immediate invasion crisis passed, the Auxiliary Units continued to expand and, in July 1942, the Auxiliary Units received their own training manual. This guide to applied mayhem was a top-secret document and, considering that many Auxunit recruits operated under the cover of their reserved agricultural occupations, it was disguised as an agricultural supplies diary – *The Countryman's Diary, 1939*. Its cover read: 'Highworth's

Fertilisers. Do their stuff unseen until you see RESULTS!' It came with the compliments of Highworth & Co (Highworth, near Swindon, was where Coleshill House was situated) and promised, 'You will find the name Highworth wherever quick results are required.' Its forty A5 pages were crowded with the distillation of the previous year's research and exploration. Though Gubbins was now well established at SOE, its pages clearly included examples of the type of sabotage and demolition devices and ambush booby traps that SOE agents used within occupied Europe. Various types of fuses, tube-igniters and detonators were described. Plastic explosive was 'the finest general purpose explosive in the world' but as it was in short supply, *The Countryman's Diary* warned that it could only be used to prime slower explosives. Within a chapter on 'delay mechanisms', the time pencil, the Auxunit and SOE favourite, which 'looks rather like a propelling pencil', was primed by inserting a fuse into the 'spring snout' of the pencil. 'Once it has been taken out the enemy has no way of telling the delay period,' the diary encouraged readers. A chapter included as an aid to calculate the precise amount of gelignite required to destroy a particular target ended, 'If in doubt, double the calculated charge!'

It's worth briefly pointing out here that *The Countryman's Diary* is the most well-known edition of instructional handbooks given to Auxiliers. In fact, the first text book for sabotage was *Calendar 1937*, produced in July 1940. This instructed the first generation of Auxiliers about the contents of their original sabotage packs, the stores of explosives and detonators and other ancillaries. These lethal bits and pieces were contained in heavy-duty cardboard boxes, what veteran Bob Millard called the 'Auxunit box'. Later on, the packs were issued in stronger steel boxes with a revised content.

Calendar 1938 was the second edition, published in 1942. It basically updated what went before but had one significant addition – instructions on how to use the new 'unit charge', which was to become the standard package used by Auxiliary Units.

The Countryman's Diary is actually believed to be the last version and was not issued until 1943, when the threat of invasion had passed. Because it wasn't produced, or used, in a state of emergency, it has survived to this day, when the previous handbooks have perished, and was long thought to be Auxunits' only A-Z of mayhem. It is equally unlikely that such a top-secret document would be printed with the location of Auxiliary Units' HQ emblazoned on the front cover!

So, in great haste and in the utmost secrecy, in the summer of 1940, Britain established the Auxunits – the world's first resistance organization ever to be established in advance of an invasion. There was no doubt that its leaders and volunteer recruits had a wide range of effective techniques with which to compromise the Nazi invader. And we also now know that the Operational Patrols were supplemented by the Special Duties Section, the intelligence gathering and radio communications cadre. John Warwicker wrote this about them:

> A network, absorbed in July 1940 from personnel originally recruited by officers of Section D as saboteurs. These were civilians to be left behind in their normal jobs, trained to collect and communicate intelligence.

John is also to be thanked for clarity about the role of the scout sections of Auxiliary Units, those units comprised of Regular soldiers seconded to Auxunits for regional and localized training purposes.

For the moment, however, all eyes were turned skywards. The British people knew that the defence of the United Kingdom was now in the hands of the young pilots of Fighter Command, for it was their job to deny the Luftwaffe the opportunity of air superiority, and this was the prerequisite of amphibious invasion. Ironically, the Battle of Britain would be decided above the fields and woods of southern England in which the Auxunits were preparing their own reception.

Chapter 3

Raiders from the Air

In this hour I feel it to be my duty before my own conscience to appeal once more to reason and common sense, in Great Britain as much as elsewhere. I consider myself in a position to make this appeal since I am not the vanquished begging favours, but the victor speaking in the name of reason. I can see no reason why this war must go on!

'Last Appeal To Reason', broadsheet
by Adolf Hitler, 19 July 1940

The Third Reich's battlefield use of bombers, notably the Stuka, in the close support of German ground forces during the campaign in Poland and Western Europe signalled a revolution in offensive air power. It was now the Luftwaffe's task to wrest air superiority over England from Fighter Command in order to prepare the way for the Navy's invasion flotilla and to provide an aerial umbrella for the landings by the Army. Amphibious troops are at their most vulnerable when disembarking from their invasion craft (as the Allies were to discover during the D-Day landings) and in 1940, the Germans, who had hastily requisitioned and converted Continental canal barges, were unable to support their invading troops with specialized purpose-built amphibious landing craft.

The Luftwaffe forces earmarked for operations against Britain and intended to soften up the home defences, paving the way for an amphibious invasion, appeared invincible and seemed more than sufficient to guarantee success for the Nazi invader. In Normandy, Guernsey and on the Cherbourg Peninsula the Luftwaffe had stationed three bomber *Geschwader* (squadrons) and three Stuka *Geschwader*, which were in turn supported by four Me 109 fighter *Geschwader*. By May 1940, the Luftwaffe had more than 5,000 aircraft, most of them (3,900) in Luftflotte 2 and Luftflotte 3. On the Pas de Calais, the nearest Luftwaffe bases to England were home to eight fighter *Geschwader* – the

In apparent defiance of RAF fighters, these Me 109s fly in formation above Channel waters.

famous 'Abbeville Boys' of ace Adolf Galland. Slightly further behind them, a further five bomber *Geschwader*, whose aircraft could operate over a greater range, stood ready to attack the RAF airfields.

In order to build up the Luftwaffe quickly, Hitler had accepted that he would have to do without heavy bombers and concentrate instead on fighters and dive-bombers. These would be supplemented by twin-engined medium bombers as these required a shorter incubation period than four-engined heavies. However, the medium bombers lacked effective defensive armaments, as was proved during the Battle of Britain when few RAF fighters fell to the machine guns or Heinkel He 111 and Dornier Do 17 gunners, neither of which had modern power-operated gun turrets. Moreover, although aircraft such as the Me 109 were superb in many respects, it had a comparatively short range, especially when it was forced to burn fuel flying throttled back and weaving in close support of the Luftwaffe's bombers. However, the Me 109 was equipped with 20mm canon in addition to its 7.9mm machine guns (at the time the RAF's canons were still in prototype form), so it packed a punch. The streamlined twin-engined He 111 bomber, whose vulnerable pilot and crew sat within a completely glazed cockpit in the aircraft's nose, the Dornier Do 17, nicknamed the 'flying pencil' by the British because of its ultra-thin fuselage, and the

Ju 87 Stukas suffered such a mauling at the hands of the RAF during the opening phases of the Battle of Britain that they were quickly withdrawn from the campaign.

Convinced of its superiority, Goering called the Me 110 his 'Destroyer'. In reality this twin-engined fighter-bomber was no match for Spitfires and Hurricanes.

high-speed Junkers Ju 88 dive-bomber completed the Luftwaffe's twin-engined bomber force. The heavy and graceless Stuka (Ju 87) was soon withdrawn from the battle after mounting losses. Another Luftwaffe aircraft that was a consummate failure was the twin-engined Messerschmitt Me 110 fighter. Goering loved this aircraft. He nicknamed it the 'Zerstroyer' (Destroyer). But apart from a few occasions – one when Me 110 skilfully intercepted a trainee RAF squadron that was circling prior to landing and shot down one after another of the fledgling pilots in the circle (each thought that the Me 110 behind them was a friendly RAF Blenheim, which it vaguely resembled – this aircraft was outmatched by Fighter Command's Spitfires and Hurricanes).

One advantage the Luftwaffe employed was a more relaxed attitude to combat flying. Me 109s flew in small groups known as 'Schwarme', or what the RAF termed 'finger four formation'. The Schwarme comprised two groups of two fighters, each pair being known as a 'Rotte'. This combination – leader and wing man – enabled German pilots to concentrate on scanning the skies for targets and attacking enemy. RAF pilots, on the other hand, had their time taken up by concentrating on their instruments and the position of their wing tips in order to remain in rigid formation with their colleagues. Many young pilots probably went to their deaths without knowing what hit them.

The RAF, however, had its own advantages. It was not only defending its own territory at close range but it possessed a sophisticated early-warning radar system – the first and only one in existence in the world – about which the Germans knew precious little. By July 1938, this radar chain consisted of five stations, centred on Dover. It showed promising results during the air defence exercises held the following August. After the Munich crisis in September of the same year it was decided that the 'Chain Home' network, as this coastal early warning system was known, was to be completed by 1 April 1939. On Good Friday 1939, the network was switched on and commenced a twenty-four-hour watch, which continued throughout the war.

In the past Britain had developed various acoustic methods that were not much of an improvement on the giant concrete parabola, or 'sound mirrors', below which Army operators wearing headsets sat impassively, straining to differentiate the sound of local vehicles and the baa-ing of sheep from the strains of distant aircraft engines. These methods continued, partly to disguise the fact that Britain was developing radar and partly because until the Chain Home system had been tried in battle no one was absolutely sure of its worth. The decaying concrete dishes that still stand sentinel-like along the coastal ridges inland of Hythe in Kent – the remains of the Hythe Sound Mirror System – are a legacy of these times.

The 30-foot diameter sound mirror high upon a ridge within the escarpment that overlooks the English Channel at Hythe. The listening chamber immediately below the decaying concrete parabola survives but vandals have long stripped it of any equipment.

The Luftwaffe's lack of accurate intelligence about Britain's Home Defences meant that Goering's bomber and fighter pilots were rarely able to take the initiative and catch them unawares. In fact, only Erprobungsgruppe 210, which flew high-speed Me 110 pathfinder aircraft at low level and were able to slip underneath the radar curtain, were able to catch Fighter Command off guard, although, in the wake of recent successes on the Continent, the Nazi High Command was justifiably confident of the Luftwaffe's chances of success against the British. RAF fighters, protected by radar and operating from a country with the most modern air defence system in the world, would not be vulnerable to the kinds of surprise attacks that had largely caught Polish, Dutch and French squadrons sitting helplessly on their airfields. Despite regular spying trips before September 1939, Luftwaffe intelligence was largely ignorant throughout the Battle of Britain about the RAF's technical innovations or precisely which RAF airfields were the key to the air defence of Great Britain.

By 18 June, the last RAF personnel had returned from France. Since the offensive in Norway, the RAF had lost about 1,000 aircraft – 432 of these since the Battle of France began on 10 May. Dowding had refused to send Spitfire squadrons to France and Spitfires that operated in support of the retreat at Dunkirk and elsewhere operated from bases in England. Fighter Command at this time possessed barely 644 machines with about the same number in reserve and after Dunkirk, only 330 modern Spitfires and Hurricanes remained to protect England from invasion. By July, No. 11 Group had barely 200 front-line fighters and yet it was the first line of defence against the Luftwaffe's 760 single-engined and 220 twin-engined fighters. Complementing this force the Luftwaffe could scramble 280 Stuka dive-bombers and 1,200 twin-engined bombers. Although replacement fighters rapidly swelled Fighter Command's numbers to between 600 and 700 fighters by the beginning of July, the Command was nearly 200 fighters below establishment.

As Air Member for Research & Development before the war, Hugh Dowding had long been closely involved with the development and adoption of new tactics in the RAF. Principal among these was the use of radio to direct scrambled fighter squadrons to the close vicinity of enemy aircraft plotted by the new, top-secret radar. Although he was keenly aware of the potential advantage bestowed by such new British methods and was aware of the disadvantages facing enemy fighters as they burnt precious aviation fuel escorting lumbering bomber formations against dispersed targets in Britain, Dowding was by no means certain that Fighter Command had the strength to beat off repeated attacks from a Luftwaffe that had grown so dramatically in a few short years.

On 2 July, Oberkommando der Wehrmacht (OKW) issued an order headed 'The War Against England', which stated:

> The Führer and Supreme Commander has decided that a landing in England is possible provided that air superiority can be attained and certain other necessary conditions fulfilled.

Although no target date was set, it curiously included orders stipulating that preparations should be made 'on the basis that the invasion is still only a plan, and has not yet been decided on.' It was this indecision and lack of commitment that was to bedevil the entire enterprise. The British people were not unduly alarmed by the German threat. Indeed, when in August copies of Hitler's 'Last Appeal to Reason' fluttered earthwards from the bomb bays of Luftwaffe aircraft above southern England they were gratefully received by citizens suffering from a shortage of lavatory paper! But although British intelligence consistently overestimated the strength of the entire German armed forces – especially the German Air Force – things were very bleak indeed for the United Kingdom. With first Guernica (struck by the German Condor Legion during the Spanish Civil War), Warsaw and Rotterdam having succumbed to the might of the Luftwaffe, the British assumed that London would be next. Perhaps the Nazis' aerial onslaught would prove irresistible.

One of Churchill's favourite maxims at the time was, 'Hope for the best, but expect the worst.' Homes with gardens could apply for one of the corrugated iron Anderson shelters, named after Sir John Anderson, the then Home Secretary. Once they had been partly buried and covered in a thin layer of earth, which was soon worn off as children started using them as a garden slide, the flimsy structures, though damp and dingy, were surprisingly capable of protecting occupants from anything but a direct hit. City dwellers and those living in flats congregated in community shelters. Some community shelters were in requisitioned buildings with convenient basements or large cellars, others were purpose-built and sited on city street corners. All communal shelters were supervised by members of the ARP, whose black-painted service-pattern steel helmets, or 'Battle Bowlers', were emblazoned with the white-stencilled words 'Shelter Warden' or 'Shelter Marshal'. Citizens soon got used to the shout, 'Put that light out!' But people lived in most fear of the ominous 'click, click, click' of the Warden's rattle, signifying a German gas attack! Curiously, the 'all-clear' for gas was communicated by the ringing of a hand bell.

The three letters 'ARP' were uttered almost as regularly as 'RAF' when civilians discussed the air war. British citizens were encouraged to be vigilant and to keep a sharp eye out for the silhouettes of unfamiliar aircraft in the skies above England. Aircraft spotting was all the rage as the public became increasingly 'air-minded'. ARP pamphlets were everywhere. One, called 'Spot them in the Air!' was published by the *Daily Mirror*. It had a foreword by 'Cassandra' that said:

Now that you've spent one thin sixpence on this book, you've done two rather good things. You've bought yourself about a bob's worth of interesting information and you've done a good turn to people who really deserve it.

Cassandra said that profits from the sale of the booklet would be used to buy dartboards for the troops. The foreword finished with:

If you have a friend who doesn't know the difference between a Blenheim and a Junkers 88, tell him he ought to be ashamed of himself, fine him sixpence on the spot and then buy him a copy of this book all for himself.

The official ARP handbook said that:

The Government would use every endeavour on an outbreak of war to secure an undertaking from the enemy not to use poison gas as this was contrary to the Geneva Gas Protocol of 1925.

This did not stop John Langdon-Davies from telling readers of his book *Air Raid* that:

One of the most dangerous results of an air raid is the sense of hopelessness that it gives to any waiting person.

H.M. Hyde and G.R.E. Nuttall in *Air Defence and the Civil Population* said:

Many of us have a picture of the sky darkened with ominous wings and the deafening roar of aeroplane engines overhead.

They continued with a sense of foreboding:

It is significant that, as from 1 January 1937, the insurance of war risks in Great Britain has been dropped from all policies underwritten by way of private business.

The British Government took a more sanguine view. In the 1940 pamphlet 'Air Raids. What you must know. What you must do', price 3d, the Ministry of Home Security said:

Whatever form aerial attack takes, damage of some kind is inevitable, and the lives of many civilians will be endangered, unless certain essential elementary knowledge is previously gained, and a number of simple precautions observed.

Pity the poor citizen, for this pamphlet was directly contradicted by another, 'Defence Against the Night Bomber', which was scornful of the 'Futility of the blackout and the AA barrage'.

A further Ministry of Home Security booklet, also distributed in 1940, said:

When a high explosive bomb falls and explodes a number of things happen. ... Anything very close to the explosion is likely to be destroyed. ... Fortunately, the zone of destruction within which this danger exists is very small. ... In fact, houses afford a great deal of protection against blast and splinters – as well as against aerial machine-gun fire.

In response to popular entertainment such as films like *Things To Come*, which sold well as Britain faced what was known as its 'Air Peril', the Government tried to be encouraging, stressing, 'Houses do not collapse unless the bomb falls on them or very close to them, and the chances of your house being the unlucky one are very small.'

In fact, throughout the entire period of the 'first' Blitz (in 1944 there was another when Hitler launched his 'vengeance weapons' – the V1 and V2, against London), only 30,000 people were killed from night bombing – far fewer than anticipated. Most died during the fearsome London Blitz. In other British cities such as Coventry, which was devastated by deadly accurate bombing on the evening of 14 November 1940 by Luftwaffe crews guided to their target by the new electronic 'X-Great' beam system, life and production went on. In Coventry's case, all the city's factories were back in full production within a week.

German and British historians have always disputed the start of the Battle of Britain. RAF pilots who served in Fighter Command between 10 July and 31 October are considered to be veterans of the battle, whereas German records consider it commenced with the 'Eagle Attacks', or *'Adler Angriffen'*, in August. Regardless, Luftwaffe attacks on England proper began right at the beginning of July, starting with sporadic raids on airfields, factories and ports. Convoys in the Channel were also permissible targets. Goering and his planners wrongly assumed that, by attacking them, Dowding's Fighter Command would be drawn into the mêlée, leaving their home bases and England's industry unprotected.

The first objective of the Luftwaffe was to close the English Channel to British shipping and on 4 July, Convoy OA 178, consisting of fourteen merchantmen, was attacked by Stukas. Four freighters were sunk outright and a further six were badly damaged. After this no more large freighters entered Channel waters. However, Churchill was determined that Hitler wouldn't deny Britain entry to its own waters, so small convoys, escorted by armed freighters, continued to ply Channel waters. Between 4 July (when Luftwaffe Stukas also killed 176 British seamen at Portland naval base) and 1 August (when his bombers vainly scattered Hitler's 'Last Appeal to Reason' leaflets over England), the pattern of enemy attacks remained consistent.

As July changed to August, however, Luftwaffe tactics also changed. Hitler knew that time was running out for Germany if it was to attempt an invasion of England in 1940. On 1 August, the Führer and Supreme Commander of the Armed Forces issued a further 'War Directive', No. 17, from the Führer Headquarters in Berlin. Its opening lines were chilling:

> In order to establish the necessary conditions for the final conquest of England I intend to intensify air and sea warfare against the English homeland.

Hitler ordered the Luftwaffe to 'overpower the English Air Force with all the forces at its command, in the shortest possible time.'

Syd Weller, who joined the Horsham Post Office branch of the Home Guard as soon as he was old enough, especially remembers the Battle of Britain because of the extra work created repairing all the damage to the overhead telephone wires. 'The Germans machine-gunned up Billingshurst High Street, which broke a lot of wires that needed a great deal of repair work.' His job meant travelling throughout the district, putting him in a good position to judge the mood of the times. He recalls the general fear of invasion in 1940. 'We kept saying, "Why don't they come?". The Government sent out pamphlets that didn't say "If the invader comes", they said, "*When* the invader comes". We were all ready for him to come. We were certain he would.'

He remembers cycling through Horsham and pausing to see the air battles taking place overhead. The sky was swarming with what he remembers as 'moths' heading for London and passing over the anti-aircraft belt positioned on the North Downs to benefit from the height of the chalk ridge. 'Flying towards us and directly overhead were all these planes in formation. There must have been 100 of them. They were flying along so unmolested that I thought they must be some of

This Luftwaffe nose emblem on a preserved Ju 88 at Hendon clearly shows that the Nazi regime had it in for Britain.

When compared to the rather aggressive emblem on the nose of the Luftwaffe bomber on the left, I think this humorous postcard from Bamforth & Co, famous for their saucy seaside postcards, ably characterizes Britain's self-deprecation and sense of irony. Foolishly naïve perhaps, but this exhortation to register for membership in ARP services shows just how 'terrified' the average citizen was of Nazi threats.

ours! It was incredible.' Syd remembers the racket of the RAF Brownings as dogfights took place overhead. 'It was like shrapnel rattling onto a tin roof. An incredible noise with those eight machine guns blazing. I always remember two Spitfires flying alongside a German bomber that didn't look to be disabled but it obviously was and the RAF pilots had gestured "Go down, or we'll put you down!" He landed intact over Redhill way. He never fired a shot. I don't even think he was crippled. There was no smoke or anything.'

By the beginning of August the Luftwaffe had lost 200 aircraft, at a two-to-one ratio in favour of the RAF. But now the German gloves were off and Fighter Command was to be crushed. On 3 August, the Luftwaffe Chief of Staff, General Jeschonnek, ordered that the British radar masts 'be attacked by special forces of the first wave to put them out of action.' From 11.30 am on this day Portsmouth harbour was attacked by more than sixty Ju 88 bombers. Fifteen of these peeled off to attack Ventnor Radar on the Isle of Wight. Ventnor, part of the Chain Home network, was a vital component of Britain's early warning system and covered the approaches to Portsmouth and the Fighter Command Sector Station at Tangmere. After the attack, however, British technical ingenuity and presence of mind came to the fore and a transmitter was hastily rigged up and set to transmit pulses of sufficient strength to

Der Adler (*The Eagle*), the Luftwaffe's own magazine.

persuade Luftwaffe eavesdroppers that the radar station was back on line. Pevensey and Rye radar stations suffered similar punishment, but the latticework construction of the 350ft-tall masts dissipated the blast. The ruse of Ventnor's dummy transmitters and the fact that the tall latticework towers seemed bomb-proof wrongly convinced the Luftwaffe that the radar stations were virtually indestructible.

On 6 August, Goering called a conference at Karinhall, his country estate deep in Germany near Berlin. '*Adlerangriff*' (Operation Eagle Attack) was to begin and '*Adler Tag*' (Eagle Day) was set for 10 August. Eagle Day was intended to be the first of the Luftwaffe's knockout blows. Goering was confident that if he could unleash the full force of his combined air fleets against Fighter Command the RAF's annihilation would be a foregone conclusion. So confident was he that, after *Adlerangriff* had begun, Goering estimated that the Luftwaffe would neutralize the RAF within four days and eradicate it as a fighting force within a fortnight. Enigma decrypts first revealed the term *Adler Tag* to the British on 9 August. The following Sunday, Churchill told his private secretary, John Colville, that '*der tag*' might be imminent and added that, if it was, 'Hitler must fail. If he fails he is bound to go east, and fail he will.'

The Luftwaffe needed fine weather for Eagle Day to be a success and in anticipation of a high-pressure system above the Azores that was heading for England, it was postponed until 13 August. Interestingly, another postponement took place around this time when, from 12 August, Luftwaffe Jagdgeschwader and Kampfgeschwader were directed to try their luck with the RAF's forward airbases and forget about targeting the 'radio direction towers'. In fact, Ventnor's 'Jerry-rigged' transmitter was unable to receive and, though they didn't know it, the Luftwaffe had successfully pierced the British radar chain for eleven precious days.

When it dawned, however, the weather on the 13th was still not ideal (in fact, the weather throughout August 1940, contrary to British folk memory, was often dull and certainly not perpetually sunny). Still, 'orders were orders' and Goering's air fleets dutifully took off to deal the intended hammer blow on southern England that *Adler Tag* promised. Despite the frantic efforts of Luftwaffe ground controllers who tried to recall the first units as it became clear that not all Luftwaffe squadrons would be airborne simultaneously (Goering had insisted on a concerted attack by his air fleets), some Luftwaffe crews headed for their allotted targets before all the designated formations had been properly assembled. In this way Eagle Day went off like a damp squib rather than with the explosive force that had been intended. But, despite the Luftwaffe's organizational and technical problems, Fighter Command bases at Manston, Hawkinge, Lympne and Detling suffered heavy punishment, and Eagle Day served as an ominous portent of what could happen once the Luftwaffe co-ordinated its attacks and operated all-out from dawn to dusk.

Eagle Day 'proper' took place on 15 August, when Luftflotten 2 and 3 were supported by Generaloberst Hans-Jurgen Stumpff's northerly Luftflotte 5 based at Stavanger in Norway. The full panoply of Luftwaffe might was at last thrown against Fighter Command's defences and, for the first time, the attack continued well into the evening. In total they shot down thirty-five RAF fighters (seventeen British pilots killed, sixteen wounded) but lost seventy-five aircraft themselves. Eagle Day was quickly named 'Black Thursday' by Luftwaffe crews.

Churchill phoned his predecessor, Neville Chamberlain, who was by then the Lord President of the Privy Council, to proclaim his joy at what he called 'one of the greatest days in history'. But Dowding realized that if Fighter Command continued to lose precious pilots at such a rate his Command would quickly bleed to death. Goering also reviewed the day's business and concluded that, due to the savaging the Stukas had received at the hands of RAF fighters, from now on his dive-bombers would require close protection from Me 109 fighters. This change of policy was crucial to the outcome of the battle as it prevented the German fighters from ranging free on the lookout for Hurricanes and Spitfires before these could intercept the bomber formations.

Still, 15 August was a real turning point for Britain and for 'Stuffy' Dowding, whose prestige increased dramatically in the eyes of Winston Churchill, who declared, 'We must regard the generalship here shown as an example of genius in the art of war.' On that day the Commander-in-Chief of Fighter Command's policy of rotating tired squadrons and exchanging them for fresh units that had been temporarily removed from the heat of battle was vindicated. It had far-reaching effects when on one occasion seven RAF fighter squadrons that had been temporarily withdrawn from the south intercepted a formation of unescorted Heinkel bombers approaching the supposedly undefended north-east coast of Britain. One can imagine the horror of Goering's crews, who had been assured that the RAF didn't have sufficient machines to cover the entire country, to find themselves engaged by such a force. The raiders were savaged. Thereafter German bombers seldom flew without a fighter escort. This, of course, put further strain on Luftwaffe resources.

On the 16th and 17th, the air battles were not so intense. However, RAF airfields continued to be attacked. Tangmere in Sussex received a savage raid. Nobby Kinnard, a local woodsman and rabbiter, witnessed the inferno from his home at Patching on the South Downs. He recalled, 'We certainly knew the Battle of Britain was real.' A stricken RAF fighter ploughed through the undergrowth of nearby Myrtle Grove Farm and smashed into a hillock of juniper bushes, despatching dozens of rabbits from the warren concealed within. Mr Kinnard said the Luftwaffe 'had accomplished a fortnight's work in a single stroke!'

On 18 August, Fighter Command's sector stations at Kenley and Biggin Hill were attacked. RAF satellite airfields on Thorney Island at Gosport and at Fort were also hit, as was the radar station at Poling. On successive days, RAF Hornchurch, Manston and West Malling, and airfields and aircraft production facilities at such diverse targets as Middle Wallop, Croydon, Shoreham, Bristol, Yarmouth and Crewe, were struck repeatedly. At the same time the vital Fighter Command bases at Biggin, Kenley and Tangmere received yet more raids. Meanwhile, Churchill told the House of Commons:

> The gratitude of everyone in our Island, in our Empire, and indeed throughout the world, except in the abodes of the guilty, goes out to the British airmen who, undaunted by odds, unwearied in their constant challenge and mortal danger, are turning the tide of war by their prowess and devotion. Never in the field of human conflict was so much owed by so many to so few.

Since mid-August, the RAF had lost 231 of its young pilots; they could not be replaced – the training reserves were already depleted. Over a two-day period on 30 and 31 August, for example, twenty-four RAF fighter pilots were killed. On 30 August, a total of thirty-nine base personnel were killed and some twenty-six injured at Biggin Hill after a Luftwaffe bombing raid had breached the airfield's perimeter defences. Vital airfields like Tangmere and Kenley were in ruins. Between 24 August and 6 September, nearly 300 RAF Fighters had been lost and 171 seriously damaged, though new aircraft were reaching the airfields faster than fresh pilots to fly them were graduating from their training courses. On 7 September, for example, Fighter Command's available machines had actually increased since the dark days of Dunkirk. Dowding's hard-pressed command was shored up by the addition of fifty-six naval pilots from the Fleet Air Arm and thirty more 'borrowed' from Bomber and Army Co-Operation Commands. Polish and Czech pilots joined other fresh pilots from the British Empire who had already been recruited.

After the Eagle attacks failed to finish off Fighter Command, the Luftwaffe pressed home its attacks further inland, ranging far and wide trying to destroy other RAF airfields and fighter production facilities in an effort to interfere with the nationwide organizational structure and quell the flow of replacement Spitfires and Hurricanes at source. This change of tactics indicates that Goering and the Luftwaffe were seeking any opportunity to detect a flaw in Britain's defences and were lacking a clear and determined strategy.

A view through the glazed nose of an He 111, the principal Luftwaffe bomber used over England during 1940.

The Luftwaffe was gradually succumbing to the attrition of the air battles of August and September 1940, and what amounted to nearly five months of more or less constant combat since the campaign in the west commenced with action over Norway. Still the initiative was with the attacker and, unless a miracle happened to allow the British a breathing space, as at Dunkirk, a German invasion seemed inevitable. Bizarrely, the miracle was delivered from the bomb bays of an errant Luftwaffe bomber. On the evening of 24 August, Heinkel He 111 crews of KG 1, attempting to locate oil storage targets at Rochester and Thameshaven, dropped their bombs on London by mistake, in direct contravention of the Führer's orders. Churchill ordered Bomber Command to retaliate by striking at Berlin. Despite the fact that Bomber Command was ill-equipped to send a force on the round trip of 1,200 miles, several RAF Wellington bombers dropped their bombs on the German capital. Goering had boasted to the German people that if one British bomb fell on Berlin they could call him 'Meier', a Jewish name. Hitler saw no humour in the situation. Incensed, he immediately ordered that London was to be 'wiped out'.

This was the turning point that Britain so badly needed. Instead of continuing to pummel Fighter Command's airfields or hitting Ministry of Aircraft Productions (MAP) factories, thereby completing the destruction of the RAF, the Luftwaffe was now diverted to London. The Blitz had begun. In his memoirs, Luftflotte 2's commander, Albrecht Kesselring, said of the shift in Luftwaffe priorities:

> Although we gained air superiority within a restricted area for a short time at the beginning of September, we failed to keep it consistently after we began to raid the London zone. But sure it is that outside the island itself we could move as freely as in peacetime, which points to the absolute inadequacy of the British bomber crews. They were also far from formidable as a defence against invasion; the Wellingtons were too little battle worthy and the German AA too strong and practised.

However, despite this negative assessment of their abilities, British bombers had made enough of an impression on the gathering invasion fleet to force the German naval staff to delay Operation Sea Lion again, until 21 September.

The start of the nightly blitz on London in September 1940 also marked the last period when weather conditions favoured the invader. Because the British had not lost absolute air superiority, its military commanders could relax for the first time since Dunkirk, although Churchill told Hastings Ismay (his representative on the Chiefs of Staff Committee) that he 'felt like a man trying to go to sleep on a very cold night with a blanket that was too small for him.' When a German attack came from one direction and was countered, this created a gap in the defensive system elsewhere. But Churchill need not have worried, for it soon became clear that the Nazis had not planned Operation Sea Lion in sufficient detail.

Hitler was unprepared to press on if Germany no longer had the upper hand. Back in August, Ironside had confidently written in his diary:

> I have no reason to believe we are being depressed by this air attack. ... We are all convinced that we shall win air superiority one of these days. ... There can be no doubt we will win in the end.

When asked if the paintings in the National Gallery should be moved to Canada for safekeeping in case Trafalgar Square should fall into German hands, Churchill would hear nothing of it. He preferred to let them be removed to quarries in Wales because he never really thought Britain would fall. And although there was a secret plan, codenamed the 'Black Move', to evacuate the Government, Churchill never seriously considered flight. The King also refused to go to Canada. Queen Elizabeth told reporters that the King's duty was as sovereign to the British people and in Britain he would remain. The King made few concessions to the emergency and would travel daily from Windsor to London, despite the bombing. When Buckingham Palace was struck by Luftwaffe bombs the Queen murmured, 'At last we can look the East End in the face.' The King insisted on the same rations as his subjects and shunned the use of an armoured limousine that came complete with close-combat weapons, just in case a Fallschirmjäger snatch squad intercepted it in a lightning attack. Churchill decided that if the King didn't want it, he would have it, as he was frequently making visits up and down the country. Hastings Ismay summed up the mood:

> Early in November, Goering switched his attack from London, first to the great industrial cities and then to our principal ports. I have never understood his reason. One would have thought that to continue to concentrate on London would have paid a better return. But if he imagined that the inhabitants of his new target might not show the same fortitude and adaptability as the Londoners, he was grievously mistaken. They were one and all completely undaunted.

The switch in tactics had taken the pressure off the RAF. Its airfields were repaired and its worn-out pilots had less to do during the hours of daylight. On 14 September 1940, Hitler told his Chiefs of Staff that the Kriegsmarine had now completed its preparations for Sea Lion but that, although the Luftwaffe had so far achieved 'enormous successes', the conditions were still not good enough to guarantee a safe crossing for the Wehrmacht, and so the invasion date was moved back to 8 October. In fact, as early as the period between 26 August and 7 September (the day before the night-time blitz 'officially' commenced), the Luftwaffe had lost 100 of its bombers. Admiral Raeder was quite sure that Goering could not guarantee air superiority before 24 September, the next date when tides would favour the invader. Hitler, on the other hand, wanted the date for the 'landing phase' of Operation Sea Lion to be no later than 27 September. The Führer said that the decision to proceed or postpone an invasion attempt would be made on 17 September. In the meantime, the Luftwaffe would have to redouble its efforts.

Battle of Britain Day commemorates the air battles fought on 15 September 1940. On this day the Luftwaffe threw in everything for one last great daylight offensive. Dowding's tactic of patiently waiting to see where the real threat was and ignoring Luftwaffe feints paid dividends. For once Leigh-Mallory's much vaunted 'Big Wing' worked. This was a formation that combined several of No. 12 Group's squadrons operating from Duxford simultaneously and at last they had sufficient time to get into position to effect maximum destruction

Reconstruction at the Imperial War Museum's famous outstation of No. 12 Group's sector control room at RAF Duxford.

on the enemy. Luftwaffe losses amounted to sixty aircraft and were the highest since Black Thursday on 18 August. From both Raeder's pronouncement earlier in September that air attacks should proceed 'without regard to Sea Lion' and Goering's later insistence that Sea Lion must not interfere with Luftwaffe operations and its 'subsequent attacks spread all over Britain', it became clear that Hitler's High Command was no longer confident about taking on the British in their homeland. Because of repeated bombing by the RAF, the transport fleet assembled to deliver the invading troops and the support infrastructure of Operation Sea Lion began to be dispersed from 19 September. On 2 October, Hitler ordered that all measures taken to support the invasion of Britain were to be 'largely dismantled'. Between 10 July and 31 October, despite inflated claims in the British press of 2,692 German raiders shot down, the Luftwaffe actually lost a still massive total of 1,733 aircraft. RAF losses amounted to 915 aircraft.

On 21 November, Hitler issued 'Directive No. 18'. Beginning with a scheme to 'seize Gibraltar' and have German forces 'made ready to invade Portugal should the English gain a footing there,' the directive only alluded to Operation Sea Lion in its penultimate paragraph. It said:

Luftwaffe fighter pilot. He is wearing the canvas summer helmet, tinted goggles and *Sauerstoffmaske* (oxygen mask).

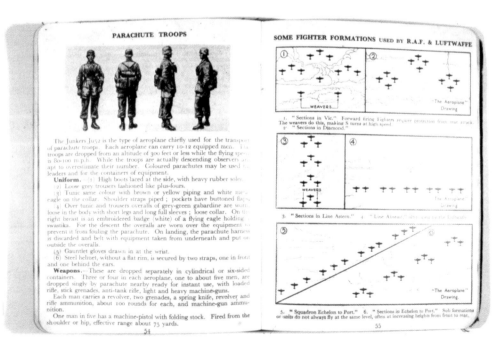

The public had a voracious appetite for advice about Nazi paratroops, the Fallschirmjägers.

Battle of Britain period RAF flying clothing. The pilot on the left is wearing an extremely rare B-type helmet, Mk III goggles and a D-type oxygen mask. His Mae West life jacket is painted bright yellow to aid visibility. The squadron leader on the right wears Luxor type goggles on his B-type and his RAF pattern Service dress can be seen clearly.

> Since changes in the general situation make it possible, or necessary, to revert to undertaking Sea Lion in the spring of 1941, the three branches of the Armed Forces will make every effort to improve in every way the conditions for such an operation.

By spring of 1941, Hitler's attention was elsewhere. His greedy gaze was fixed on his one true enemy – Soviet Russia. On 22 June 1941,

Civil Defence contamination crew figures by Taylor and Barrett. This rare set is redolent of the anxiety about chemical warfare, which even found its way into 1930s' toy boxes.

'Operation Barbarossa', the invasion of Stalin's empire, began. This was to be an altogether more massive undertaking than Sea Lion, which as we have seen might have started with a Luftwaffe paradrop of only three divisions. The Germans launched Barbarossa with 200 divisions!

So, what would have happened, for example, if the Nazis had taken advantage of the loophole created by the breach in Britain's Chain Home network and the Luftwaffe had dropped both bombs and Fallschirmjägers on the Isle of Wight? Well, my opinion is that the immediate landing of two or three German airborne divisions would have paid dividends for the invaders. Kesselring considered that an immediate airborne operation might work. The readers of *Parachutes Over Britain* knew what to expect. Its author, John Langdon-Davies, sitting in a garden not 2 miles from where 'a great beacon which would have been lit, if Napoleon had invaded England in about 1803', mused, 'Perhaps by the time these words appear in print, England will have been seriously invaded again, the first time in 834 years.' Leonard Mosley's *Parachutes Over Holland*, whose cover blurb screamed, 'I saw them drop!' said that the actions of the German paratroops he saw in the Low Countries were, 'characterized by a hard ruthlessness.' He said he had witnessed 'the dreadful work they did on the ground, work from which Chicago gangsters in their hey-day might have recoiled.' Britons had a lot to fear.

Securing an airstrip is a vital prerequisite of invasion. As we shall see, the fledgling British resistance, the Auxiliary Units, were designed to exploit the sense of confusion or 'jitteryness' that invading forces feel soon after they have made landfall and while they are attempting to secure a bridgehead. With no aircraft carriers in the Kriegsmarine and no steel matting of the type that Americans later used so adeptly in the Pacific, the Luftwaffe had no choice but to make an early attempt to secure one or two of Britain's coastal airfields if German forces were to be sure of speedy reinforcement and supply. Following RAF Tangmere's bruising after a successful Luftwaffe Stuka attack and the smashing of Ventnor Radar, Hitler had an ideal opportunity to grab not only the Isle of Wight but an inland RAF sector station as well. If he had managed to land Fallschirmjäger in enough numbers to also capture the Royal Navy dockyard at Portsmouth, the effect on British morale would have been incalculable.

Chapter 4

Fighting on the Beaches

The Germans threaten to invade Great Britain. If they do so they will be driven out by our Navy, our Army and our Air Force. Yet the ordinary men and women of the civilian population will also have their part to play.

'If the Invader Comes', pamphlet issued by the
Ministry of Information in co-operation with the
War Office and the Ministry of Home Security, July 1940

S-Day, the landing phase of Operation Sea Lion, would only occur if the Luftwaffe had secured air superiority in the skies above England. If this had been achieved, the full might of the Wehrmacht's ground forces would have been thrown against the meagre British defences. Although Hitler had started to demobilize some army units since the fall of France, sending some conscripts back to civilian life, the German Army was still a formidable fighting force. In addition to the regular infantry, artillery, engineers and other units common to most armies, the German Army also included a uniquely Aryan fighting force – the SS. Unlike many other German soldiers, the Waffen SS had a fanatical belief in Nazi superiority and Germanic purity: their mission was to reassert German prestige after the humiliation of the 1918 Armistice. It was soldiers like these, and the political 'militia' of the SS – the black-clad Allgemeine SS – that British soldiers would have fought if the Nazi invasion had taken place. Before the unthinkable actually happened, however, the Nazi hordes had to first get ashore in Britain.

Germany's navy, the Kriegsmarine, without any reference to either the army or air force (and this lack of inter-service co-operation was perpetually to bedevil the effectiveness of Germany's armed forces throughout the Second World War) came up with a plan for the invasion of England. Not surprisingly, Oberkommando der Marine (OKM, Nazi Germany's Naval High Command) recommended a seaborne invasion route across the North Sea. The plan stressed certain prerequisites: the Royal Navy's fleet had to be contained; coastal forces in the vicinity of the landings (then envisaged to take place on England's east coast) had to be eliminated; strong anti-submarine measures had to be prepared; and the RAF had to be neutralized before the invasion force could safely set sail. The report concluded that the plan would 'in all probability result simultaneously in the complete collapse of her [England's] will to resist; thus a landing, followed by occupation, will scarcely still be necessary.' Perhaps this ambitious summary, whose findings were probably correct, revealed that OKM considered it unlikely that such fantastic preconditions could ever be met and, if they were, the 'English' might as well be left alone anyway. In December the baton was passed to Oberkommando das Heeres (OKH, Army High Command). On 13 December the Army Commander-in-Chief, General von Brauchitsch, asked his planners to commence 'an examination of the possibility of a landing in England'. This plan, which called for the use of paratroops but was also based on the east coast of England, aroused the scepticism of the Kriegsmarine, which was curious to know from where Brauchitsch's planners expected to procure the requisite number of transport ships. The Luftwaffe was equally unenthusiastic about 'Study North-West', as the German invasion plan was called at this time. The Luftwaffe maintained that, unless the invasion armada could be guaranteed air cover and conditions of absolute surprise, the venture would be too risky.

The Kriegsmarine had always been sceptical about an invasion attempt against a maritime power of Britain's size. After the Norwegian campaign Hitler's navy had been badly damaged. Only the heavy-cruiser *Admiral Hipper*, three light cruisers and eight destroyers were combat ready. The *Graf Spee* had been lost the previous year when it was scuttled after the Battle of the River Plate and his two new pocket battleships, *Bismarck* and *Tirpitz*, would not be ready until 1941. In their revised feasibility studies the OKM concluded that a successful seaborne invasion of southern England could only effectively be mounted from occupied ports along the Channel coast. By July 1940, this condition had been met.

It was not until 21 May 1940, with France nearly vanquished, that Hitler first asked to see the plans that his commanders had drawn up for continuing operations against England. He studied Raeder's OKM plans but was unimpressed by them. He decided instead to temporarily increase the stranglehold on Britain's supplies by encouraging an increased naval blockade. On 20 June, Raeder informed the Führer that invasion preliminaries were still being organized and the Kriegsmarine's Merchant Shipping Division started

Details of German Sea Lion land campaign map. These maps are especially fascinating because of the detail they display regarding specific assembly, or *Armee Parke und Lager*, areas.

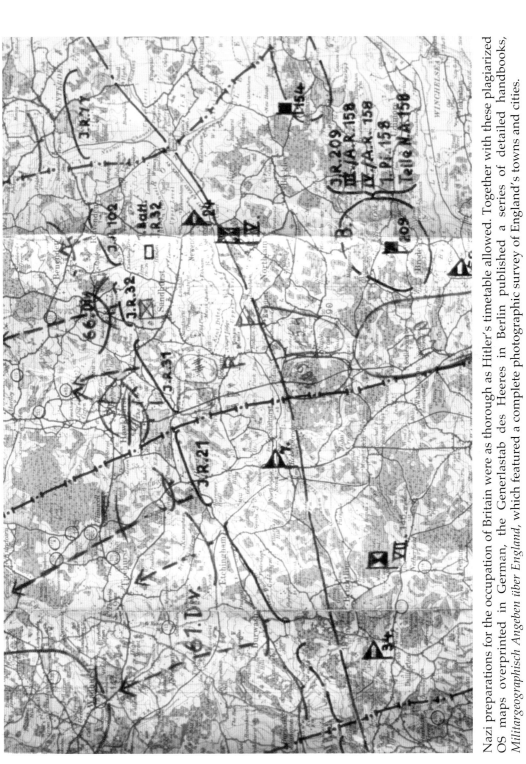

Nazi preparations for the occupation of Britain were as thorough as Hitler's timetable allowed. Together with these plagiarized OS maps overprinted in German, the Generalstab des Heeres in Berlin published a series of detailed handbooks, *Militärgeographisch Angeben über England*, which featured a complete photographic survey of England's towns and cities.

to evaluate the problem of gathering sufficient vessels to transport an army and its supplies across the seas. Furthermore, now that the coast of France was in German hands, OKM could safely initiate topographical studies of south-eastern England – the shortest and most direct assault route from the newly captured coast.

On 3 July, General Beaumont-Nesbitt, the Director of Military Intelligence, reported to the COS that landing craft had been seen at Kiel and that Luftwaffe bomber units based in France were being stockpiled with fuel and supplies in likely preparation for a new campaign. He summed up by saying that there was a considerable body of evidence pointing to an invasion at an early date. On 6 July, Churchill asked Colonel Jacob in the military wing of the War Cabinet Secretariat for a report 'of any further indication of enemy preparations for raid or invasion'. By 7 July, the British Chiefs of Staff had accepted the likelihood of a German invasion and ordered that all enemy shipping in occupied Channel ports was to become a priority target. The same day, Churchill wrote to the Admiralty inquiring about the apparent ease with which the Nazis moved vessels along the coast of occupied Europe. 'I cannot understand how we can tolerate the movement at sea along the French coast of any vessels without attacking them,' he said. He further asked if it was true that British mines that had been dropped in an attempt to impede the movement of German shipping had become defective after only ten months. In a note to Ironside, Dill and Ismay on 10 July, Churchill contradicted this to some extent by saying that he had seen no evidence of suitable invasion craft being massed on the German-occupied Channel coast. He said that, if they did, in fact, exist, he was confident that the Royal Navy's 'numerous armed patrolling vessels', manned by 'competent seafaring men', would be more than a match for a Nazi invasion flotilla.

The Third Reich could count on deploying strong forces against Britain if Operation Sea Lion took place. The overall military command of German ground forces for Sea Lion was entrusted to Field Marshal von Rundstedt, the aristocratic Prussian soldier who had been brought out of retirement to successfully lead Army Group South in the Polish campaign and command Army Group A in France, which had forced the crucial bridgehead that had finally destroyed the resolve of the French Army at Sedan. For the invasion of England, Rundstedt's Army Group A was to take the lead again. Rundstedt assigned three infantry divisions and one mountain division from Generaloberst Busch's 16th Army and four infantry divisions and another mountain division from General Strauss's 9th Army to take part. The 17th Infantry Division and the 6th Mountain Division (for scaling the cliffs around Dover) were earmarked for the initial assault phase against the south coast of

England and the 16th Army, sailing from ports between Rotterdam and Boulogne, was assigned to attack the Hythe, Rye, Hastings and Eastbourne area. The 9th Army, sailing from ports between Boulogne and Le Havre, was detailed to attack between Brighton and Worthing.

Originally the German Army had favoured an assault across a wide front, spreading from Ramsgate to Lyme Bay, but, because of the Kriegsmarine's inability to guarantee protection, a narrower beachhead between Hythe and Worthing was selected instead. On 16 August, Field Marshal Keitel (who, in overall charge of OKW, was virtually Hitler's war minister) ordered that 'preparations for a landing in Lyme Bay will be suspended.' He further altered the plans for the narrow front on 27 August, when he told his planners that the German assault preparations taking place at Le Havre that were aimed at the sector between Brighton and Portsmouth should be scaled down. On 3 September, Keitel circulated a new timetable in which the earliest departure date for the transport ships would be 20 September 1940, and which moved S-Day to 21 September 1940. The operation was to commence with ten days' notice but the final decision about the precise 'S' time (when the landings actually commenced) would be taken at the latest three days before the set time. These instructions warned, however, that the decision to scrap the undertaking would be reserved until the last moment – twenty-four hours before 'S' time. Nazi indecision right up to the wire!

After all the wrangling about the original operational details for the invasion, the so-called 'Basis Plan', which called for the broader assault, the attack across the narrower front was chosen. This reduced front relegated General Bock's Army Group B, based in Cherbourg, to the reserve. Army Group B, which was originally to accompany Army Group A, included the Sixth Army, which, should conditions develop favourably, would land later and extend the frontage of Sea Lion to include an area that extended westward to Weymouth and Lyme Bay.

The initial seaborne invasion would involve some eleven German divisions. This force totalled 180,000 men in the first wave alone. They would pass between prepared channels marked in newly-sown German minefields. The flanks of these swept channels were further secured by patrolling U-boats. The second wave would consist of another 160,000 troops. Dover would be subjected to attack on its landward side by 10,000 Fallschirmjäger airborne 'shock troops' from the Luftwaffe's 7th Flieger Division who would co-ordinate their arrival with the landfall of the first-wave amphibious assault troops. The German paratroops were to attempt to surprise and outflank the entire British defences of this strategically important harbour. With the addition of the tanks of four panzer divisions and the vehicles of two motorized infantry divisions, the total number of German troops that would have been involved in the three stages of Operation Sea Lion would have numbered well in excess of 350,000. However, throughout the entire assault phase Nazi land forces totalled only twenty-five divisions, some five divisions short of the thirty originally considered to be the required minimum. But now that they were invading across a narrower front and the Kriegsmarine was more confident it could provide sufficient merchant vessels to support it, the invasion force was considered sufficient.

Unlike the Allied invasion of Europe four years later, which established a centralized command and control structure for the entire enterprise, there was no attempt made to establish a single HQ for the combined military command of the three German services engaged in Sea Lion. All Hitler asked was that the command posts of each service was no farther away from his own battle HQ, which would be in a castle, Schloss Ziegenberg, near Frankfurt-am-Main.

After Army Group A's divisions had forced a bridgehead, all the invading combat troops were to proceed to a line that ran roughly from Canterbury through Ashford and on to Arundel. One week later, the invaders were to proceed to Gravesend, Reigate and Portsmouth. This was to be the first objective. London and other important towns and cities, which included Bristol, Southampton, Oxford, Guildford and Salisbury, south of a line between Gloucester and Ipswich, were second-stage objectives. They could be isolated and captured later and would only be secured once the Wehrmacht had arrived in such strength and with such material that Nazi hegemony could no longer be resisted by the British defenders. The entire operation was rather optimistically assumed to take from between four to six weeks.

Germany's Fallschirmjäger airborne troops – literally, 'Falling hunters' – were the world's special forces elite in 1940. The Fallschirmjägers of the 7th Fliegerdivision were to add the surprise punch to Sea Lion. Though their Ju 52 transports would show up on radar screens, the advance warning offered to defending troops would be minutes rather than hours. Fallschirmjägers were the one German military component that Britain's High Command really feared and sought to emulate.

At a time when Britain was still considering setting up its own airborne forces, the Fallschirmjägers were already well established in Germany and they had become a veritable army in their own right. One year later, their crowning achievement would be the capture of an island actually defended by British troops – Crete – which they successfully invaded in May 1941. But in the summer of 1940, their star was, literally, still in the ascendant. In their distinctive helmets, unique camouflaged smock, which covered their Luftwaffe pattern blue-grey flying blouse, and rubber-soled jump boots, these fighters made an imposing sight. If they were dropped in force on England they would have presented a formidable foe. Ironside would have been forced to commit his reserves too soon, potentially leaving the way clear for a breakout from Sea Lion's first linear objective, the assembly points south of London.

Originally, German military intelligence, the 'Abwehr', had assumed a defending force of some twenty British divisions. German planners must have been heartened by the sight of so much of Britain's arsenal lying strewn on the beaches and dunes of Dunkirk. They were no doubt confident that soldiers of the calibre of the 9th Army's 7th Panzer Division and the Grossdeutschland infantry division of the 16th Army, both in the second wave, would give a good account of themselves. The 7th Panzer was still smarting from the British counter-attack near Arras on 21 May, one of the few occasions during the Battle of France when the BEF really surprised the Wehrmacht. The 7th Panzer was keen to exact revenge.

In the days before the savagery on the eastern front tarnished their names to a large degree, the SS Leibstandarte Adolf Hitler (LSSAH, Hitler's personal bodyguard) and the Grossdeutschland Division, both

Sentry on a coastal beach amid coils of barbed wire, a characteristic scene in southern England in July 1940.

in 16th Army and both earmarked to rendezvous in southern England, were considered Germany's elite. The Grossdeutschland Division had employed the only battery of the new Sturmgeschütz 75mm armoured self-propelled guns in support of its units during the attack on Sedan in May. For Sea Lion it could expect to deploy further batteries of this formidable self-propelled armoured tank-killer. The Sturmgeschütz was a turretless tank – virtually a steerable high-velocity assault gun, based on the new Panzer Mk IV chassis. With its low silhouette it would have proved a difficult target for British gunners and it would have lent powerful support to the Wehrmacht's advancing soldiers.

Opposing them, the forces in England, though still pitifully weak, had grown stronger by September 1940 during the three months since the evacuation from France. Indeed, after the war, Kesselring, one of Hitler's ablest commanders (who later switched services, joining the Army and became one of the Reich's best land commanders) said, 'For the energy with which the British Government raised the defence potential of the island I have only admiration.' However, he didn't think that the Home Guard posed much of a threat. 'I cannot believe in any special combat value on the part of bodies like the Home Guard,' he said. 'The Voksturm (Germany's equivalent of the Home Guard) had a great propaganda effect, yet even though it was better armed than the Home Guard it turned into a fiasco.' Clearly Kesselring had never heard about the reception that was in store for the invaders from the Auxunits armed with state-of-the-art weapons like plastic explosives. He hadn't seen Churchill's memo to Ismay dated 18 June that suggested:

> There ought to be at least twenty thousand [British!] Storm Troops of 'Leopards' drawn from existing units, ready to spring at the throat of any small landings or descents. These officers and men should be armed with the latest equipment, Tommy guns, grenades, etc., and should be given great facilities in motor cycles and armoured cars.

Because most of the Regular British Army escaped unscathed from the enemy but had abandoned most of its vehicles and equipment, Churchill was more interested than most about the speed of replacement of the lost weapons. On 18 June he had written to Ismay asking to be kept informed about the state of coast defences and he again stressed that enough troops should be kept in reserve for the 'mobile columns', 'brigade groups' and the 'general reserve'. He also, rather irritably, reminded Ismay that he didn't want to hear that new tanks were going to storage depots as they came off the production line. He urged that they go instead to the 8th Tank Regiment, for example, to whom he had promised fifty-two new tanks.

British production, now stepped up and part of a war economy, was surprisingly more efficient than that of Germany. In June, Britain's aero factories, under Lord Beaverbrook's enlightened management at the Ministry of Aircraft Production (MAP), actually built 446 new fighters. The best Germany could manage in the same month was 220. Of Beaverbrook, the Labour politician Emmanuel Shinwell said, 'No one can underrate the Canadian press lord's contributions to the war effort, notably in the production of aircraft, but after the extreme emergency of the Battle of Britain period his successes were counterbalanced by failures in other ministries by his quixotic and unpredictable manoeuvres.' 'Manny' Shinwell conceded that Beaverbrook 'had a genius for improvisation, precisely what Churchill needed.' Beaverbrook made such an impression on Churchill that in 1941 he was made Minister for Supply and given responsibility for tanks as well as aircraft. Lord Nuffield, better known as William Morris, was another business dynamo who threw his lot into helping the war effort. His 1,414 acre site at Castle Bromwich in Birmingham turned out Spitfires by the hundred. He subsequently became Director General of Maintenance and headed the Civilian Repair Organization (CRO). Under Nuffield's stewardship the CRO engaged the considerable might of Morris Motors Ltd in the recovery, repair and redistribution of battle-damaged or unserviceable aircraft.

This increase in British production was not achieved without cost. The factories now employed scores of women and the emergency demanded long shifts. Mass Observation noted that, unless something was done to inspire and encourage the new army of workers that were drafted in to support the war economy, 'the increase of effort called for by longer hours will very rapidly decline.' Soon, workers' canteens echoed to the sounds of Tommy Handley of *ITMA* (*It's That Man Again*) fame. *ITMA* was a title that poked fun at the Government's fascination with initials, such as ARP, LDV, WRVS and FANY. The government-sponsored ENSA (another acronym – this time for the Entertainment's National Service Association) ensured that live concerts and visits by celebrities provided sufficient distraction to make the tedium and fatigue of the twelve-hour shifts more bearable.

The Royal Navy had to reckon with both the Luftwaffe's expertise with dive-bombers as well as the threat of mines. At the time Admiral Sir Charles Forbes' Home Fleet protected the waters of the English Channel and also looked after the 'Northern Approaches'. During the winter of 1940, more than half of the Royal Navy's ships lost to enemy action (twenty-eight out of a total of forty-eight) were destroyed by German magnetic mines. Typically, the bullish Albert Kesselring wasn't too worried about the threat of a superior Royal Navy. After the war he said that with all the means at Germany's disposal the Third

Denn Wir Fahren Gegen Engelland (now we are marching against England), a Nazi sea shanty.

The sight of *schnorkel* – adapted Nazi Pzkw IV tanks – rising from the depths would have no doubt quickly wiped the smiles from the faces of these defending British troops.

Reich 'could have paralyzed even these superior forces.' Although the British Admiralty did warn the Prime Minister on 12 July that 'It appears probably that a total of some 100,000 men might reach these shores without being intercepted by naval forces,' in an article titled 'Our Sure Shield', published in the August 1940 issue of *The Navy: The Official Organ of The Navy League*, Vice-Admiral Harper expressed his confidence in the Royal Navy as an impregnable bulwark:

> Our Navy, assisted as it is by an incomparable Air Force, must see to it that, in spite of the enemy being at our gates, our supplies from overseas are maintained and our shores guarded from invasion. ... Invasion, to be successful, must still rely on the safe transport by sea of troops, munitions, guns, tanks, and supplies of every description ... it is the duty of the Navy, assisted by the Air Force, to prevent such a catastrophe overtaking us. The Navy can do it. The Navy will do it.

The following summary of British coastal forces from *The Oxford Illustrated History of the Royal Navy* suggests that Admiral Harper had good reason to be confident:

> By September 1940, the Navy had thirty-eight destroyers and seven Kingfisher and Shearwater-class coastal escorts based at Immingham, Harwich and Sheerness. These were backed up by the cruisers *Manchester*, *Birmingham* and *Southampton* at Immingham and *Galatea* and *Aurora* at Sheerness. The Commander in Chief, Portsmouth, had at his disposal another nine destroyers and five Free French torpedo boats backed up by the cruiser *Cardiff* and battleship *Revenge*. A further 700 smaller craft were also deployed with 200 or 300 at sea at all times to provide early warning.

The Chiefs of Staff replied to Churchill's 15 August minute with a document entitled *Defence against Invasion*. It stressed that all commands had been told about 'the paramount importance of immediate counter-attack upon the enemy, should he obtain a temporary footing on these shores.' The COS report reminded the Prime Minister that British reserves situated north and west of London could easily be directed against an enemy incursion in either East Anglia or the South East. It added that the reason there were so many home defence troops in the south – making that region seem 'slightly over-insured' – was principally because these troops could be easily protected by Fighter Command's 'umbrella'.

Shortly after this reassurance, however, British Intelligence became aware of German barges assembling along the coasts of France and Holland. Intelligence sources also reported that two German mountain divisions with mules were reported to be assembling near Boulogne. It was obvious that the white cliffs adjacent to Folkestone and Dover were to be a target. Churchill realized that the situation had been rapidly transformed.

On 25 June, General Sir Edmund 'Tiny' Ironside presented his plan for the anti-invasion defence of Great Britain to the combined Chiefs of Staff. Aware that England's coastline was especially vulnerable anywhere between Folkestone and The Wash, Ironside made his dispositions accordingly in a brave attempt to ensure the integrity of these areas.

By the end of June, Ironside's command consisted of only fifteen infantry divisions. Four of these were training divisions and eight of them were stationed on coastal defence duties. Armoured divisions didn't exist until the war started and after the retreat from France there was only one complete armoured division in Britain – 2nd Armoured. This was based in Lincolnshire and had 178 light tanks. 1st Armoured Division was despatched to France as late as 21 May, in a last-ditch attempt to avert the collapse of the BEF. It was reformed in Surrey and with its eighty-one 'mediums', 100 'lights' and ninety 'heavies' (the new Matildas), 1st Armoured Division quickly became the most powerful force in the United Kingdom. Ironside's three infantry divisions (one Canadian and two Scots) completed his reserve. However, his forces were further depleted on 8 June, when the 1st Canadian and 52nd Lowland Divisions were landed at Cherbourg in an abortive attempt to reintroduce the BEF to the French battlefield.

Ironside's defence plan featured an elongated 'crust' of beach defences that combined anti-tank mines and static beach obstacles with miles and miles of barbed wire. Beach exits were mined but having, in an effort to prevent local inhabitants from being accidentally maimed, an identifying clump of earth on them, they were also obvious to any enemy. Rover mouths and estuaries were effectively part of this outer crust and they were also mined. The heavy artillery of 'the Emergency Coast Batteries' mainly consisted of First World War vintage guns and their mountings taken from ships that had long been scrapped. Shells were in such short supply, however, that gun crews were forbidden to fire even a single practice round.

Behind the outer crust a succession of 'stop lines' radiated, often following natural obstructions such as river courses. These were strewn with tank traps and pillboxes. Railway sleepers were slotted into pre-sunk apertures and could be hastily erected to block roads thought to be likely invasion highways. Further inland the stop lines led back to the GHQ line, which consisted of a trench 20 feet wide and 10 feet deep that stretched across England from the Bristol Channel to the Wash and dog-legged south of London to protect the capital. The GHQ line featured yet more anti-tank traps and obstacles, with belts of pillboxes spaced at intervals of 1,000 feet. Beyond this redoubt sat the GHQ Reserve, comprising Ironside's three infantry divisions and his single complete and unbloodied armoured division. The GHQ Reserve was to wait patiently in preparation to plug an enemy breach of any of the static defences.

Though there were many in high office who doubted that the invasion would happen, Ironside was obviously not one of them. On 6 July he wrote: 'Personally I think the Boche must have a go at us, and they will be sure to make a determined effort when they do.' On 9 July, he added, 'I have so many factors to take into account.' Indeed he had. Ironside was continuously juggling with the various different demands that placed a strain on his overstretched command, including the actual beach defences, the training of the reserve, its mobility and the availability of first-rate fighting troops to staff it, and the state of the troops who manned the static defences of the coastal crust. When he

Pillbox cunningly disguised as Hansel & Gretel's cottage.

was replaced by Alan Brooke on 19 July, General Ironside was confident he had 'done his best' for the defence of Britain.

The various halt lines manned by Regular troops were supplemented by Local Defence Volunteers (LDV), the forerunners of the Home Guard. The LDV's name was changed on Churchill's insistence as he considered 'Home Guard' a more appropriate and inspiring title considering the emergency. Local mobile reserves, some in 'armoured cars' converted from Ford, Hillman or Alvis saloons, weighed down with appliqué armour fashioned from boiler-plate, stood ready to rush forward to check any incursion. Guarding the RAF's airfields waited vehicles such as MAP's 14hp 'Beaverette' light armoured car, preserving their precious fuel in anticipation of an enemy glider or parachute attack. Airfields were further protected by Picket-Hamilton forts. These were small armoured turrets armed with machine guns that were sunk below ground level within an airfield perimeter so as not to obstruct taxiing aircraft. The raising mechanism was originally based on an ingenious system of mechanical counterbalances but later it was activated by compressed air so that the 'disappearing pillboxes', as they were often known, could rapidly pop up from the ground and offer any unsuspecting enemy a painful surprise. The smooth steel domes of 'Alan Williams' turrets provided further protection for beleaguered airfields and were another testament to the capabilities of British engineering in an emergency. Once the gunner had dropped inside and closed the armoured hatches behind him he was able to traverse his armament through 360 degrees and could fire at targets on the ground or quickly switch to the AA mode. GOC Southern Command, General Auchinleck, definitely thought the Alan Williams turret was an excellent design, saying it was 'a preferable alternative to a pillbox for machine guns as it is lower and more easily concealed'.

Circling London, the 'Outer London Defence Ring' consisted of another continuous line of pillboxes. The capital was further protected by roofed-over 'Emergency Batteries' of coastal artillery at Coalhouse Fort, Shornemead, Shellness and Shoeburyness, which covered the approaches to the Thames Estuary. They were supported by up-gunned Victorian coastal forts and by nearby submerged booms that physically obstructed the entrance to the Thames and the Medway.

On 25 July, Churchill wrote to the Admiralty, under the heading 'Action This Day', to push his idea of laying a curtain of mines behind the German invasion flotilla, thus containing it within a trap. His note said:

> If an invader lands during the night or morning, the flotillas will attack him in the rear during the day, and these flotillas will be heavily bombarded from the air, as part of the air battles that will

be going on. If, however, when night falls a curtain or fender of mines can be laid close inshore, so as to cut off the landing place from reinforcements of any kind, these mines, once laid, will not have to be guarded from air attack, and consequently will relieve the flotilla from the need of coming back on the second day, thus avoiding losses from the air and air protection.

If the soldiers of the Wehrmacht had actually landed, the British defenders would have been in for a very rough time since by then they would have lost the luxury of air cover. With no tactical air support Britain's soldiers would have had to rely on their wits to survive. About the only weapon the British infantry had to fend off the screaming Stuka was the trusty company Bren, which could be attached to its rather spindly AA mounting.

If they had survived the preliminary softening up of salvoes from German shore-based artillery firing from occupied coasts and repeated sorties of Luftwaffe bombers operating a 'taxi rank' type of offensive strategy around the clock during the pre-landing phase, some of Lieutenant General Sir Frederick Pile's weaponry might have been employed on the developing invasion battlefield. His Anti-Aircraft Command had some 1,700 3.5-inch and 4.5-inch anti-aircraft guns and more than 4,000 searchlights. These weapons would not have been of much use tied to the static AA defence of Britain's cities and factories after the Nazis had landed. They would have been better employed firing HE (high explosive) shells horizontally across the open countryside once the German invaders had secured a bridgehead.

Home Guards were encouraged to take note of new ideas such as those described in the series of 'Victory' pocket books published by Bernard's. These cost only 1/- and were each 'a mine of information'. As the threat of invasion approached it is likely that men of the Home Guard, soldiers in the Regular Army and particularly the volunteers of the Auxunits snapped up copies of a paperback called *Guerrilla Tactics*. This book was full of illustrations describing the myriad ways an invader could be stopped. It showed a plucky infantryman thrusting a rod-like implement into the drive sprocket of a panzer – 'Destroying Track of Enemy Tank by Means of Crowbar'. Presumably the German crew, despite having had nearly a year of combat experience, had forgotten to check their vehicle, even though it was in enemy territory!

Throughout the summer and autumn of 1940, Churchill chaired a series of 'Invasion Conferences'. The Army was represented by a single delegate – Commander-in-Chief Home Forces (Ironside, then Alan Brooke), but the Royal Navy, with five commands (Home Fleet, the Nore, Portsmouth, Plymouth and Western Approaches), each with its own commander-in-chief for Fighter, Bomber and Coastal Commands, easily outnumbered the soldiers. At times there were suggestions that a supreme commander (like Eisenhower at D-Day) should be chosen who would lead Britain's armed forces if the Germans actually secured a landing. However, Ismay felt that there was no one better than Churchill capable of simultaneously directing both military and civilian operations if the crisis worsened.

The English landscape was quickly transformed as anti-invasion precautions sprang up across the country. 'Dragon's teeth' (concrete anti-tank pyramids), anti-glider poles and beach obstacles proliferated. Fields were further made safe from glider assault by the addition of row upon row of rusted and disabled cars. Towed from breakers' yards, they became a surreal addition to the English landscape.

Pillboxes of three basic types were built. Some can still be found with the evidence of their hasty shuttering still preserved in the concrete that was used to erect them. Major-General Taylor of the Directorate of Fortifications & Works was in overall command of British pillbox construction in 1940. The smallest pillbox type had walls 15 inches thick and was for the protection of small groups of riflemen. The next size up had 42-inch walls and shielded Bren guns and their crews. The largest housed either 2- or 6-pounder anti-tank guns.

Until the National Road Research Laboratory initiated careful research into what were the best construction methods and, later in the war, formulated regulations for design and production co-ordination, British pillbox quality was not high. Few would have been able to contend with shots from the formidable German '88. This German all-purpose fieldpiece was ubiquitous throughout the Wehrmacht and Luftwaffe (it was originally designed purely for the anti-aircraft role). It could rapidly shoot a close group of eight armour-piercing shells through 6½ feet of concrete at a great distance.

'A Popular Guide to the German Army', published by the General Staff of the War Office, graphically showed the defenders what was in store for them if the Nazis invaded. Its cover showed German paratroops tumbling from Luftwaffe aircraft. Inside it said:

> Parachute troops are picked and trained by the German Air Force. They are young and fit. They volunteer for adventure and know that they stand a good chance of being killed. But if they try to use them against trained determined troops, WHO ARE TRAINED IN VIGOROUS AND SPEEDY COUNTERMEASURES AND ARE NOT TO BE CAUGHT OFF THEIR GUARD, then the only result will be the annihilation of the attackers.

The leaflet further warned that speed was the essence of defence, 'because a parachutist who has just landed is defenceless until he can get rid of his parachute harness.' British soldiers were warned, however, that their ruthless enemy 'has been known to carry on his

This photograph was taken in June 1940 and shows one method of preventing an enemy glider's safe landing. A cheaper and easier method was to simply erect scores of anti-glider poles in thick plantations across open fields.

Deep rows of concrete dragons' teeth anti-tank obstacles were supposed to prevent panzers from breaching the GHQ Line.

person hand grenades, a knife, an automatic pistol, and in some cases only, a Tommy gun strapped to his back.' It continued, 'Air-landing troops will have machine guns ready to shoot from the windows of their aeroplane as it comes down and will lose no time climbing out and adopting battle formation. Watch as the [parachutist's] container lands and get him as he goes to open it.' The words, 'He has no defended post. Stop him getting one' were cold comfort to the lonely men of an infantry section sitting passively in their newly-built pillbox. It must have felt strange for the occupants of pillboxes situated only yards from the relative normality of a town or village railway station to contrast their lot at the hands of the invading armies (pillboxes would be priority targets) with that of the civilians who went about their normal chores only yards away.

General Thorne's XII Corps was situated in the most threatened sector of Southern Command now commanded by General Auchinleck, based in Wilton, in Wiltshire. Thorne's command was covered on its northern flank by XI Corps and further protected by VIII Corps to the west. By now, two divisions from the Empire had been entrenched in the south-east – one Canadian division and one division from New Zealand. The First Motor Machine Gun Brigade was also stationed within General Thorne's sector. Not counting the General Headquarters Reserve (Ironside's three divisions) that was stationed to the north-west of the capital, nine Regular infantry divisions protected the south-east of England. A further five infantry divisions, stationed throughout the West Country and East Anglia, could have been called upon if things became too desperate. The entire southern half of Britain was protected by only three armoured divisions, however: the 21st north of Portland, the 2nd in Somerset and the 1st and 2nd in the south-east of England.

Because of the recent failure of the 'static' Maginot Line, Ironside's thin coastal 'crust' defence, which relied on a mobile component (the GHQ reserve) rather than strong static coastal defences, was favoured by many, including Churchill. The premier thought the Germans were capable of penetrating any fixed defences and he reckoned that they were particularly good at exploiting a fixed front at several points. Ironside's plan with its 'mobile reserve', a hard-hitting force that was expected to rush to the scene of any breach in the crust to 'plug' the gap, was expected to take account of the speed and changing nature of the modern battlefield. Montgomery supported this idea too, even going as far as requisitioning southern counties buses for use as troop carriers! Auchinleck and the Vice CIGS, General Sir Robert Haining, however, thought the idea of adopting a system that would allow the Nazis to gain a foothold was folly. They preferred to resist the invader on the beaches, believing that it was here that the battle would be decided. Events in Normandy four years later during the D-Day operations were to bear out the wisdom of their argument. The

Germans failed to prevent the Allies from establishing a bridgehead and could do little to stop the build-up of Allied reinforcements. Due to continual Allied bombing, German reserves were unable even to get as far as the rapidly advancing front line.

Auchinleck thought that the idea of a defensive line being manned by a mixture of artillery men, Allied soldiers, Territorials and Home Guards, with the cream of Britain's Regular Army garrisoned as a *'corps d'élite'*, as he termed it, was divisive and wrong. He felt it smacked of snobbery and that it ignored the fact that many Territorial units were superior to some of the Regular ones. The 'Terriers', as they were known, were not always commanded by Colonel Blimps. In fact, the Territorial units often managed to recruit officers of a higher calibre than those that joined the Regular Army. Many Territorial officers were well used to leadership and management in their professional careers.

Auchinleck was not much liked by Montgomery, who had the ear of the Prime Minister and who preferred to keep 'fighting men' separate from part-timers. In fact, since Auchinleck's promotion to GOC Southern Command, Montgomery (who had assumed command of Auchinleck's previous command, V Corps), continuously questioned his predecessor's methods. Montgomery proved more successful than Auchinleck in earning plaudits: it is often forgotten that Auchinleck was responsible for stemming Rommel's advance by winning the first battle of El Alamein.

On 5 September 1940, Brooke sent a message to Auchinleck:

> There are indications that Hitler may intend in the near future to carry out a direct attack against Great Britain. The most favourable areas for landing would be between Southwold and Shoreham. Conditions are most favourable for invasion about 12 or 13 September.

He warned that, if weather conditions improved, the Germans could come 'at any time after the 6th'. On the 6th, Brooke actually issued orders to all his commanders, including Auchinleck, which warned, 'Attack probable within the next three days.' Southern Command's forces were put on their highest state of alert – eight hours' readiness. On 7 September, the codeword 'Cromwell', the alarm for a German invasion, was inadvertently issued to some of GHQ's forces, notably members of the Home Guard. The ringing of church bells, prohibited since 13 June, caused further consternation in some areas as this was the signal that the German invasion had started. Auchinleck's units remained at Cromwell alert for some weeks. Shortly after the Cromwell false alarm it was decided to introduce an intermediary warning stage, 'Stand-To'. However, the drama of 7/8 September did at least realistically check that Britain's invasion defences were in order.

The German ground troops would have been transported in a vast assortment of vessels scoured from the ports and harbours of Nazi-occupied Europe. The German Navy's Merchant Shipping Division, the Schiffahrtsabteilung, was the organization tasked with assembling the invasion flotilla. This job was made all the more difficult because nearly 1,000,000 tons of the Reich's shipping had been interred in neutral harbours around the world when the war started. A third as many again had been sunk by the British, who had imposed their own blockade on Germany since hostilities commenced in September 1939. The recent campaign in Norway had highlighted the importance of the Scandinavian iron ore route and it was impossible to divert German vessels that were engaged in carrying this precious cargo, especially during the summer months when the ports along the Norwegian coast were largely ice-free. The heavy losses in warships suffered by the Kriegsmarine during the Norwegian campaign further weakened Germany's maritime capability and highlighted how precarious naval operations could be. However, Germany had captured about 2 million tons of freighter capacity from French and Dutch ports. Combined with the tonnage the Schiffahrtsabteilung had scraped together, this meant that Hitler's support and supply fleet for Sea Lion grossed about 750,000 tons.

Although the German assault troops in the first wave would have hit ports like Newhaven in Sussex fast and hard in an attempt to capture them intact, OKW and OKM were under no illusions about the real likelihood of securing an operable harbour on S-Day. Much thought was therefore given to finding alternatives to capturing British harbours intact. At a Führer Conference on 21 May, two concepts were outlined by Admiral Raeder. One, the brainchild of Gottfried Feder, an executive within Germany's Ministry of Economics, was a scheme to prefabricate harbour installations and take them to England after the first wave assault had established itself. Although the proposal diverted resources away from the manufacture of the concrete fortifications that were then being speedily erected as part of Hitler's 'Atlantic Wall' along the Continental Channel coast, the idea was given a hearing. Feder suggested that the sections of strong points could be adapted to float, 'caisson-like', and could then be towed across the Channel and sunk to form artificial breakwaters and quays. It is interesting to note that the Germans considered this four years earlier than the Allies, who created the famous Mulberry floating harbours, which were dragged to the beaches of Normandy on D-Day. The other inventive scheme was for the construction of special high-speed tank-carrying hydrofoils that would cross the narrow waters and unleash portable self-powered pontoon sections that would race on to the landing beach. The main craft would then return to its base in France and collect another light tank prior to commencing the return journey.

If Churchill had had an inkling of these schemes he might have been less confident about the chances of resisting the invader.

Transporting tanks and soldiers was a problem that greatly occupied German planners during the early summer of 1940 and a Major Siebel in the Luftwaffe proposed the introduction of pontoon ferries powered by airscrews! In fact, Kesselring had great faith in the Siebel ferries 'in which I had travelled myself,' he said, 'large numbers of which could be easily assembled armed with three 8.8cm Flak and light guns; they could also protect the crossing against attack by British light naval forces.' Although he admitted that Kriegsmarine High Command was reluctant to try anything new, he thought the Siebels were 'an excellent means of transporting troops across the English Channel, as they later proved for Germany when they ferried materials between Sicily and North Africa.' Though hasty and imperfect (the floating harbour and hydrofoil ideas never went into production), German invasion preparations in the summer of 1940 were all made in deadly seriousness. On the Ems estuary between 25 July and September, the Germans even trained 51,000 assault boat coxswains for Operation Sea Lion.

Regardless of Germany's engineering genius, the Third Reich was steadily running out of time and resources to be capable of launching the invasion of England. It was decided that the only way forward was to hastily convert the many freight-carrying barges that plied Europe's inland waterways to troop transports. In all, nearly 2,500 barges, or *prahme*, were converted. Floors were reinforced by the addition of longitudinal strengtheners and the bows were cut away to be fitted with removable bulkheads so that an internal ramp could be unfolded to allow the passage of troops and vehicles. Not all these vessels were simple inland barges as has often been assumed. At the time the British press made light of the threat of thousands of seasick steel-helmeted 'Jerries' crammed together in open barges of the sort that are towed on the river Thames, being pitched about in the English Channel as their vessels were slowly towed to the coast in a huge daisy chain formation. Many of the *prahme* had their own internal power. Neither were the *prahme* all expected to make the entire crossing themselves from coast to coast. A large number were intended to be used simply as lighters that would make repeated trips to unload the numerous larger seagoing freighters that were unable to venture into Britain's shallow coastal waters. Type 'AS' armoured barges, intended to transport infantry close to the beaches during the initial assault, were also included in the Nazi invasion flotilla. Reinforced by the addition of concrete, these more robust powered *prahme* had a reduced load-carrying capacity of only 40 tons. They were intended to release their human cargo as they neared the beaches. Storm troopers, packed into inflatable rubber *sturmboote* of the type that had successfully carried

Hitler's troops silently across the Meuse in May, would launch their dinghies from slides that extended from above the AS's armoured hull.

Great ingenuity had also been given to the problem of transporting and unloading tanks. German planners were well aware that armoured vehicles were at their most vulnerable as they were being unloaded. At the time the LST (Landing Ship Tank) of the sort that the United States later developed for use in the Pacific and at Normandy didn't exist. Furthermore, Luftwaffe reconnaissance had revealed the fact that Britain's coastal fortifications had been greatly strengthened by the addition of large-calibre weapons (though the fact that many of these were obsolete guns from scrapped First World War vessels or that the gun crews did not even have the ammunition for practice firing was fortunately not known). The Germans had two solutions for this problem. Firstly, they discovered that, with the addition of floats and rudimentary waterproofing, the Panzer Mk II tank was seaworthy and could power itself to the beach by engaging a simple propeller driven from the vehicle's tracks. However, the newer and heavier Mk III and Mk IV tanks required a more ingenious solution. The answer was the revolutionary introduction of an extendable *schnorkel* device that allowed the diesel engine to vent and breathe while several metres below the surface. This idea, now commonplace in the world's armies, was first tried out by volunteer crews at Westerland on the Jutland island of Sylt. The submersible tanks could operate at a depth of 15 metres, and by virtue of an onboard gyroscopic compass, they were able to navigate blind. There were some accidents and at least one fatality when exhaust gases backed up inside the driving compartment, but generally the vehicles worked. What defending British troops would have thought when they were confronted by field-grey German tanks, streaming sea water, suddenly emerging with their engines running from the murky Channel waters is best left to the imagination.

There also existed a huge variety of pontoons and ferries capable of carrying non-essential items, such as stores and heavier equipment, to be used after a bridgehead had been secured. Some of these could be safely towed the entire distance if sea conditions were favourable. In fact, the Germans intended to tow heavy field artillery across the Channel. Howitzers and flak artillery would simply be floated across on rafts constructed of lashed-together pontoons. The Luftwaffe supplied enough parts to construct 150 rafts that were to be powered by their Siebel aero engine. One idea for a landing craft was based on the captured parts of British engineer assault bridges left in France by the BEF.

Soon the various conversions began to leave their workshops throughout the Reich and started to converge on the various occupied ports chosen for the disembarkation of the invasion flotilla. On just one day, 30 August, the harbour at Emden released sixty camouflaged and armed motor fishing vessels, thirteen motor boats and two 'command' boats to Le Havre and Boulogne – just two of Sea Lion's embarkation harbours. This traffic continued apace and on 12 September, for example, 516 invasion barges, more than 500 converted trawlers, seven armoured assault barges, 143 tugs, twenty-one 'group leader' boats and an assortment of transports for carrying *schnorkel*-equipped tanks had commenced the penultimate stage of the proposed landing phase. It has since been estimated that if Sea Lion went ahead the line of invasion barges and their supporting motor vessels would extend out to sea some 12 miles! Sympathy should be given to the problems faced by Germany's logisticians. These men had to draw up a plan that demanded literally thousands of sailors and soldiers to pilot, load and repair the huge armada. Things were so desperate that Kriegsmarine reservists were called up in an effort to feed the monster that Sea Lion had become.

Should the invader actually have landed, the RAF was prepared to convert some of its Tiger Moth biplane trainers to drop bombs full of newly developed gases (such as the exotic sounding 'Paris Green') on the enemy. Though a last resort, the situation was so desperate that even Churchill was prepared to 'drench the invasion beaches with mustard gas.' A former wartime chemist at Porton Down (Britain's chemical defence establishment in Wiltshire) told me that Britain was always worried that the enemy might use chemical weapons. A great deal of energy was expended at Porton by scientists trying to ensure that Britain's armed forces were sufficiently protected from chemical attack. This fear was exacerbated by the fact that the Germans were known to have cornered the world's available arsenic supplies. If Britain did decide to use gas its own soldiers were to be warned of its presence by the addition of patches of chemically impregnated yellow fabric, which when attached to the service respirator case would change colour if gas was in the air. Similar steps were taken to avoid any mistakes involving British armoured vehicles succumbing to attack from their own side. If invasion happened, all British tanks and lorries were to have a large white circle painted on top and RAF pilots were to be briefed to make sure they didn't attack vehicles thus marked. Later, when the Allies invaded Normandy during the D-Day landings, all Allied vehicles were marked with the white US star for the same reason.

As early as 1938, at the time of the Munich Crisis, the British Government had compiled a register of all the available scientific brains – student and professor alike – who would be held in reserve from military service should war break out. In 1939, British Intelligence reports confirmed the suspicion that the Nazis could deliver gas shells containing arsenicals small enough to penetrate the filter of the standard British respirator. The expanded team of scientists at Porton soon conceived a project, codenamed 'Arthur', to develop a special additional filter that was proof against this new threat from arsenic trihydride. It was feared that the Germans might also use tear gas, which could be fired at tanks and drawn in through the ventilation system, and much attention was given to gas-sealing the new British tanks.

On 15 June 1940, advocating the pre-emptive use of low-level gas spraying above the invasion beaches, Sir John Dill, Chief of the Imperial General Staff, wrote:

> At a time when our national existence is at stake we should not hesitate to adopt whatever means appear to offer the best chance of success.

He recognized that resorting to gas warfare before the Germans did would alienate many, especially the Americans, who were more than sympathetic to Britain's plight, but was convinced that, in view of the critical circumstances, there was no alternative but to resort to chemical weapons.

In support of its conventional fixed defences and its regular and volunteer fighting services, Britain considered some bizarre and desperate measures. One of the most memorable was the 'Flame Barrage', a scheme that involved setting England's coastal waters alight. In the *Big Lie*, author John Baker White (who in 1940 formed a special unit within the DMI to broadcast propaganda to the Germans) said, 'I am convinced that one rumour, one deception, that above all others, discouraged the Germans from launching their invasion attempt in 1940 consisted of eight words: "The British can set the sea on fire."' After a display of Britain's 'Flame Barrage', whereby specially constructed pipes fed a continuous stream of petrol into the sea off Dover's St Margaret's Bay, the rumour was given impetus by two chance occurrences. Firstly, after a particularly effective RAF incendiary raid on German invasion-barge formations at Calais, trains of badly burned soldiers (who had been on board the vessels practising embarkation) started to pull in to the railway termini in Paris. Not surprisingly, their specific burn injuries caused French tongues to wag. 'How did they get so badly burned?' Second, eight German prisoners were captured after one of the Royal Navy's regular forays into enemy waters. These were regularly mounted to gain intelligence and snatch unsuspecting enemy troops who might reveal useful secrets about German invasion preparations. Surprisingly, the German prisoners, though stationed on the same armed trawler, all happened to be from different units. This proved to be a bonanza for the Political Warfare Executive (PWE, formed in July), which quickly broadcast that the soldiers had been 'rescued from the sea' by the benevolent British. The PWE broadcast was quite detailed. It gave the names of each one of the prisoners and revealed their differing unit designations, suggesting that they had all been captured from different places across a wide area. 'We knew nothing of the fate of their comrades,' the broadcast solemnly added. The ruse obviously worked for, as soon as the broadcast was heard (it was also communicated through what was called the 'pipe-line' of channels in neutral countries such as Sweden, Spain and Portugal), Germany's Chemisch-Physikalische Versuchsanstalt at Wilhelmshaven, after tests involving 100 tons of a petrol-oil mixture that burned for more than twenty minutes, confirmed what Germany's office of Naval Operations first noted on 10 August – 'The British might use oil as a coastal defence.' Churchill commented on the rescue of the soldiers: 'This was the source of a widespread rumour that the Germans had attempted an invasion and had suffered very heavy losses either by drowning or by being burnt in patches of sea covered with flaming oil! We took no steps to contradict such tales, which spread freely through the occupied countries in a wildly exaggerated form and gave much encouragement to the oppressed populations.' As late as 18 September, Churchill wrote to Ismay asking him to make 'inquiries whether there is no way in which a sheet of flaming oil can be spread over one or more of the invasion harbours.' The premier went on to remind Ismay that this idea wasn't new, it was 'no more than the old fire-ship story … that was tried at Dunkirk in the days of the Armada.'

If the German invader had landed, Churchill's War Cabinet could have expected to endure a troglodyte experience in underground bunkers, much like the hundreds of Auxunit volunteers dotted throughout England, Scotland and Wales in their damp and claustrophobic OBs. The MPs' anti-invasion hideout was the Cabinet War Rooms in Whitehall. Built secretly in 1938, at the height of the Munich Crisis, these reinforced bunkers were the last ditch defences of the government of the day. No expense had been spared to ensure that they were proof against all known forms of conventional attack. They were shielded at ground level by a girdling concrete apron, which was intended to be proof both from direct gunfire and bomb blast. The entire complex (formerly the basement chambers of Whitehall's Office of Works) was further protected by a metre-thick concrete 'slab', which was added in 1940, when it was realized that a direct hit by a 300lb bomb would penetrate this vital national nerve centre. The first cabinet held in the bunker took place under Chamberlain's administration in 1939. In July 1940, Churchill held the first meeting of his cabinet there, having room 65A assigned as a combined office and bedroom. On 29 July, the Advanced HQ of Britain's Home Forces was established within the building. On 11 September, he made his first radio broadcast to the nation from the War Rooms, of which he had previously declared, 'This is the room from which I'll direct the War.'

Throughout the summer of 1940, Britain braced itself for the worst. But time was on the nation's side. Every passing day brought the natural protection of inclement weather closer. Churchill's much vaunted 'Channel fogs' would soon cloak British coastal waters and hamper enemy navigation. The invasion barges and their crews, some unfamiliar with service on the open seas, might not have coped with seas that are at best unpredictable but in winter can be treacherous. All the time, the British Army and Air Force were growing stronger. So much so, in fact, that soon British commanders would become relaxed enough to remove Auchinleck and trained troops from Southern Command to counter the German threat in North Africa.

As autumn approached, it became increasingly obvious to Hitler that he might not have to invade Great Britain in order to destroy it. He was confident that Britain could be brought to her knees by a combination of night bombing and the strangulation of an overwhelming naval blockade. Although the Kriegsmarine possessed few battleships it had plenty of submarines. By November and December 1940, German U-boat successes began to take a heavier and heavier toll of British merchant shipping. 'No doubt this is largely due to the shortage of destroyers through invasion precautions,' Churchill wrote to the Admiralty on 4 August 1940.

In February 1941, Churchill decided to concentrate Royal Navy forces in the north-western approaches and took the unprecedented step of moving the Admiralty's command of Britain's sea lanes from Plymouth to Liverpool. A new Battle of Britain was about to be fought. Not on or above British soil, but on and below the surrounding seas.

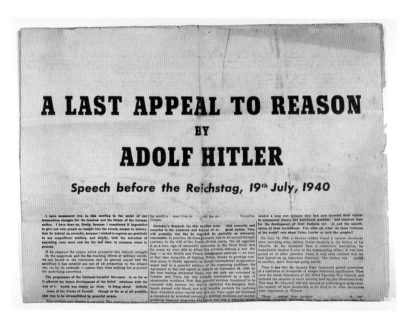

The Luftwaffe vainly scattered thousands of Hitler's 'A Last Appeal to Reason' over Britain. Hitler genuinely believed that a negotiated peace was possible.

Chapter 5

The Balloon Goes Up

Lecture on Bren Gun. Canadian, at Bishopstone, 1800-2200 hrs. Lecture on Bren Gun Carrier by Canadians. Rode over hills to Firle, back to Bishopstone by road. 0900-1300 hrs. Meet at Mary's farm under Capt. Bond, for attack on tanks in Stanmer Park. Firle patrol successful. 1900-0030 hrs. Night scheme with Canadians. Firle and Bishopstone patrols got through without meeting enemy. 1800-2300 hrs.

Bill Webber, Auxunit Patrol Leader
'Firle Patrol', diary entries, winter 1940-41

Bill Webber (centre) with Mr and Mrs Tom Smith.

Bill Webber and his friend Tom Smith are the only survivors from the four-man Firle Patrol in Sussex that was responsible for the downland area north of Brighton. In a diary entry from the summer of 1941, Bill Webber reveals that Auxunit patrols were not only concerned with enemy infiltration of their patrol areas. Sussex was heavily garrisoned by Canadian troops during 1940 and, although they largely had a cordial relationship with their British allies, sometimes it was too close for comfort from the secretive Auxunits' point of view, as the following diary entry testifies:

> Visit from Corporal Heaseman who went through patrol personal gear. Received the schedule for June training. Patrol visited OB and found the emergency entrance had been opened and our operational ration run had been ransacked. 2000-2230 hrs. 20 May 1941.

Auxunit patrols were to remain concealed in their Operational Bases for the first two weeks of a German invasion, allowing time for enemy spearhead patrols to push forward and for GHQ Home forces to determine the direction of the main enemy thrust and to identify the

This photograph shows how superbly camouflaged SS soldiers were. The SS first adopted printed camouflage patterns in 1937. The smocks were reversible and designs such as Oakleaf, seen here, and the later Plane Tree were screen-printed onto water-repellent duck cotton.

immediate Nazi objectives. As the first German troops ashore would have included elite detachments from the Waffen-SS there would have been little the Auxunits could have achieved by attempting to resist the invader head-on. Time and time again, Auxunit veterans impressed upon me that it wasn't their duty to directly engage the enemy. They could do more damage behind the lines when their small numbers and stealthy abilities would have been a distinct advantage. The Auxunits would gather covert field intelligence and disrupt the build-up of enemy forces by any means that came to hand. This might involve polluting enemy water or fuel supplies or capturing an unwary German sentry and sending him to the rear for interrogation by British military intelligence. As the German Army consolidated its bridgehead and started to break out further inland towards its first assembly points it would need to establish supply dumps, field hospitals and theatre HQs. To attack these, the Auxunits were equipped with a formidable arsenal of explosives, including plastic explosives, or

The slightest noise would cause German patrols to halt. Auxunit booby traps were lethal.

'marzipan', as the French resistance later named it, as well as an assortment of ingenious fusing and detonation devices to set them off.

S-Day of Operation Sea Lion called for a combination assault by Nazi land and airborne troops. The immediate German objective was to secure the flanks and high ground inland of the invasion beaches and to land men and equipment on these beaches in force and in such numbers that a bridgehead was irresistible. In the Folkestone-Dover-Ramsgate area, for example, working in concert, the airborne troops of General Kurt Student's (the hero of the earlier drops in Belgium and the Low Countries) 7th Flieger Division and the ground forces of Busch's 16th Army hoped to lay claim to a pocket of territory that included vital port facilities and the RAF base. As soon as these objectives were secured the Germans could do two things with confidence. Firstly, of course, they could start the immediate resupply of their forces by air (it was assumed that the port of Dover and the harbours at Folkestone and Ramsgate would take some time to repair and make serviceable). Secondly, reinforced and re-equipped invaders could begin to break out further inland. Impending Luftwaffe operations on captured British airfields and hampering the progress of the German march inland was where the Auxunits would have come into their own. The airfields would have soon become home to Me 109s and to fleets of J 52 tri-motors – the same aircraft that would have dropped sticks of Fallschirmjägers early on the morning of S-Day. As soon as conditions allowed, Auxunit saboteurs would have slipped under airfield perimeter wire in an effort to sabotage Luftwaffe aircraft in the manner they had previously employed while on exercise against RAF fighters. Although now they would be using explosives against the tails of aircraft – not government-issue adhesive labels!

For close on a year, Britons had been regaled with stories testifying to the German Army's achievements on the field of battle. Many people assumed that Hitler had employed alchemists' skills to create a new kind of warfare to which resistance appeared futile. Some, however, questioned the apparent invincibility of the Wehrmacht. In *Landmarks of Modern Strategy*, W.E. Liddell Hart said he intended to 'dispose of an illusion that has tended to break the nerves of opponents.' It might well have been one of the worthy tomes that Auxunit intelligence officers turned to for guidance when training their men to impede the steady progress of the German war machine.

One of the keys to German success on the Continent was the 'dissected march', which enabled them to progress steadily through enemy territory. As Hart himself said, 'The form of marching employed by the German General Staff since the beginning of the war is called a 'dissected marching order' and this form probably comes nearest to an efficient solution of the vital problem of approach.' The

Pillboxes would prove little defence to an enemy that had overcome the strongest fortresses in Belgium and France.

German Army of 1940 had to develop a new method of advance to support the relative speed of its new armoured *blitzkriegs*. Panzers could punch holes through the front-line defences of Nazi opponents but only the rapid advance of supporting infantry could exploit such opportunities. In fact, the Nazis fielded the first professional army that successfully applied the doctrine of 'fire and movement', a theory that appreciated the significance of armour's ability to extend rapidly the front deep into enemy territory. In 1929, the British War Office said, 'The AFV [Armoured Fighting Vehicle] acts by fire and movement with the intermediate object of creating an opportunity for decisive action and the ultimate one of securing a concentration of superior force at the decisive point.' Regardless of the German superiority in tanks, assuming, of course, that they actually managed to put all their designated vehicles ashore, the 'opportunity for decisive action' would only exist if the infantry was able to keep up with the Panzerwaffe. The dissected march meant that the Wehrmacht had mastered the technique of continuous battlefield movement, enabling supplies and reinforcements to keep pace with spearhead units. This new method meant that 'des Heeres' was unimpaired by the traditional weaknesses of fatigue and absence of logistics support that often hampered other modern armies.

The dissected march that enabled the German Army to exploit its initial successes on the battlefields in Poland and France, and the one they would have exported to the rolling downland of Kent and Sussex, had several advantages. Firstly, it proceeded in a progressive, almost rhythmic manner, ensuring that advance troops seldom got too far ahead of their reserves and allowing the whole formation to arrive complete and on time. Forward troops were continuously replaced, daisy chain-like, by fresh units from the reserve behind. In this way, no troops went into combat with the enemy immediately after they had completed a forced march. Secondly, as parts of the attacking column were at rest as they waited to be reinforced it was never clear to the defenders exactly where the objective lay, as it would have been if the entire column was marching towards a particular location.

To ensure that the advance worked, three components were integrated within the dissected march: an advance guard consisting of motorized and mounted formations that acted as a scout formation and was used for reconnaissance purposes; a formation called the *Corpore Celere*, an Italian invention adopted by the Wehrmacht that integrated fast-moving units of motorcyclists with machine-gunners, strong anti-tank units and motorized engineers that were capable of breaching obstructions; and finally, the bulk of the division, which could march with confidence, sure that the way ahead had been scouted and prepared. Generally this final element would march under cover of darkness.

'Time is a vital factor,' urges Liddell Hart in *Landmarks of Modern Strategy*:

> It is the essence of modern attack that at the beginning a passage is vital for the successful continuation of plans, but the ultimate aim of breakthrough having been accomplished, the subsequent shape of this passage is of secondary importance. The defence, if given sufficient time, would carefully prepare the counter-attack with armoured forces at this point.

It was the job of Auxunits to buy time for the defenders by preventing the Wehrmacht from preparing a 'passage' through which it could confidently deploy the three elements of the dissected march.

Hart said that in the massed assault of modern armies one element above all others, 'surprise', was 'essential for decisive success in the offensive. It ensures success; the more complete it is, the more difficult and prolonged is any recovery on the part of the defence.' Although Operation Sea Lion wouldn't have been a surprise for the defenders (the German invasion flotilla would have been easily seen on the Channel horizon), the arrival in the first wave of airborne units from the 10,000-strong 7th Flieger Division, tasked with securing Dover and Hythe from landward approaches, would probably have achieved some level of surprise. Some, like the Fallschirmjägers of the 19th and 20th Parachute Regiments, would jump from Junkers Ju 52s; others would have landed in their DFS 230 gliders, towed from France. General Ironside's 'crust defence' relied on a strong counter-attack by British forces to repel the invader inland if a successful landing had been accomplished. The German airborne forces might well have secured certain objectives because they had surprise on their side but they would have needed reinforcing soon by the main bulk of the foot-slogging infantry. The weakness of lightly-armed airborne troops in the face of concerted infantry and tank assault was ably demonstrated at Arnhem some four years later, when British paratroops of the 6th Airborne Brigade were defeated by conventional German infantry and supporting Panzerwaffe forces because the reinforcing armour of Britain's 30 Corps was unable to relieve them in time. Similarly, troops from Germany's 7th Flieger Division would have depended on the rapid support from the regular Wehrmacht troops that had been

Even the sight of the relatively puny Panzer Mk Is bearing down on defending British troops would have struck fear into their hearts.

disgorged from the *prahme* along with the amphibious panzer Mk IVs that would have clambered up the beaches breathing air through their ingenious *schnorkel* devices. Surprise would have been crucial during the second phase of the landings – the enemy's attempt to break out from its bridgehead. The Auxunits reconnaissance skills would have been invaluable at this time.

Although he wouldn't have known about Auxunits at the time, Hart's writings seem to have been predicting the creation of such a force. Uncannily, he urged for the formation of 'a special and rather independent reconnaissance formation [that could] watch the lines of communication leading towards the area about to be penetrated by the attacker.' This was precisely what Auxunits were intended to do. As was their ability to grind down the invader by a combination of psychological attrition and to infiltrate rear areas inhabited by second grade support troops, 'the theory that most fully exploits the advantages of defence is known as the strategy of exhaustion.' Liddell Hart goes on to consider the consequences for the Germans of a failure to break out of their bridgehead: 'If the German High Command were able to establish a major bridgehead on the British coast for a main thrust through the country, they would do their utmost to feed this thrust, and if they should encounter strong British resistance in time they would be forced to go on feeding their first-line forces until losses had become overwhelming and evacuation was forced upon them.' In concert with regular forces, the covert hit-and-run attacks that the Auxunits would have mounted were intended to encourage uneasiness amongst the German invaders and for them to think that Britain was unconquerable.

In the earliest days of Auxunits, Operational Bases didn't follow a standard pattern. They did, however, have certain things in common. Most were hidden off the beaten track, deep in woodland. Care was taken to ensure that woodland sitings were chosen in areas of mixed vegetation, in order to avoid undue exposure in autumn and winter. The treeless marshlands of southern Kent and East Anglia posed more of a problem. Here, excavations were made into stream banks or underneath the basements of derelict buildings. In Sussex there were problems too: its naked chalk downs, being so close to the potential invasion beaches, were ideal locations for OBs. One solution was to ask Bomber Command to jettison a stick of bombs in an area of uninhabited downland. The Luftwaffe would naturally be blamed and the area could be cordoned off in case of UXBs (unexploded bombs). Under the cover of bomb disposal work, work could begin to further excavate the bomb crater nearest to natural cover as a site for an OB.

One thing most OBs had in common was an escape route. Auxunit planners never underestimated the Wehrmacht and it was appreciated

Recreation showing an Auxiliary emerging from the trap that led to the concealed OB at Tottingham.

that, however well concealed, OBs might be discovered. Even during the early period, OBs featured some kind of escape tunnel (later on, Royal Engineers furnished them with emergency exits made from sections of the then newly invented prefabricated concrete piping). Escape tunnels might run for several hundred yards and often exited in hidden locations such as muddy river banks or gorse thickets. It was reckoned that if a German soldier was brave (or foolish) enough to use the main entrance to an OB, which often meant entering a trap door only big enough to accommodate one torso and then a lonely descent down a vertical 10ft shaft, the occupants would have time to beat a speedy retreat. Especially if the first German soldier had been stabbed with a Fairbairn knife as he dangled from the surface trap. Escape tunnel entrances were generally within a small ante-chamber and were therefore shielded internally by the presence of walls or partitions that acted as blast walls and prevented the decimation of the entire patrol if a cautious enemy lobbed a stick grenade down the entrance before entering.

An average OB would be home to up to seven men. Some early ones were simply holes that had been excavated and then shored up with timber supports and panel-clad walls beneath an earthed-over roof. Some consisted of little more than an arched chamber made of corrugated galvanized steel, looking like an oversized Anderson air raid shelter or Nissen hut, of the type familiar to generations of British servicemen. Generally, OBs were buried below the surface and connected to it by a concealed access shaft. Entrance to this shaft often involved manipulating a series of ingenious mechanisms involving counterbalances that, when activated, would cause the entrance to swing or slide open. A popular method for concealing the entrance was to construct the trap door 'lid' as a shallow tray that could be filled with earth and vegetation similar to the surroundings. Once in place the entrance was invisible, even close up. As a further precaution against unwanted entry, OBs generally featured a concealed lookout post from which a lonely Auxunit sentry would be able to monitor any comings and goings. A marble rolled down a concealed length of rusty drainpipe that entered the OB was often a signal that an Auxunit member wanted entry. A series of bunk beds, a 'map table' (often an upturned box), a water tank with attached tap, an Elsan chemical lavatory (as used in Bomber Command aircraft), cooking facilities and a storage area completed the layout. Because of their danger, explosives were often concealed in a dry store external to the main OB. Some OBs, such as the one under the cellar of Tottington Manor in Sussex (the HQ for Auxunits in the county) were built to a much higher standard. Later in the war, existing OBs were reinforced by the addition of concrete breeze-blocks and sturdy RSJ supports. Often, local Royal Engineer detachments, told that they were building secret storerooms in case of invasion, would be brought in to provide professional help. On occasion, civil contractors were also drafted in, but these would be firms from outside the local area. Damp was an ever-present problem and many OBs featured simple floor grilles that allowed excess water to drain away. Auxunit commanders took a lot of trouble to ensure that OBs were well ventilated and that the fumes from Primus stoves and paraffin lamps neither choked nor revealed the occupiers.

Auxunit veteran Sid Gaston was only twenty-one years of age when he was in the Auxiliaries. According to Gaston, initially the newly formed units in Sussex still went by the nomenclature 'XII Corps Observation Unit', like the original patrols established in Kent, and all the new recruits came from the Regular Royal Sussex Regiment, Gaston from a detachment in Herne Bay and others from the regiment's depot in Chichester. 'When we were trained [they spent about a fortnight at Coleshill] my unit, all Regulars, was one of two "Scout Sections" in Sussex, one covering eastern Sussex and the other [Gaston's], further west. I was based at South Stoke, near Arundel, and our HQ was at Tottington Manor, near Henfield.'

In all there were ten Auxunit patrols in West Sussex. Nine of them were recruited from the Home Guard and Gaston's 'scout section' from

Sid Gaston in his Royal Sussex Regiment 1937 pattern battledress at the outbreak of the war. Notice the absence of unit insignia, bar the Royal Sussex cap badge, and the fact that all the tunic and trouser buttons are fly-fastening. This tailoring luxury was soon abandoned as material shortages took bite.

Awaiting an enemy tank attack one Home Guard shoulders the Boys anti-tank rifle in anticipation of its fearful recoil (the half-inch calibre weapon was virtually a hand cannon). The other Home Guard prepares to fit the weapon's box machine.

the Regulars. 'We covered a wide area: Tangmere Aerodrome, Ford Aerodrome, West Hampnett and Poling radio location (radar) station. Our OB was in Arundel Park. I could get from Arundel Park up to Whiteways Lodge and through the Royal Woods as far as Goodwood without crossing a road. We would then make our way to a big OB at Stanford Park. Then we could come along the coast (a combined journey that avoided habitable areas) right round and back. One of my places to blow up was a petrol dump at Tangmere.' After Sid Gaston's men had been fully trained, local farmers formed separate patrols because they knew the local countryside intimately and were better suited to establishing new rural patrols. Sid Gaston's scout sections were equipped with the standard Auxunit weaponry but, unusually, they had portable foldaway bicycles too. 'When we first started we didn't have PHE [plastic explosive], we had gun-cotton and Nobel's 808 [gelignite]. Later, we did have some plastic – the black one was the best. We also learned exactly how detonators worked. We learned that ours were made of 'ASA' [based on aluminium], not the standard fulminate of mercury, which all went to the Navy [for shells].' His job at this time obviously made a lasting impression on him for, without prompting, Sid Gaston was able to reel off the long list of explosives and their properties that he had first learned more than fifty-five years earlier: 'There was Amonol, Baratol, gun cotton, Noble's 808 and plastic,' he said. He remembered that the deadliest explosive was plastic and could still remember that it turned from solid to explosive gas at a rate of 8,000 metres a second! 'My scout section never had a mishap with the Mills [grenade] because in the Regular, full-time Army we were so highly trained. We used to practise with a 4lb lump of concrete. We would lob them about to see if we could throw far enough.'

Auxunit patrols, however, would have resorted to the use of noisy weapons only as a last resort. 'We didn't go up the road to kill somebody,' Sid Gaston told me. 'We didn't lay an ambush to catch somebody, we had a specific job: to be a general bloody nuisance and to stop the Jerry getting the advantage. We would be told of a target and we had to go that night because it was causing trouble. We would go and blow it up or turn it over. Why did we want to kill somebody and give our position away?' If they were to kill the enemy, and I have no doubt that brave men of Sid Gaston's calibre would have been perfectly prepared to, Auxunits were well trained in the use of the trusty Fairbairn fighting knife. After my interview, I was under no illusions about the darker side to organized resistance against an invader as ruthless as Nazi Germany would have been. I was told that if Gaston's patrol had had the good fortune to capture two or three enemy soldiers for interrogation, the method used to get them to talk involved slitting open the mouth of one of the prisoners and waiting.

It is probable that the Auxunits would have been used to take care of domestic as well as foreign enemies. With the fate of the nation at stake, the British authorities would have taken a very dim view of any collaboration or over-friendly behaviour that took place within the enemy-occupied invasion zone. Sid Gaston told me, 'I know of one section where they were prepared to kill the head of police because of the information he had. I must admit that every so often we would have a talk with our intelligence officer down at South Stoke if we were concerned about a gardener or caretaker who saw too much. He would say, "Well, what do you think?" He would never say, "Shoot him," but perhaps he would have vanished one day!'

There was a lighter side. Sid Gaston also told me, 'I know of one Auxiliary who asked, "If there is an invasion, will it be all right for me to bring my wife and kids down into the OB?"' There was more trouble with the wives who didn't know anything about the Auxunits, especially those married to a volunteer recruited from the Home Guard, because he knew the local woods well and was regularly sent on night patrols there. Sid Gaston again: 'His neighbour's wife might ask his wife, "What's happening with your George? My Bert is wearing the same Home Guard uniform and he didn't have to go out last night." He got accused of going out with another woman – having an affair. And the two women had a punch-up! Some funny things happened like that. Most of us in the scout sections were twenty to twenty-five. We were young and bloody silly. We didn't have a care in the world.

'When the invasion was imminent we used to lay low. We used to go to ground. If Jerry had come over we would have laid low for about fourteen days. When Jerry had come forward we would have come out. Remember, we usually only worked in groups of two or three and we could easily move about the country. Nobody stopped us, providing we were in army surplus and picked up a shovel or a hoe – we looked like farm labourers. Nobody stopped us; you could walk across anybody's field.'

'Kipling' was the codeword allotted to Sid Gaston's patrol to signify that the invasion was actually happening. 'We were also able to see the "Golden Rain" fireworks that were fired from the coastal defence sites throughout Kent and Sussex. It didn't go "bang!" or anything like that. It was just a big shower of sparks and was used in all the OBs in the Hastings area – a big fat skyrocket, a special one not an ordinary one.' It is thought-provoking when one considers that the Nazi invasion of England would have been heralded with a dramatic firework display – a type of communication more normally associated with festivities but now a portent of doom. 'We would only come out after they had passed over us,' he reiterated, 'not to fight a rearguard action but for sabotage. You can cause a lot of trouble simply by turning a train on its side. But when you do blow things up like that you don't do it to destroy them because you're hoping that one day your own people will come back. If any of us had fought a rearguard action we would have all been caught within weeks. When we went to ground we had enough food for a month. We thought that if we did come out after a fortnight we would probably have been caught if we tried to go back.'

Sid Gaston spent some time at the Sussex HQ at Tottington Manor. Before the pre-cast concrete escape tunnel was installed there he remembers that the first emergency exit was through the cesspit of a country house! Another recollection has curious parallels to Colonel Field's memories of the period when he took over from Peter Fleming at The Garth in Kent: 'At Tottington we had two RAF blokes. Nobody knew what they did except for cooking our food. But they may have had their own radio and were probably there for another purpose, but we never knew what it was.'

Typically, Auxunits were most active at night. 'At night-time we went out to Tangmere Aerodrome, for example,' Sid Gaston told me. 'We stuck sticky economy labels on the tails of all the planes and they went flying across the grass the next day with all the labels stuck on! Or we might go to Poling [the nearest Chain Home radar station] and tie blocks of wood to all the pylons. We didn't just go on the off chance. The station CO at Tangmere, for example, was told to expect a break-in and to keep his men on their toes. We went down there one day and were shown how to blow the tail off a fighter. You simply removed two screws and undid an inspection plate on the tail. A small amount of plastic, as big as your fist, would blow the tail off. There was no need to worry about engines if every plane had lost its tail. The next day, after we had "been in", our intelligence officers (Captains Bond or Fazan) would go to Tangmere and tell them there had been a raid. "Proof? – have a look at your aeroplanes and see all the economy labels on their tails!" At Poling the commander would say, "You never got in here last night!"

'"Well," they would reply, "look at the pylons. See the blocks of four by two tied to them?" At one army place, we broke in at night and pinched all their boots! We used to lay a lot of "drain traps" in the area around Chichester. These were linked to the aerodromes at Tangmere and Ford. By connecting two wires you were able to detonate distant targets.'

'Pipe mines', capable of ripping long furrows through potential German glider-landing fields, were laid in profusion by Auxunit patrols. Sid Gaston took great delight in showing me a video of a local television news report and a local newspaper report entitled 'Rise and shine, it's bomb disposal day!' which proudly claimed that a series of still-live pipe mines had been found near Goodwood Airfield that had to be deactivated by Army bomb disposal engineers and were thought to be relics of the Canadian troops stationed there in 1940. These were surreptitiously laid there some fifty years previously by his own patrol! Indeed, a pock-marked weather vane attached to the spire of a nearby church has also traditionally thought to have been a target of boisterous Canadian soldiers. In fact, it proved an ideal target for the silenced high-velocity rifle of Gaston's patrol. Another article in a local paper that amused Sid Gaston told of the surprising find of a mysteriously forgotten 'air raid shelter' that was found in the back garden of a house in Rottingdean, Sussex. The opportunity to be the first to enter this underground chamber was auctioned for charity and the money presented to a local children's hospital. The story ends with the delighted hospital manager saying, 'We've come across some pretty unusual means of raising money but this has to beat the lot,' and the paper finishing with 'A further mystery remains. Was the shelter once connected to gun emplacements on the nearby cliff face?' It was, of course, an Operational Base.

An Auxiliary Units fighter who thought that dogs might have been the most formidable weapon the Germans could employ to root out Auxunit volunteers from their OBs was Frank Penfold. Born in 1913,

The invading German troops would have soon become aware of the inaccuracy of their own maps. Captured British soldiers in possession of any potential worthwhile field intelligence would have been subject to ruthless and speedy interrogation.

Penfold was an agricultural contractor in a reserved occupation with his family firm, James Penfold Ltd, established in Arundel in 1833. Since the time of Frank Penfold's great-grandfather, the family had been heavily engaged with country matters all over Sussex so they knew the lie of the land really well. 'We did most of the contract threshing in Sussex. For example, I had eight sets of threshing tackle, giro-tillers – lots of things. We also supplied agricultural machinery to farmers and we installed plant such as grain silos and grain dryers in farmsteads, and combines when they started to come in.

'We only had Regulars as officers. ... We had a Regular officer who covered a whole area, let's say West Sussex, and all the people below that, the patrol leaders, were rated as sergeants and the rest were privates. Originally I was in the local HG, and then I went to Leslie Drewitt's Goodwood Patrol at Eartham before I formed my own in 1942. Leslie Drewitt, a former friend of mine, said, "Would you like to come and join my mob?" I said, "Yes, I would" – I was a bit browned-off with the rather unexciting parades of the local Home Guards. He told me roughly what his lot [Drewitt's patrol] got up to. So I was joined into his lot. I didn't know anything about the nature of it until I joined.' (Leslie Drewitt, a farmer at Oving, had his first OB in Eartham Wood. Frank Penfold's was on Bury Hill in Combe Wood, along a track to Langham Farm (now Houghton Forest). It no longer exists as the spot was felled and replanted with conifers after the war.

'A common expression [for Auxunits] used by the HG people [who, of course, were unaware of their real name] was the "Home Guard Commandos". And then when I got into it I found they called themselves the "Intelligence Unit". Nowadays we seem to call them Auxiliaries, which was a name I don't remember being used at the time. Intelligence Unit seemed to be the sort of standard phrase – we were still in effect enrolled in the HG except that we had to sign the Official Secrets Act.' (He had never heard of Colin Gubbins!)

Frank Penfold told me how being in Auxunits affected his routine. 'I lived at Walburton. I worked all day, so Auxunits was an evening and weekends job – a spare-time occupation. I went to Coleshill for a course, but most of our training was done either individually or in our patrol. We had chaps from the Commandos and from the Parachute Regiment who came and gave us lessons in various things. We had weapon training, we had field craft, and we had thuggery – unarmed combat. The one thing I've got left is the Fairbairn-Sykes fighting knife.

'Coleshill was a "grand style" house. We had a weekend there and the men in charge were Colonel Lord Glanusk of the Grenadier Guards and Captain Lord Delamere of the Welsh Guards, of Kenya fame. Most of the time we were engaged in field craft. It was some little time after I was enrolled that we were sent to Coleshill. We had to get ourselves

Frank Penfold reluctantly brandishing his Fairbairn-Sykes fighting knife.

together and organize our OB. We first had local training and then in due course we went up there.

'All patrol leaders were sergeants – I was a sergeant. When I was in Leslie Drewitt's patrol based in Eartham Wood they decided on an expansion programme. They commonly selected internally for leaders of new patrols that were part of the expansion programme. The officer was Lieutenant Fazan – he was our leader, our Army liaison. He said, "Would you form a patrol for a new OB we are going to set up between here and there?" I said, "All right, I suppose I can find some chaps." So I received half a dozen chaps locally – mostly the same age as me, including the chap who was running the Arundel Forest for the Forestry Commission. There was my blacksmith and the welder from my works – all reasonably powerful people. Physically fit sort of chaps. George Cross, the forester, was a very big chap. Twice my size. I visibly remember having unarmed combat with him – a bit tricky to throw, of course!'

The handle of Frank Penfold's Fairbairn fighting knife was bound with plastic tape during the war because this type of weapon (later made famous by its association with the Commandos) featured an all-metal handle, which would have had a tendency to slip when covered in blood! Covering the handle with tape also made it bigger and consequently easier to grip. Mr Penfold was clearly a pragmatist. He struck me as a man in the mould of Peter Fleming or perhaps Wilfred Thesiger or Paul Gallico. He is a traveller and explorer for whom the Auxunits was merely a brief interlude and an opportunity to hone and refine his knowledge of the great outside. Living rough with his patrol in their isolated OB was probably no great challenge to an individual whose sympathies and experience already lay with the natural world.

Frank Penfold's OB was constructed by the Royal Engineers. It had an entrance shaft going down, which was framed in timber and surrounded by corrugated iron. A ladder led down to the bottom of the shaft where there was a tunnel that opened out into a couple of rooms. The far room was a kind of magazine and equipment store and the other chamber contained the metal bunk beds. Ammunition was kept in dustbins. A slice of tree root, covered in moss, was fastened to the entrance 'lid'. When you closed it you 'wouldn't know the OB was there. It was just a wooden lid – no more than you could lift up. We didn't have an escape tunnel but about 40 yards away we had a one-man hole equipped with a field telephone and whenever we were operational this sentry with a field telephone would warn us of impending trouble.'

Damp was an ever-present problem in OBs. 'We had the explosives in a galvanized iron dustbin with some silica gel, I think, to act as an absorbent. But our OB was pretty dry, actually; it was built on solid chalk and was quite dry. The main problem when we stayed overnight was our own breath [condensing on metal surfaces etc.]. One of the ideas was to attack German command headquarters. At one time early on we were trained to attack tanks. We had Sticky Bombs, which were to be stuck on the reduction gear or on the tanks' drive sprockets, and the idea was that this would wreck the tank.'

When asked if his Auxunit ever had run-ins with local Army commanders risking compromising the secrecy of his organization, I was told, 'Only once. On one occasion we had an exercise against the Arundel Home Guard. People were dashing around doing this, that and the other, and there wasn't any scoring [to keep track of who was "killed"]. We would be called up by the local HG commander but they didn't know what we were up to exactly. It's surprising today to learn how little one got to know about what was happening in Worthing, for example [barely 10 miles from Arundel]. Only a few miles away, but you didn't have the radio or the television blasting out the same news ten times an hour – it was silence. If houses were bombed at

Littlehampton we may have seen the smoke and heard about it but if houses were bombed in Worthing we didn't know!'

Did he ever think there would actually be an invasion? 'I think we did in the early stages but that was before I was in it. In fact, we were talking about the possibility at the time of Dunkirk. By the time the Russians were involved the danger of invasion had passed.' I asked him if he actually witnessed any of the air battles of the Battle of Britain, given that he farmed and worked in such a heavily contested sector of southern England. 'Oh yes, it was taking place all over us. I was right on the edge of Tangmere Airfield when the first Stukas dive-bombed it. It was absolutely amazing. Our thrashing tackle was working in a barn right on the edge of the airfield and I went to my employees on my normal rounds to take them their food or money, or whatever, when suddenly there was this row going on in the air. A lot of Hurricanes – more Hurricanes than Spitfires in those days, in fact, I'm not even sure there were any Spitfires – and we were just watching this with some interest. You heard screaming as planes dived and so on – all taking place overhead. Then the first Stuka started to dive down and they employed a deliberate shrieking noise. It was quite frightening as they swooped down like gannets diving. Suddenly these "milk churns" started to fall out! We thought, "What the hell are they?" Then we realized that they were, of course, bombs. We had never seen any before. They came down only a few hundred yards away and smashed up all the buildings at Tangmere.'

In fact, at the time, Tangmere was home to Nos. 43 and 601 Squadrons. Nearby at Westhampnett was No. 145 Squadron. All were Hurricane Squadrons – the aircraft Frank Penfold saw. On this day, 16 August 1940, the Stuka attack had completely wrecked all Tangmere's hangars, killed thirteen base personnel and injured a further twenty. It also destroyed three Blenheim bombers on the ground, and seriously damaged another three Blenheims, seven Hurricane fighters and a Miles Magister trainer.

'And then, of course, there were bullets flying around in all directions,' Frank said, 'and you didn't know whether to sit out and look because it was so interesting or to take cover. We did a bit of each. I think we dashed in and out of this barn. Then there were disabled planes crashing in the fields all around. You saw smoke pouring out of an aircraft coming down and it crashed a few fields away, that sort of thing. When they bombed Ford aerodrome I was in an ARP repair squad (in 1940 I was not yet in the HG). If things – roads and bridges – got smashed, we went out to mend them.' His father was a superintendent in the Special Constabulary and had nominated Frank for ARP duties.

With his Mauser KAR 98 shouldered and his steel helmet replaced by the more comfortable *Feldmutze*, this fully equipped veteran of the Great War pauses for a smoke while his superior officer receives the latest intelligence regarding British strengths and dispositions.

The raid on the Fleet Air Arm base at Ford took place on 18 August 1940. The Luftwaffe hit the station's fuel stores, sending thick palls of smoke high into the sky.

'On one day, two Spitfires were "dicing it" above us ... just exercising, when suddenly they hit one another. Both blokes fell out and came down close to us ... about two fields down the road. They didn't have a chance as they were so low. I can remember one of them now. Every bone in his body was broken. He was just a sack of wheat. When he was moved his impression was left in the surface of the soil of the pasture field. Things like that did happen. Once a Heinkel came over Walburton and a German airman came out and landed in a tree and was taken prisoner. I can't really recall any racial element in that we hated the Germans per se, but they were the aggressors. They were the enemy. They had to be destroyed. But it was much more rational than "the sour *Boche* will mutilate you if you're captured," anything like that.'

Being a countryman, Frank Penfold, like the majority of the other Auxunit volunteers recruited in rural areas, was well suited to the outdoor environment that was the natural habitat of these British guerrilla fighters. 'We would do night walks across the countryside. A townsman would have probably got into a mess but we knew our countryside. If I had to go from our OB to the coast or inland to Storrington, for example, I could do it in the middle of the night with no trouble at all. We had our own private cars and I would park mine up there and walk to the OB after picking up my chaps. This didn't arouse any attention as I used my car for my work.'

Frank Penfold's unit had a sizeable collection of side arms. 'A genuine Tommy gun – not a Sten gun, which was what the HG got. We also had an assortment of side arms: 4.5 Webleys, Webley automatics, Colt automatics [a 4.5 Colt and a 3.2 Colt]. A telescopic sighted 2.2 rifle to knock off German Alsatian guard dogs. I reckon dogs were our biggest menace, actually. We were particularly concerned about dogs and we always reckoned that the silenced 2.2 was our best defence against them.'

Frank Penfold was asked if he carried any suicide pills to take if captured and avoid being shot out of hand as a *Francs-Tireur*. 'I can't remember. We did often carry explosives though.' Several Auxunit veterans have told me that, if caught and able to detonate the explosives load they were carrying, they would have preferred to blow themselves up along with their captors, rather than be taken alive. 'One idea was that you filled a bicycle tyre with it and slung it around your shoulder – plastic explosives, that is. We had quite a lot of TNT, which is tricky stuff because after a time it starts to go off. It leaks and becomes sensitive. We didn't like that very much but there was quite a lot of that about.'

Meeting Frank Penfold was a revelation. It struck me as a very real paradox that such a charming and hospitable individual had once been prepared to fight in such unorthodox ways within an organization that would have given and expected no quarter from its enemy.

I asked Eric Johnson, one of the six-man Ashburnham Patrol, if local people were ever suspicious of his activities. He reminded me that all this took place at a time when people simply didn't ask questions in case they were mistaken for enemy agents, and he added, 'Both Wilcox [the Patrol Leader and a fellow farmer] and I were in the regular HG in different sections from different villages, and we just said we had been seconded for other purposes. … We always felt there was a little bit of bitterness about it but nobody knew exactly what we were doing.'

Eric Johnson joined the Local Defence Volunteers within a couple of days of Eden's broadcast. 'At that time we definitely thought there would be an invasion … we were on high alert for some six months after Dunkirk – we were very much on the edge. In 1940 you couldn't help feeling that there might be an invasion – it was close. … There was a general suspicion and hatred of the Germans at the time. There was one person in the area who was one of our prime targets. He was very German oriented; we didn't trust him anymore. He was pro-Hitler.

Had the Germans come in, any potential Fifth Columnists would have been dispensed with.' I asked him whether he had any qualms about 'dispensing with' potential targets. 'I didn't have any qualms,' he said, 'I'm not squeamish.'

I met Dick Body at one of the various Auxunit reunions that took place some fifty years after the organization was disbanded. In 1940 Dick Body was a Territorial soldier and was prevented from joining the Regulars because of his reserve occupation. He was a farmer in the Romney Marsh area of Sussex. On 14 May 1940, four days after the Nazis bombed Rotterdam and landed troops throughout the Low Countries signalling the start of the Fall Gelb *blitzkrieg* in the west, Dick Body applied to join the newly formed Local Defence Volunteers.

'It must have been in 1941 that I was approached by a Captain Allnatt, who I had served under in the TA and who, like me, had returned to civil occupation. He said, "I have a job for you, I think you will like it, but I cannot tell you what it is. Can you find six more men to come in with you? The main thing is that they must have good local knowledge." As a result seven of us went on a Sunday morning and, after reading and signing a copy of the Official Secrets Act, were then told that we were in the secret British underground army. All I will say here is that our training was good and a watertight base below [marsh land] was quickly built by a contractor from out of the district. Three were built in the marsh and two are still there.'

Dick Body's unit was codenamed 'Mushroom Patrol'. Their OB, situated in a sheep pound at Snargate, about 600 yards from Body's house, still exists but is often full of water as the original entrances are in poor condition and the ventilation shafts have been removed. Dick Body remembers that it cost precisely £300 to build.

The likelihood of an invasion not only meant that, for the first time, GHQ Home Forces became an operational command and also required the hasty establishment of a communications network in mainland Britain that would enable distant Army commands and headquarters to keep in contact should the public communications network operated by the GPO fall into Nazi hands or be irreparably damaged by enemy action. GHQ Home Forces became an operational HQ that controlled a series of regional HQs throughout the British Isles. This necessitated a massive reorganization of the British Army's internal communications network and signal capabilities. The importance of wireless communication on the battlefield, which had undergone rapid development in the 1930s, was reflected in the expansion of the Royal Corps of Signals from 34,000 to more than 150,000 by the war's end.

Modernization of battlefield communications naturally extended to Britain's newest and most secret field force – the Auxunits. OBs contained an abundance of weaponry and the necessary survival rations required to support the individual patrols but they were devoid of radio sets. Wireless communication in the field and the all-important link with GHQ Home Forces was provided by Auxunits Signals. Auxunits Signals was such a secret component of Britain's clandestine resistance that when in 1994 Auxunit veterans Peter Wilcox and Geoffrey Bradford set about organizing the first reunion, to be held some fifty years after the organization was disbanded, they were largely unaware that the men that provided their communications link were actually part of their own teams.

Arthur Gabbitas was one of the few surviving Auxunit Signals members to hear of the plans for a reunion and he had first to persuade the organizers that he should be invited to the exclusive gathering. Fortunately, Gabbitas had retained his field passes and certificates from the period, which proved conclusively that 2355011 Corporal Gabbitas, as a part of 'GHQ Auxiliary Unit Signals' was cleared for 'Special Transport Duties'. Like most men recruited into the top-secret British resistance during the early war years, Arthur Gabbitas is not entirely sure why he was selected but as he had been drafted into the Royal Corps of Signals at least he was involved in work for which he had been trained. He doesn't think that he and his Royal Corps of Signals colleagues merit any special recognition for their time associated with Britain's guerrilla fighters but, because scores of civilian volunteers completed the complex communications net that fed Auxiliary Units HQ and GHQ Home Forces, he feels it is time that their work was recognized. Much of his time was spent visiting the many civilian outstations that worked hand-in-hand with Auxunit Signals personnel recruited from the professional Army.

Arthur Gabbitas told me how the complex communications network designed to supplement the work of the Regular forces actually operated. 'Auxunit Signals comprised around 100 men and officers of the Royal Signals and forty-three women of the ATS,' he told me. 'After initial training as wireless operators at Catterick, five of us were sent to Auxunits at Coleshill.' At Coleshill Gabbitas and his colleagues were shown the results of the intensive R & D that had gone into developing the resistance's unique communications network. In 1941, small radio telephony sets were specially designed and built by enlisted radio hams. These sets had to be simple to use and capable of withstanding the damp conditions of covert operation in the fields and woodlands of England. The sets were enclosed in 15 x 6 x 5-inch wooden cases. They operated on ultra high frequency and were powered by large 6-volt accumulator batteries. A 'vibrator' boosted the limited 6-volt power supply and apparently Auxunit personnel knew where to 'bang' the vibrators when the sets got out of tune! Because of their relatively low power the radio sets were barley capable of transmitting beyond the

With no road signs to guide them and possessing maps that were woefully inadequate and incorrect – General Thorne's XIV Corps, thought by the Nazis to be in Wales, was actually in the front-line of Kent – progress for the Wehrmacht through the English countryside would have been very hazardous.

visible horizon and thus required a string of relay stations. Headquarters for Auxunit Signals was in Suffolk, at Bachelors Hall, in Hundon, where Signals personnel were fully trained in the operation and maintenance of the sets.

There were approximately thirty control, or 'Zero', stations established in key positions around the coast from Scotland to Wales. These were manned by Auxunit Signals personnel and featured installations above or, if invasion came, below ground. Each control was fed, via one of the newly developed Auxunit radio sets, by between five and ten civilian outstations that collated information they received from a number of trusted couriers known as 'runners' or 'cutouts'. The control stations in turn retransmitted the signal to the appropriate defending force in the threatened area. The civilian outstations were often concealed in the roofs of country buildings. One was at the top of a 'folly' in Brocklesby Park, Lincolnshire. Another was in a bunker hidden beneath the outside privy seat of a chicken farmer in Devon. One outstation transmitter was said to be hidden in Lincolnshire's famous Boston Stump church tower.

The communications chain started with runners – individuals who kept an eye out not just for signs of invasion but for any enemy

German soldiers had a healthy respect for British rifle drill ever since they had clashed with the Old Contemptibles of the first BEF in 1914. On that occasion, on the receiving end of fifteen aimed rounds per minute from the redoubtable .303 Lee Enfield (seen here), the Kaiser's advancing troops had been convinced they were being confronted by machine guns.

espionage activities in their area. The runners would deposit their messages in a variety of weird and wonderful ways. Messages deposited in the chicken farmer's converted privy, for example, would be concealed in a split tennis ball. These would then be coded and passed on to the nearest three-man unit.

Each three-man Auxiliary Unit Signals detachment comprised two wireless operators and an instrument mechanic. Day-to-day work took place in a hut on the surface but hidden in the woods close by was the typical underground OB of the Auxunits, a 'small Nissen hut underground with extra proofed chamber for charging the batteries and underground privies,' as Gabbitas described it. 'The tunnel taking away the generator gases was also an escape route,' he told me. His daily duties included changing the accumulator batteries and attending to the copper wire aerials hidden in the branches of surrounding trees. These featured thick down leads that were concealed behind the bark of tree stumps. Traces of these down leads can still be seen in surviving trees – mysterious deep ruts that run the entire length of the trunks.

Barbara Culleton was one of the women who joined Auxunit Signals and who provided an essential reinforcement to the organization's radio net. The female Auxunit signals component was commanded by Senior Commandant Beatrice Temple, a niece of the then Archbishop of Canterbury, who after the war became Mayoress of the Sussex town of Lewes.

After enrolling in the ATS/TA with a friend in 1938, Barbara Culleton was called up for wartime service on 1 September 1939. In June 1941 she was recommended for a commission but shortly afterwards was summoned to undergo voice tests 'somewhere in Essex'. After these were completed it was explained that radio operators were required for a secret organization and 'because of the emergency' she was asked to attend a shortened OCTU (Office Cadet Training Unit) course. Shortly afterwards, on 7 September 1941, she was posted to Auxunits Signals.

'Our radio sets were particularly sensitive to sunspot activity and thunderstorms, when a great deal of interference was experienced,' she told me. When asked if the specially designed Auxunit radio receivers were ever used to pick up other radio traffic, such as the radio 'chatter' of RAF air crews, I was told, 'Recognizing the call signs and codenames [changed frequently] of our own stations, and on occasions those used during Army exercises by tank commanders etc., was all we were interested in. ... The urgent task of establishing a nationwide radio communications network appeared to have belonged jointly to the Royal Signals and the Intelligence Corps. ATS officers posted to Auxunits were attached to the local Signals HQ and lived in civilian billets. Signals personnel trained its ATS members in radio operation and maintenance procedures and gave instruction in the use of firearms [not issued] and survival techniques. They positioned aerials, laid field telephone lines, ferried operators to and from sites to their billets and arranged transport on relocation.'

The location of the radio station was always some distance from the operators' billets and only Signals personnel knew its exact whereabouts. Before more substantial bunkers were established transmitter/receiving stations were usually located at the edge of a wood or in a field that was partially concealed by tree coverage. As was often the case with Auxunit OBs, the location of many of the radio stations manned by the female operators, dubbed the 'secret sweeties' by some, was in the grounds of large country houses. 'One was in the summerhouse in the grounds of a stately home!' Barbara Culleton told me. 'As soon as one network was functioning, no time was wasted,' she said. 'It was up and away to another part of the country, often, like me, working alone, with very little notice. In addition to setting up the network some parts of the daily watches were devoted to listening out for enemy agents. The time and dial readings were immediately relayed to Intelligence (via the field telephone) if any were heard but

Eerie remains of the Thorveton Patrol's OB in Devon.

we were never told of the outcome. Once my operational duties came to an end I was despatched to Auxunit HQ to act as Admin Assistant to Senior Commandant Beatrice Temple, who had been appointed CO of the ATS side, which was about to expand. Our living quarters were at Hannington Hall, a short distance from the HQ at Coleshill House, Highworth, where we participated in the exercises held there for the mobile patrols.'

The late Bill Webber, a sprightly eighty-seven years young when I interviewed him, was typical of the resourceful, pragmatic and unflappable men found in Auxunits. He insisted on leading me to the site of his wartime OB, on top of Firle Beacon in Sussex, near Lewes. Apart from the fact that he virtually exhausted the author, who was trailing behind with cameras and notebooks, it soon became clear that Bill Webber had lost none of the observation skills that made the ideal Auxunit volunteer. As we got nearer to the copse within which the remnants of the OB were to be found, Bill Webber suddenly cautioned me to stop in case I should disturb a badger run. I had to look very closely to find any evidence of the run, but, sure enough, it was there.

Born in Brighton in August 1908, Bill Webber moved to Firle in 1931. His mother had died in 1914, when aged only thirty and after having five children. Bill's father was killed the following year. Bill and his siblings were brought up in a local home, set up in 1916 for 'Kitchener's War Orphans'.

The entrance to the model OB in the grounds of Coleshill House, in Wiltshire.

Bill Webber on Firle Beacon sitting in the depression made by his wartime OB.

The similarity in construction to the famous Anderson shelters explains why surviving OBs are often mistaken for air raid shelters.

His friend Tom Smith had an equally hard youth. Tom was born in 1913 and came originally from the Forest of Dean. His mother died when she was just forty-five and, like Bill Webber, his father was an infantryman in the British Army in the Great War. Tom came south during the depression of the 1930s, aged twenty-one, and desperately seeking work. When war was declared in 1939, they were both employed in Firle as market gardeners – a reserved occupation. But they both wanted to join the Regular Army, like their fathers.

I asked them how they felt about being selected for Auxunits. Bill Webber told me, 'I wasn't very keen on drilling, to tell you the truth. So we jumped at it. We didn't realize what we were going in for but we soon adapted ourselves.' Their patrol was codenamed 'Badger One' and based at Bishopstone. Bill Webber was the leader of the four-man patrol. 'I've got William Webber, Jack Cornwall, Jack Pilbeam, and

Together with their most vital task, gathering intelligence, another crucial function of Auxiliers was simply to buy time for regular troops, who, like this Bren gunner, were relatively lightly armed but desperate to know to where they should rush, confronting the Nazi invaders with the strongest response.

Tom Smith. That was our four,' said Bill. Pilbeam was a farm-hand and Cornwall a painter; at the time both men worked on the Firle estate. 'Then there was Lionel Willett, Frank Turner, Jack Clark and Fred White, and then Woolmer came in later.' They formed another patrol, Badger Two. Mr Willet, who had a van, was the patrol leader. He was a farmer at Bishopstone. 'He was a good leader,' said Tom Smith.

'Yes, marvellous,' agreed Bill Webber. 'He was a first-time officer in the Army. He was very blunt though,' he said.

'They gave him some stripes as sergeant,' Tom told me. 'He said what we had better do with them is cut them up and have one each.'

Bill Webber remembered, 'The best feat we ever did with a compass was when we went straight through this forest with streams and ponds and we came out the other end within 50 yards of a pub! We didn't get orders all the time – we just trained. We had our training books and knew what to do. One time we took the newest bombs to pieces and put them together again. … Lionel Willet went out with about twelve Mills bombs and a revolver – that's all he wanted. He said he felt safer with Mills bombs than anything else. I quite agree with him.'

A British Bren gun position on a bridge above a stream in the Weald of Sussex.

Tom Smith told me about how destructive these small anti-personnel bombs could be. 'Say there were five or six Germans, you threw one of those amongst them – that would be the lot.'

I asked them both if they ever came across other patrols active in the Firle Patrols' area. 'We used to meet them,' said Tom Smith.

'Only in their area,' interjected Bill. 'There was the Cooksbridge Patrol, Lewes, Rodmer …'

I asked them if there was any rivalry between patrols. 'Oh, no,' said Bill, 'we used to have competitions. I've got that in the diary. We would have won easily but I couldn't hit the target with the Tommy gun! We were first in everything except that; it let us down.'

'We used to practise [with a revolver], over at Willet's,' said Tom. 'He fixed up a revolver with a battery in the grip and a bulb in the barrel and when he pointed it the spot of light used to come up on the target. And that worked well – good practice that was. Yes, he was a very clever man, Mr Willet. We did have a Bren gun, during the latter part, because it was the most accurate gun you've ever shot out of. In fact, it's too accurate to be a machine gun, I think.'

I asked them if it was the Royal Engineers who maintained their OB. 'No, we did,' said Bill. 'Once they had built it, we had the first bit first and then they put the escape exit in afterwards.'

'When they dug the hole they carried all the chalk and tipped it all a hell of a way from there. It was done properly,' Tom added.

'The Army used to change the rations every month,' said Bill. 'Great long tins of corned beef.'

Tom Smith and Bill Webber, in common with all the other Auxiliary Units veterans it has been my privilege to meet and interview, were about as far away from the Captain Mainwaring and Private Pike stereotypes immortalized by *Dad's Army* as I can imagine. It is clear from the characters of all those I have met that, although they were recruited in haste and in obvious secrecy, the process was nevertheless rigorously selective. I have no doubt that if any of these men had been pitted against the ruthless and battle-hardened Third Reich war machine they would have 'given the enemy a bloody nose.'

Chapter 6

Nazis in London

Germanization. The colonization of lesser breeds has been in
time past a thorn in the Aryan Reich.

The Racial Conception of the World, Adolf Hitler, 1938

Once, Nordic Vikings went out into the world. Of course, they
were robbers like all other warriors, but they dreamt of Honour
and State, of domination and creation. And everywhere they
went they gave life to a particular culture: in Keiff, Palermo,
Brittany and England.

Mythus, Dr Alfred Rosenberg, 'Kultur' Minister

Nazi ideology was well established by 1940. An engineer by
training, Alfred Rosenberg had become the leading Nazi
pseudo-philosopher. He had met Hitler in Munich in 1920 and
was immediately made the editor of the Nazi's 'house paper', the
Volkischer Beobachter. His first pamphlet from this period, *The Trace of
Jews in the History of the World*, laid the foundations of Nazi anti-Semitic
theory. Throughout his period in office he published reams of such
malicious verbiage and reissued out of print publications of similar
'scientific' work that concurred with Nazi ideas of racial purity and
Aryan supremacy. Notable amongst the books Rosenberg
enthusiastically reprinted was the infamous forgery, *The Protocols of the
Elders of Zion*, circulated throughout Europe for more than half a
century. It was used as 'evidence' of Judaism's determination to
overthrow Christianity and destroy the Aryan race.

In 1933, Hitler despatched Rosenberg to London and charged him
with explaining the peaceable, righteous nature of the new German
regime. Other than to organizations like The Friends of Europe (a pro-
Nazi pressure group that numbered the Duchess of Atholl MP among
its members), Rosenberg's visit was not a success. His magnum opus,

Nazi regalia such as these martial banners would have decorated British streets if a German invasion of Britain had succeeded.

Mythus (*Myth of the Twentieth Century*) subtitled *A Valuation of the Spiritual and Intellectual Conflicts of our Time*, was a bestseller, second only to *Mein Kampf*. It quickly became the Nazi 'bible', speaking as it did of 'the awakening of the Soul of Race, which, after a period of long slumber, victoriously put an End to racial Chaos.' From 1934, Rosenberg was given responsibility for instructing new recruits into the ways and theories of the Nazi Party. No doubt in 1940 he would have been responsible for 'converting' those impressionable Britons attracted to the glamour, pageantry and theatre of Nazidom after Sea Lion had taken place. By July 1941, Rosenberg had been made Reich Minister for the German Occupied Territories and was key to the Germanization of these lands. He supervised the organization of slave labourers from occupied territories prior to their despatch to Germany and was closely involved with the Final Solution. He was hanged at Nuremberg.

The British could expect a hard battle ahead of them if the Germans did break out from a secured bridgehead. Even before France fell, 'Pug' Ismay had told Churchill that he assumed the Germans had considered the prospect of an invasion of Britain with the thoroughness and attention that the Third Reich had already exhibited as a character trait and a prerequisite to any military action. Ismay was confident that

Hitler had planned things 'to the last detail'. He further said, 'We can be sure that Hitler would be prepared to sacrifice ninety per cent of the whole expedition if he could gain a firm bridgehead on British soil with the remaining ten per cent.' With coastal airfields captured the Germans might not even need to capture a port. The possible fate of the Royal Navy was preoccupying the governments of Canada and the US. At a secret conference on 24 May between the Canadian premier Mackenzie King's government and President Roosevelt's administration, Britain's navy was top of the agenda. Both governments were concerned to prevent the Royal Navy's numerous ships from falling into German hands once Britain was 'forced to sue for peace.' US Ambassador Joseph Kennedy had been supplying his president with consistently pessimistic reports about Britain's chances of resisting invasion. Although Roosevelt knew that many Britons would consider the flight of the Royal Navy to safer waters as abhorrent and shameful, he decided that arrangements should be made 'for the remnants of the British fleet to be sent out to South Africa, Singapore, Australasia, the Caribbean and Canada.'

Anti-tank gunners in training. 'AA gunners are now spending hours daily to develop lighting-like speed in setting up and dismantling their mobile guns,' proudly boasts the original caption.

Once the Germans had invaded and the Auxunits had begun to carry out sabotage and assassination, the Nazis would have begun rounding up civilian hostages in an attempt to flush them out. Innocent citizens would probably have been accused of complicity with the resistance and the British, unused to being host to an occupier, are likely to have fared badly. The traditional British stoicism would have soon tried Nazi tempers. In occupied Guernsey, for example, a special free edition of the island's oldest newspaper, *The Star*, published on 1 July 1940, sported a message from the German Commandant warning citizens that, although the Nazi occupiers would respect the population, 'should anyone attempt to cause the least trouble, serious measures will be taken and the town will be bombed.' The local British authorities reiterated this warning by asking the public to 'be calm, to carry on their work in the usual way, and to obey the orders of the German Commandant.' On the British mainland, however, it is likely that the tense stalemate would have been broken by repeated clandestine night raids by Auxunit saboteurs.

As evinced later on the Continent at Oradour-sur-Glane and Liddice, reprisals for armed resistance to Nazi rule in England would have been swift and terrible. Ashford, straddling the Dover to London road and a nodal point in Kent on the likeliest invasion route, might well have been one of the first towns to suffer the full force of Nazi retribution. Just how long Colin Gubbins' resistance fighters would have held out after they had heard that Ashford had been systematically razed, its menfolk shot and women and children deported to the Reich's hinterland is best left to the imagination.

As soon as the invading German forces felt confident enough to attempt a breakout from their principal invasion bridgehead in the Dover area their likely route inland would pass along the A20 via Canterbury in the vicinity of Ashford and Maidstone, which coincidentally was the site of one of the strongest parts of the GHQ Line and adjacent to the position of XII Corps Observation Unit, Peter Fleming's pioneering British Resistance patrol. It is unlikely that German forces would have moved forward until they were entirely confident of possessing numerical superiority to their British opponents and by now the attacking forces would have included a complement of the new Pzkw Mark IVs from Erwin Rommel's 7th Panzer Division.

Villages and settlements along the routes of stop lines, such as Ashford, were integrated into the entire static defence and could become substantial obstacles to an invader. They were known variously as nodal points, anti-tank islands, keeps, defended locations and hedgehogs. Because of their size and extended location such nodal points presented opposition to an attacker across a much larger area, threatening his forces from the flanks and (especially after defeated troops had gone to ground in the basements of houses or amongst the debris that followed an artillery bombardment) the rear.

The British, fighting from prepared positions along the various stop lines and principally within the GHQ Line's boundaries would enjoy all the natural advantages bestowed on the defence. Matilda, Cruiser and Light tanks from 1st Armoured Division and the 1st Tank Brigade would have moved into position in Kent from their depots in Surrey and have prepared to fight in concealed 'hull down' positions. Once located in this way (with the thinly armoured and vulnerable tank belly bedded behind an earth embrasure) the British Matildas, especially, would have had nothing to fear from the less powerful guns of the German Mk IIIs and IVs. Even if spotted the Matildas would have been all but impervious to enemy shots, which would have been unable to pierce the British tanks' strong frontal armour. Quickly the air would have resonated to the shrieks and whizzes of ricochets and rebounds as German armour piercing rounds simply bounced off. However, the enemy had a distinct advantage in the ease with which it could call upon batteries of the dreaded mobile 88s, which could destroy any British tank with ease with its armour-piercing rounds. These guns and their experienced crews (many of them had been in action in Poland in 1939 or had seen more or less constant action since April 1940), with the advantage that long range and mobility confers could take their time picking off the British targets. The gun's flexibility meant that it was equally adept at lobbing high-explosive shells onto the tanks that couldn't be reached with direct shots. Those tanks that were hit and unable to be immediately recovered would be lost to the advancing Germans who would have had the advantage of forward movement. In fact, the British were hopelessly short of recovery vehicles and, especially, spare parts throughout the entire early war years (as some of the sorry tales of the BEF tank units in France confirm) and disabled vehicles would have been ready prey for marauding Luftwaffe Stuka units.

It is likely that most of the decisive engagements on the British mainland during the first week of Sea Lion would have taken place in Kent, the region defended by General Thorne's XII Corps. XII Corps' key sector included Major General Liardet's 1st (London) Division, which was one of the new 'motorized' formations that had been mobilized the previous September. Close by was 2nd (London) Brigade, prepared to counter-attack the airfields of Lympne and Hawkinge, wresting their control from the air mobile Nazi Fallschirmjägers and any advance parties of Gebirgsjäger (mountain troops) if they had managed to capture these stations. In the Dover area Major General Hyland's 6th Anti Aircraft Division possessed eighteen mobile 3.7-inch AA guns and a small quantity of AP ammunition for use against advancing panzers. One battalion of

A soldier of the Royal Engineers prepares to meet the invader. He sports a crudely fashioned sniper's mask and wears non-regulation sewn-on shoulder titles. The muzzle of a nearby Lewis gun can clearly be seen. Thousands of these were pressed into service to make up for the loss of so many newer Bren guns in France.

infantry (1st London Rifle Brigade) from Liardet's division was also detailed to support the counter-attack against Lympne and Hawkinge.

If a successful Nazi invasion had taken place, England could have expected to receive similar treatment to that shown to other occupied countries. It should be remembered that by 1940, the full horror of the Third Reich had yet to be exhibited. Prior to Operation Barbarossa in 1941, Germany had not demonstrated its ruthless belief in Aryan superiority over the Slavic peoples of the East. Neither had it commenced the systematic destruction of the Jewish people – the Final Solution. Whilst operation Sea Lion would have been executed with the single-mindedness and the efficiency that is a hallmark of German organizational management, the British could have expected to receive better treatment than that which the citizens of the Ukraine, for example, received eighteen months later.

It is clear from Hitler's pre-war writings that he regarded France as the deadly enemy and not England. Indeed, as we now know, Hitler would have preferred a settlement with England. In a pamphlet issued by The Friends of Europe, Hitler wrote:

Only with England to cover our rear, would it have been possible to begin the new Teutonic march. To gain England's favour no sacrifice should have been too great. We should have denied ourselves colonies and sea-power, and have spared British industry from our competition.

Although he considered the British Empire bourgeois and decadent and was sure that its financial institutions were under Jewish control, he was curiously in awe of Britain's achievements and world stature. His repeated attempts to find a compromise with Britain confirm his reluctance to fight her.

In any case, expansion eastwards, not westwards, was Hitler's real dream. Only then would he be able to fulfil his, and Germany's, destiny. He had made no secret of his ambition for more territory. In the long and rambling *Mein Kampf* he had written:

It was the soil that was profitably Germanized in our history, the soil which our ancestors acquired by the sword and settled with German peasants.

England had forced the Führer's hand, however, and, as he saw it, made a Nazi invasion inevitable. Because Britain, and especially Churchill, had proved so belligerently steadfast in the face of German might, it is possible that it would have been singled out for special punishment and used as an example of the Third Reich's superiority. Equally it might also have been used to demonstrate Hitler's magnanimity. He hoped that certain territories, such as Holland and the Channel Islands, might be held up as examples of the Third Reich's fairness when it came to administration of civil affairs.

Security in Nazi-occupied Western Europe was the responsibility of the HSSPF – the Höhere SS and Polizeiführer (High Command of the SS and Police). Several SS Totenkopfverbände (SS Death Heads Units) were established in western occupied territories. Counter-intelligence and espionage was the province of the Abwehr (Wehrmacht counter-intelligence service) and the Geheime Feldpolizei (GFP), the Secret Military Police. After the campaigns in Scandinavia, France and the Low Countries, a few Police Regiments were formed, such as the two regiments in Norway (NordNorwegen and SudNorwegen). The Allgemeine SS established national branches in those occupied countries where Germanization occurred. Volunteers for foreign Waffen SS units were invited from each newly occupied land. The Waffen SS also established volunteer combat units within occupied countries.

Home Guard in 'battle order' in characteristically mismatched denims. He wears the HG's BAR pouches, originally made to carry ammunition for the Browning automatic rifle, although he is armed with a P17.

To encourage occupied countries to comply with Nazi demands the Third Reich possessed a massive and sophisticated secret police and espionage establishment. Himmler's SS (Schutzstaffel) were Hitler's elite guard and dated back to the blood purges of the 'Night of the Long Knives' in 1934, when Ernst Roehm and his rival SA Storm Troopers were liquidated in the struggle for political ascendancy that consumed the Nazis during the first year of the new order. The SS surfaced from the turmoil as the elite police arm of the Nazi party. It was split into two main components – the black-clad Allgemeine (or general) SS, whose dubious honour it was to organize the Nazis' more unsavoury business, such as politically motivated killing and the implementation of the Final Solution (the industrialized murder of Jews and other 'undesirables'), and the Waffen (or armed) SS, the renowned and fearless camouflaged soldiers who supplemented the regular army in the field. The intelligence branch of the SS, the SD (Sicherheitsdienst, or security service) was supposedly under the control of the Minister of the Interior, Wilhelm Frick. In reality it was commanded by Himmler's gifted prodigy, the handsome model Aryan SS Obergruppenführer Reinhard Heydrich. Himmler decreed that the SD would 'discover the enemies of the National Socialist Concept' and 'initiate countermeasures through the official police authorities.' Directed against the 'enemies of the state', the SD included a Security Police Branch, the SIPO, and a Criminal Police Branch, the KRIPO.

If established in Britain, the full panoply of Heydrich's SD would have swung into action and the country would have been quickly sown with Nazi agents and informants. Those patriotic Britons who had adopted Ironside's 'Stand Firm' policy promulgated throughout southern England by a poster campaign that said, 'Every citizen will regard it as his duty to hinder and frustrate the enemy and help our own forces by every means that ingenuity can devise' would have to contend with infiltration in the neighbourhoods by SD 'A' Men (*Agenten*) and 'Z' Men (*Zubringer*, or informants). In due course they would come to especially loathe the 'H' Men (*Helfershelfer*, or secondary informants) and the 'U' Men (*Unzuverlässige*, or unreliable), for these were the paid informers. A twitch of a neighbour's net curtains could indicate that she was in either of the last two categories. British householders living under Nazi occupation would learn to live in fear of a knock at the front door that revealed a SIPO officer investigating a report filed for reward by a nosey 'H' Man. In fact, during Germany's *Anschluss* with Austria in 1938, the absolute power of Heydrich's SD was demonstrated when 67,000 'enemies of the state' disappeared after arrest. Any legal opposition to SD arrest would be as pointless in Britain as it was on the Continent, for Heydrich made sure that his organization included some of the best legal brains, who could legitimize any of his rulings. Magistrates' courts in England would soon feature a complement of SD officers ready to transport a convicted defendant (and once accused, few were ever acquitted) either to factory labour in the Reich hinterland or to slow death in a concentration camp.

Perhaps the single Nazi organization that would have struck most terror into British souls was Amt IV of the RSHA (Reichssicherheitshauptamtor, Nazi Central Security Agency), which dealt with the investigation and combating of opposition (Gegnererforschung und Gegnerbekämpfung) and was better known as the Gestapo (Geheime Staatspolizei, or Secret State Police). The RSHA was established on 17 September 1939, with Heydrich at its head, and the Gestapo became its most feared department. The Gestapo also actively supported organizations outside Germany that were sympathetic to Nazi policy and it recruited collaborators among Nazi sympathizers in Norway, Denmark, Belgium and Holland. The

International Military Tribunal at Nuremberg specifically linked the SD and RHSA and declared that from its single headquarters on Prinz Albrechtstrasse in Berlin and via its own command channels it had worked 'both in Germany, in occupied territories and in the areas immediately behind the front lines … for purposes that were criminal under the charter involving the persecution and extermination of the Jews, brutalities and killings in concentration camps, excesses in the administration of occupied territories, the administration of the slave labour programme and the mistreatment and murder of prisoners of war.' Gestapo, SS and SD personnel who were members of any of the organizations during the years 1939-45, and involved in the 'active planning of war crimes and crimes against humanity connected with the war' were declared war criminals at Nuremberg. Members of another secret police force department, the GFP (Geheime Feldpolizei, or secret military police), who wore yet another uniform that Britons would have come to recognize and loath, were one of the few Nazi secret police departments to escape this blanket condemnation.

After the war a variety of documents fell into the hands of the advancing Allied armies as they swept through Germany. Many were prepared by Generaloberst Franz Halder, OKW's Chief of Staff, and some of the surviving documents were ready for the signature of OKW's Commander-in-Chief in 1940, Field Marshall Walther von

Reminiscent of the classic 1940 Channel Islands photographs, an unwelcome German tourist is helped by the ubiquitous British bobby.

Brauchitsch. The Gestapo went to the trouble of preparing two handbooks to help its agents on the ground in occupied Britain. The first, *Information Sheft GB*, was a 100-page reference work detailing the geography, culture, regional idiosyncrasies, transport network and varying dialects of Britain. The second surviving booklet, *Ordnances of the Military Authorities*, for German-occupied Great Britain, was actually printed in 1941, long after the real danger of invasion had passed but during a time when Hitler had only officially 'postponed' Operation Sea Lion. It provides an interesting insight into the kind of minutiae that concerned the Nazi mind and serves as an indication that Germany was more prepared for the occupation of England than is often thought. This document was printed in German with facing translations in English throughout and it covered topics ranging from 'Hunting Rights in the Occupied Territory' to 'Exemption from Customs Duties for the German Army'. The instructions range from railways ('No removal of material shall be made from the occupied territory for the purpose of making good a deficit of locomotives or engines ...') to vagrancy ('Any woman found guilty as a vagrant and if found affected by venereal disease shall be confined in hospital until released by authority of the physician.') Under the heading 'Political Meetings' (*Politische Versammlungen*), it states, 'Although no special approval for holding meetings is now required, the German Military Authorities may forbid the holding of any meeting as they think fit. Speeches will contain nothing that is offensive to the Axis Powers or of a nature that will tend to disorder.'

A sub-section of Amt IV-'E' was headed by one Walther Schellenberg. Schellenberg was responsible for the hurried compilation in May 1940 of *Sonderfahndungsliste GB* (*Special Search List GB*). Along with a list of some 2,820 individuals targeted for immediate arrest, the book featured a gazetteer of organizations including the Amalgamated Society of Boot and Shoe Makers and Repairers, the Catholic Committee for Refugees from Prague, publishers such as Jonathan Cape and Constable, hospitals, Freemason lodges and industrial corporations, each with the reference number of the RSHA section assigned to check them out. Much of the document is dedicated to the arrest list and plenty of bland ruled pages were included so that Gestapo investigators could add to the document. It is no surprise to see Winston Churchill's name, though I doubt if he would have been staying at the address shown – Chartwell Manor! Though precisely why Noel Coward of 'London' should have been wanted for questioning is anyone's guess.

In the UK, the 41-year-old SS Colonel Professor Dr Franz Alfred Six would have led department (Amt) II of the RSHA. This department, '*Haushalt und Wirtschaft*', literally 'household and economy', took care of the internal administrative, judicial and economic arrangements within the RSHA and Six would have been the man responsible for the Gestapo arrest operations in occupied Britain. Dr Six and his forty Gestapo officers would have referred to the pages of the special search list as they travelled around Britain arresting those individuals identified in it as enemies of the Reich. Fortunately, because Sea Lion never took place, the name 'Dr Six' has never entered British history books. He crops up later in occupied Russia, where he identified Soviet political commissars amongst the hordes of captured Russian troops and despatched them to the firing squad. After S-Day, Six was to have commanded, appropriately enough, six of Heydrich's Action Commandos (*Einsatzkommandos*) based in London, Birmingham, Liverpool, Bristol, Manchester and Edinburgh. Heydrich had told him:

> Your task is to combat, with the requisite means, all anti-German organizations, instructions, and opposition groups that can be seized in England, to prevent the removal of all available material and to centralize and safeguard it for future exploitation. I designate London as the location of your headquarters and I authorize you to set up small *Einsatzgruppen* in other parts of Great Britain as the situation dictates and necessity arises.

Sentenced to twenty years for war crimes at Nuremberg, Six was released before he had served barely four years in prison.

One can speculate on what would have happened to the monarchy if the reigning king and his government had been forced to flee to Canada in the 'Black Move'. Only recently have official papers been released detailing the 'unbalanced' judgements of the Duke of Windsor, who abdicated as King Edward VIII in 1936 and who refused to budge from his house in Antibes, France, in June 1940, even as the Nazis surrounded Paris. As we know, he finally accepted the governorship of the Bahamas but then conducted a telegraphic struggle with Churchill from his new home in Spain, which culminated in the Prime Minister's warning that 'refusal to obey direct orders of the competent military authority would create a serious situation' (the Duke was still a serving Army officer). An informer recalled the Duke of Windsor during a dinner party in Spain anticipating a British collapse, a newly installed Labour government suing for peace with the Third Reich and himself returning to London to replace his brother, George VI.

A number of people spring to mind as possible heads of a puppet regime in Nazi-occupied Britain. The first, Sir Oswald Mosley, the leader of the British Union of Fascists, had been imprisoned in Brixton under the recent emergency regulations granted to the Home

Secretary. Although a confirmed fascist, Mosley was avowedly patriotic and anti-Nazi so he is unlikely to have been coerced to turn 'Quisling' (Vidkun Quisling was the leader of Norway's fascist party and grabbed power after the Nazi invasion of Norway). In *Tomorrow We Live*, the BUF's manifesto, the organization's policy was clearly spelled out and it is clear from the patriotic Mosley's writings here that he would not have been prepared to countenance surrender to Hitler:

> We will not surrender one inch of British territory to any power.
> ... We are British and before all else in our national creed we place Britain and our love of country.

But he may have been hinting of future collaboration when he added, 'but because we love our land we can understand and work with those that love their land.'

Some writers have suggested that the Conservative MP Sir Samuel Hoare may have been another candidate. Hoare had been a pre-war Foreign Secretary who had been forced from office in 1935 because of his pro-appeasement views, which led to the abortive Hoare-Laval pact concerning the Italian invasion of Ethiopia. However, considering that he became First Lord of the Admiralty after he left the Cabinet, I think it unlikely that he would have been capable of acquiescing to German demands.

A more likely candidate is John Amery, one of the sons of Secretary of State for Burma, Leo Amery. The other son, Julian, was a fearless SOE fighter who supported eastern communist partisans in their struggle against the Nazis. Paradoxically, his black sheep of a brother, John, was on the other extreme of the political spectrum. Before the war John had offered his services to Franco and was involved in gunrunning during the Spanish Civil War. At the outbreak of war he was in France as a prominent member of the French fascists, the Gagoulards. Throughout the war Amery commanded the British Legion of St George, which subsequently became known as the British Free Corps. The British Free Corps organized tours of German prisoner of war camps and endeavoured to recruit disgruntled Tommies into one of the Waffen SS foreign regiments. After a failed attempt to convince the crown that he was a Spanish citizen, John Amery was tried and executed for treason after the war. At his trial government psychiatrists described Amery as 'abnormally defective' and advised that as early as 1940, when the first British POWs captured in Norway and France began appearing in the Stalags, senior Nazis, notably von Ribbentrop, began courting Amery and his compatriots on the Continent. While trapped in Vichy France in 1940 after Germany's Western Offensive, Amery had contacted Dr Fritz Hess, head of

Hitler's 'England Service', and had offered to broadcast uncensored propaganda to England.

After the war two Germans were put forward as the Führer's nominees for the post of Reichskommissar of occupied Great Britain. One was the Nazis' arrogant and snobbish Minister for Foreign Affairs and ex-wine salesman, Joachim von Ribbentrop, who had been Ambassador to Great Britain in 1936 and 1937. He had committed the ultimate faux-pas of greeting the King with a Nazi salute. Nevertheless, the fact that he had lived as a commercial rep in Canada before the First World War, had been Hitler's spokesman at the Court of King James in London and was a self-professed expert on British attitudes and opinions (despite the fact that he assured Hitler that Britain would not go to war over Poland), made him a strong contender. The other was the 35-year-old Ernst Bohle, an under-secretary in Ribbentrop's ministry and the main architect for overseas organization of the Nazi party. Bohle denied that he ever wanted or was earmarked for the post but did admit that at the signing of French capitulation at Compiègne the Führer promised him the job of German Ambassador to Britain, which he was sure would now seek peace terms. Archive film is testament to Hitler's high spirits on the day. British propagandists re-cut footage of Hitler's exuberance and depicted him gleefully dancing a pompous jig. Perhaps on this day he was confident enough to assume that he had won the war.

We can get a pretty good idea of what occupation would have been like on mainland Britain by studying the plight of the Channel Islands, that one part of Britain that was ruled by the Nazis during the Second World War. Hitler decreed that the occupation of the Channel Islands was to be a 'Model Occupation'. This would show the world and Britain the benevolence of the Third Reich. Unlike other areas of occupied Europe, the Nazis treated the *'Juden Frage'* (the Jewish Question) with relative kid gloves. Although there was deportation of those Jews who had not chosen evacuation before the Germans invaded, and from time to time some of those left were singled out for deportation within the Reich along with other civilians in reprisal for British Commando raids on the Channel Islands, the occupying forces did not instil terror into the populace in the same way that Nazi troops did on the Continent.

However, the latest release of government documents concerning the German occupation of the Channel Islands shows that Hitler's Reich committed atrocities in the British Isles of a kind that later became commonplace in Eastern Europe. We also know that Alderney was home to a British concentration camp that the Nazis codenamed 'Sylt', after the popular German holiday resort. Half of Sylt's 1,600 Russian inmates died there. Some were crucified to the camp's gates in winter and doused with freezing water until they died of exposure for simply digging up the rotting remains of abattoir carcasses and scavenging amongst the remains of animal entrails in a desperate effort to find food. Other prisoners were used as rifle targets by camp guards or hunted down by guard dogs. While all this was going on, the occupying Nazi garrisons on Jersey and Guernsey, which, unlike Alderney, had witnessed the forcible evacuations of the civilian populations, kept up the pretence of Nazi correctness. Such was the occupier's apparent even-handedness that some Channel Islanders were happy to co-operate with the German authorities and the records tell of many petty jealousies being resolved by citizens wilfully reporting their neighbours to the occupying authorities for minor misdemeanours or insignificant acts of 'resistance'. Could all this have happened on the mainland if England had succumbed to invasion? Given that the Nazis mainly comprised thugs like Streicher, misfits like Goebbels, those who felt aggrieved and wronged by society in general like Hitler and twisted petty bureaucrats like Himmler, I have no doubt that they would have had no trouble attracting limited support from those Britons with similar chips on their shoulders. Occupying German forces would have attempted to curry favour with local British authorities and police forces and I'm sure that by employing a reasoned approach and sympathetically appealing directly to certain officials, rather than confronting or overruling them, some could have been won over. A regime so enthusiastically devoted to bureaucracy would have embraced similarly minded clerks in Britain. As they did in the Channel Islands, some local government officials on the mainland would have doubtless co-operated to the extent of turning a blind eye to the less savoury activities of the occupying regime. Some British officials might even have prospered if the United Kingdom had been conquered.

To guarantee the tenure of a Thousand Year Reich the Nazis needed to foster the same ideals in the forthcoming generations as those that had sustained party elders through the wilderness years of the 1920s. Key to future Nazi hegemony was the development of a band of young heirs to the National Socialist cause, the Hitler Youth. Hitler demanded that they comprise 'a violently active, dominating, brutal youth … indifferent to pain', with 'no intellectual training. … Knowledge is ruin to my young men.' Perhaps this opinion could have been expected from a drifter and academic failure. By 1935, less than two years after it was established, more than half of all German boys between fourteen and eighteen were in the Hitler Youth. In 1936, every German boy was expected to join. Any boy who didn't was considered, along with his family, to have violated his civic responsibilities. This system of 'press-ganging' gradually eroded the traditional family structure in Germany and the Führer increasingly became an actual, not just symbolic, father figure. The Hitler Youth wasn't simply a cadet force for future soldiers – boys were encouraged to go camping, study scale modelling, learn music and appreciate 'non-decadent' arts and crafts. Membership of the Hitler Youth soon took precedence over formal school education in Germany.

Non-martial clubs and associations dedicated to outdoor pursuits and individual health and wellbeing also abounded in pre-war Germany. In 1936, Hitler had said, 'non-political sport, so-called neutral sport, is unthinkable in the Reich,' and images of the Führer encouraging athletic young blondes from the League of German Maidens (Bund Deutscher Madel, which was set up alongside the Hitler Youth in 1933) decked out in their swastika-adorned sports kit featured in magazines as often as those of Hitler as commander-in-chief saluting rookie Storm Troopers. Shortly before the German invasion of Poland, the more famous Kraft durch Freude movement (strength through joy) organized more than 100,000 concerts, exhibitions, operas, folklore plays and film shows throughout the Reich regaling audiences with the virtues of North European racial and cultural superiority.

The League for Aeronautic Sport (Luftsportverband) encouraged civilian flying, principally gliding, and between 1933 and 1935 had been used as cover for the training of scores of the still secret Luftwaffe's fledgling pilots. Young people were encouraged into organizations dedicated to non-military pursuits like farming and building. The vegetarian and dog-loving Hitler was a keen follower of country pursuits and greatly supported the Office for Agriculture (Agrarpolitischer Apparat). No doubt Agricultural Auxiliary Service classes would have been established for British schoolchildren and, like their German counterparts, they might have taken part in the harvest during the holidays. Hitler wrote at length in *Mein Kampf* about future German expansion being by the shovel as well as the machine gun. Unlike his deputy, Goering, he never bedecked himself in flamboyant military uniforms or regalia, preferring to wear the drabbest of outfits. Martial glory was only a means to an end – National Socialism was to be achieved by concerted military and civilian endeavour: '*Ein Volk, Ein Reich, Ein Führer*'.

The Organization Todt (OT), which brought together government firms, private companies and the Reichsarbeitsdienst (Reich Labour Service) for all major Nazi construction projects, would also have been transplanted to Britain. This semi-military organization had been the key to the development of the new autobahns in Germany. After the death of its founder, Fritz Todt, in 1942, the OT was administered by Albert Speer. One can only speculate as to whether under Speer occupied Britain might have enjoyed a road system as advanced as

Street fighting amidst the ruins of British towns and cities destroyed by enemy air bombardment and artillery fire would quickly take on the quality of combat later associated with the Battle of Stalingrad. The original caption reads, 'Street fighting exercise taken at the School of Battle Drill, Lymington, near Southampton.'

Germany's if work had started in 1940. Britain's Trades Union Congress would have had to accommodate the desires and aspirations of ex-chemist Dr Robert Ley and his German Labour Front (Deutsche Arbeits Front). Ley was effectively in charge of all the German trade associations and workers' unions that had ceased to have autonomy after 1933. In 1935, Ley claimed that, under the new structure imposed by the Nazis, Germany possessed the world's first class-free society.

The British would also have been served up some purportedly progressive welfare programmes such as the generous tax deductions that could be claimed by large families. Indeed, mothers occupied a hallowed place in the Third Reich and from 1939, those with large families were presented with their own medal, the *Mutterkreuz* (cross of motherhood), in recognition of their work! Propagation enjoyed such a special position in the Reich that state-run brothels even existed, the *Lebensborn*, not merely for client gratification but, as Himmler decreed in 1939, for the procreation even 'and especially' of illegitimate children.

Another initiative that enjoyed widespread success in Germany was the popular '*Winterhilfe*' campaigns, which began in occupied territories in 1940. Millions of Reichsmarks (for the alleviation of wounded soldiers and bereaved families) were netted after the street-corner sale of special editions of stamps and plastic miniatures of tanks and aircraft. These too would have been transplanted to a conquered Britain.

These programmes, which are perhaps not widely known, would have been foisted on reluctant Britons along with the whole gamut of Nazi horrors such as state-controlled sterilization, euthanasia and murder, as well as all that was entailed in the Final Solution. In view of this macabre package, it is as well that Great Britain had the power, the courage and the good fortune to resist the Nazi invader.

Chapter 7

Stand Down

The War Office has ordered that the Operational Side of Auxiliary Units shall stand down. In view of the fact that your lives depended on secrecy, no public recognition will be possible. But those in the most responsible positions as General Headquarters, Home Forces, know what was done, and what would have been done, if you had been called upon. They know it well. It will not be forgotten.

Colonel Frank W.R. Douglas,
Commander Auxiliary Units, 30 November 1944

In September 1996, as the author was completing the manuscript for the first edition of this book, a series of press articles appeared that revealed that, although it was more than fifty years since they were 'stood down', surviving Auxunit veterans would at last receive the official recognition they deserved. Under the headline 'HONOUR AT LAST FOR THE ELITE FORCE WHOSE HOUR NEVER CAME', *The Times'* Defence Correspondent, Michael Evans, said:

> The Ministry of Defence confirmed yesterday that the Army Medals Issuing Office at Droitwich, near Worcester, would award the former secret commandos provided they could prove they had completed three years' service.

I have no doubt that most surviving Auxunit members, their friends and relatives will think this recognition is overdue. I am equally sure that some former patrol members will not be too eager to apply for the medals to which they are entitled. I am of the opinion that, in general, men of the character required for selection to this unique 'do-or-die' organization would not be bothered with all the fuss and bureaucracy required to stake a claim for a 'gong', dismissing it as bunkum or stuff and nonsense. These gentlemen knew what they were trained for and

Recognition must have appeared a long time coming for many of the Auxunit veterans who gathered at the Radnor Arms in Coleshill for their first reunion, fifty years after the Units were disbanded in 1944.

how perilous their lives would have been if the 'balloon' did go up. A medal might be a nice heirloom to pass on to grandchildren but I doubt it would make too much difference to men who had spent more than half a century without one.

Hitler's Germany didn't, of course, attempt an invasion of England in 1940. Neither did it dust off the 'postponed' plans for Operation Sea Lion in 1941 as directive No. 18 suggested it might. Hitler's war had changed dramatically in less than eighteen months since his Luftwaffe had been denied air superiority in the skies above England in the Battle of Britain. His attack on the Soviet Union in the spring of 1941 had not been the walkover some had predicted. As winter set in, his armies, ill-equipped for winter warfare in Russia, were still short of Moscow. The Führer's obsession with capturing Stalingrad would ultimately lead to the destruction of the Third Reich. Few observers could believe that, in the face of the undefeated might of Nazi Germany, the Soviet Union successfully moved its manufacturing base across the Urals and reappeared on the battlefield with the best tank in the world at the time – the T-34.

Britain's obstinate refusal to give way to Nazi authority was a beacon to the Soviets and to the rest of the world. It showed that Hitler was fallible after all and that, perhaps, Germany could not endure a long war. Certainly, Roosevelt's isolationist US was inspired by Britain's stand. And when, after the devious Japanese attack on the American Pacific Fleet at Pearl Harbor in December 1941, Hitler foolishly declared war on the US in the vain hope of encouraging his Axis partner, Japan, to help him fight the Soviet Union, it was clear that the combined strength of the Western Allies and Russia would be more than a match for Germany.

Clearly, if Hitler had not been so obsessed with destroying the Soviet Union, the seat of world communism, then further invasion attempts against England would have taken place. Only if they had, would the mettle of Auxunits personnel and the value of its organizational structure have been put to the test.

It should not be forgotten that in 1941, when many in high command argued that that Auxiliary Units' *raison d'être* was no longer viable, even Winston Churchill feared that the Nazidom might vanquish the Soviet Union, and if it did, Hitler would then undoubtedly turn once again to Britain.

But by the autumn of 1944, the Western Allies had successfully broken out from the tangle of the Normandy bocage hedgerow country within which they had remained trapped for three months following the D-Day landings. As soon as the push eastwards towards Germany began, Britain's High Command, not unrealistically, decided that maintaining GHQ's mainland home defence land forces, including the Home Guard and Auxiliary Units, was unnecessary. Accordingly they sent a letter to Colonel Frank W.R. Douglas, the Auxunits Commander. It was dated 18 November 1944 and began:

> In view of the improved war situation, it has been decided by the War Office that the Operational Branch shall stand down, and the time has come to put an end to an organization that would have been of inestimable value to this country in the event of invasion. … All ranks under your command are aware of the secret nature of their duties. For that reason it has not been possible for them to receive publicity, nor will it be possible even now.

General H.E. Franklyn, the Commander-in-Chief GHQ Home Forces, reminded his subordinate that, far from feeling deflated by this lack of official public recognition for their activities, his volunteers should regard the fact that they were involved in such an important covert organization with 'special pride'.

In turn, on 30 November, Douglas wrote to each of his charges saying:

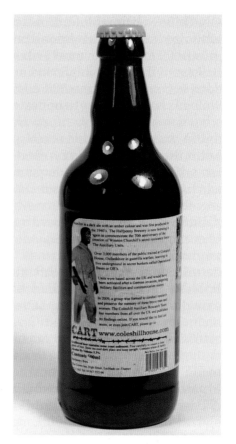

Front and rear of Auxilier Ale bottles. Brewed for the Coleshill Auxiliary Research Team (CART) by the Old Forge Brewery at Coleshill, this real ale was named by Bob Millard. This is a real souvenir because the fine brew is no longer produced!

I realize what joining Auxiliary Units has meant to you; so do the officers under my command. You were invited to do a job that would require more skill and coolness, more hard work and greater danger than was demanded of any other voluntary organization. In the event of 'Action Stations' being ordered you knew well the kind of life you were in for.

After telling them of GHQ's decision to keep Auxunits secret, Douglas added:

But those in the most responsible positions at General Headquarters, Home Forces, know what was done, and what would have been done, if you had been called upon. They know it well. It will not be forgotten.

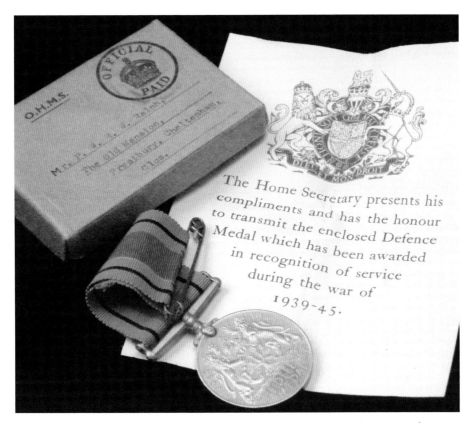

The Defence Medal (1939–45) was awarded for non-operational service. This type of service in the UK included those service personnel working in headquarters, on training bases and airfields and members of the Home Guard. Home Guard service counts between the dates of 14 May 1940 and 31 December 1944. The flame colour in the centre of the ribbon is flanked by stripes of green to symbolize enemy attacks on Britain's 'green and pleasant land', with narrow black stripes to represent the blackout.

Not surprisingly, perhaps, it was left to the resourceful Auxunit veterans to remind the world of what they were prepared to do half a century ago. For, despite the 'whistle' being blown on the organization in David Lampe's book in the 1960s and brief mentions of the organization in histories about Britain's home defence in 1940 (including a fiftieth anniversary commemorative history of the Battle of Britain written in association with the RAF Museum by this author) and a series of particularly good magazine articles submitted by veteran Geoffrey Bradford, personal details remained sketchy. Only through the initiatives of veteran Geoffrey Bradford and Peter Wilcox (the brother-in-law of Auxunit member Colin Cooke) were surviving Auxunit veterans contacted and reminded of their erstwhile kinship.

Via a series of newsletters and reunions, the first and most significant of which was held at the Radnor Arms, Coleshill, in the winter of 1994, fifty years after Auxunits were stood down, members from all over Britain came together near the site of their old training HQ. It is really only because the author and other researchers were invited to incessantly pester the survivors for details of the Auxiliary Units' structure and daily routine that the real story has surfaced.

Sid Gaston had a somewhat pessimistic view of what would have happened to the Auxunits. 'If the invasion did happen I don't think we would have survived for more than a week. If we were caught we weren't trained about what to do. Put a revolver in your mouth and pull the trigger! If we had been caught we knew we would have been shot anyway. The German dogs – the Germans were very good with dogs – would have sniffed us out and we would have been caught. Never mind "rear-guard actions".'

Frank Penfold remembered the final days of Auxunits. 'We were called to a meeting at Tottington (Small Dole, near Henfield, the Auxunit HQ in Sussex) just before D-Day and were told, "We're thinking of putting it up to the War Office that we ask for volunteers from your patrols," and asked whether we would be prepared to be dropped behind the German lines in France to link up with the French Resistance and do the sort of things you've been trained to do, like sabotage and so on. They asked for everyone who was willing to go to put up their hands. I know all my patrol did. They said you will not be trained in parachute dropping – your first drop will be your only drop. You will land with your kit and start operations immediately. But by that time most of us realized there wouldn't be a German invasion and therefore we wouldn't be in action.

'After this happened we had an inspection of my OB by General "Boy" Browning. I met him with our Army Patrol Leader, Captain Bradley, who took over from Fazan. The next we heard was that he wasn't going to use us – so whether he was sufficiently unimpressed I don't know! The excuse we were given was that the Treasury wouldn't wear it because of the pension implications if we lost our lives. Which was just as well! I don't know how much good we would have done. Certainly most of us would have lost our lives.'

There was concern that Auxiliaries, who were recruited locally and had an in-depth knowledge of the rural districts in England where they had lived all their lives, would be out of their depth in a foreign country. Resistance fighters like the Maquis and Auxunits are only viable if fighting in their own back yard. Furthermore, given that Auxunits weren't paid on the Regular Army establishment, covered by the Geneva Convention or even 'officially recognized' it is entirely

The concrete slab that reinforced the ceiling of Whitehall's Cabinet War Rooms can clearly be seen in this photograph.

After reading the 1997 edition of this book my neighbour, Joe Revill, who coincidently works for Penfold Verrall, the modern incarnation of the late Frank Penfold's family firm, told me he knew of an underground store in the woods atop Bury Hill that looked very similar to the wartime Operational Bases I had written about. It was, of course, Frank's wartime hideout and had not been destroyed. Here Joe is seen preparing to enter the supposedly long lost OB.

plausible that the tight-fisted Treasury was reluctant to insure them and pay compensation to their war widows.

The authorities sought to wind up the organization as efficiently as possible and a meeting was arranged to decide who would take charge of decommissioning Frank Penfold's OB. 'At this meeting they asked Leslie Drewitt if he wanted to take responsibility,' Frank told me. 'He said "no". So did I. A patrol leader, Cooper, was made up to a Regular captain and he had the responsibility of decommissioning the OBs etc.' This was no mean job because, as Frank Penfold told me, 'We had a hell of an arsenal. In the explosive line we had all sorts of devices like tripwires, pull switches, detonators, electrical ones operated by batteries, and, of course, time-pencils.'

In one of those amazing coincidences that sometime occur, in June 2008, while I was living in Houghton, in Sussex, my neighbour, Joe Revill, who worked at Penfold Verrall Ltd, the merger of Penfold Public Works and G.W. Verrall & Sons, told me he had met Frank Penfold occasionally. After I showed him a copy of the first edition of this book, Joe told me that when walking his dogs on nearby Bury Hill he had come across an underground 'storage' vault that looked very similar to the so-called OBs in the photographs within the book.

It sounded too good to be true! Frank Penfold told me his OB had been decommissioned and no longer existed. But it clearly did, and though not easy to climb into, Joe and I managed to get inside and the photographic results of our efforts are shown in this edition. The OB has since been secured against unwanted entry.

As his Auxunit patrol was dismantled, Eric Johnson recalled that, 'We were told it was still to remain absolutely secret. At that time one didn't know if the war was going to be really finished or if something else would crop up at a later date and whether the same sort of thing might be needed again. You didn't want everyone to know exactly what had happened. They would have a line on what defences there were, the type of defences that could be locally organized again.'

'So it was kept secret because they might need to reactivate you again?' I asked.

'Well, yes, not necessarily us personally but the same scheme, the same kind of defence.'

I asked Eric Johnson if he felt that there should have been any official recognition of the Auxiliaries.

'Well, I feel that it has been left rather too long before it was acknowledged and people who say, "You were evading military service," and all that sort of thing just didn't know what we were doing. One occasionally felt that there was a little bit of antipathy to us but it wasn't as if we weren't doing anything.'

Interior of model OB at Coleshill.

View deep inside Frank Penfold's rediscovered OB. Remains of the wartime fittings such as bunk beds can clearly be seen, as can the entrance to the concrete escape tunnel.

Eric Johnson's wife didn't find out that he had been involved in Auxunits until David Lampe's book, *The Last Ditch*, was published. She thought he was in the Home Guard all the time! Lampe's book brought it out into the open.

Arthur Gabbitas told me how he felt when the Auxunits, and specifically his branch of it, Auxunit Signals, was stood down in 1944. 'Our Commanding Officer was hoping that we might be used in embassies around the world but we were sent back to Catterick for retraining. Five of us were retained as instructors at Catterick while others were sent to various parts of the war zones,' he told me. In 1994, shortly after the Auxunits' first ever reunion, he wrote to me saying, 'No one discussed their work outside their operation. After demob, no one seemed to bother about what happened; they were only too pleased to be back home! It is only in the last few years that nostalgia has made me look for old haunts and trace old comrades. The vast majority of people knew nothing of Auxunits, not even the authorities, so no recognition was made. As soldiers we obeyed orders but I think Auxunit civilians should have a medal, either the Defence Medal or the British Legion Medal for National Service. I wrote to them but they would not help.'

Geoffrey Bradford remembered the end of Auxunits. 'There was what we called a "standing down" parade and certainly all the Devon ones met in the Guildhall in Exeter – we didn't actually parade as such.' He recalled travelling to Exeter by car on a particular Sunday and being presented with the standard HG certificate and copies of the two official winding-up letters by no less an officer than Colonel Douglas himself. When I first interviewed Geoffrey Bradford in 1990 he hoped that one day there would be a reunion. 'I'd love it,' he said. 'I would be interested to hear from any surviving members who belonged to "Highworth's Fertilizers" and would love to see a reunion in Highworth village.' The reunions that commenced four years later probably surprised Geoffrey by their size and by the interest in Auxunits they unwittingly whipped up!

In *Invasion 1940*, author Peter Fleming, who, of course, was closely involved in Britain's anti-invasion defences at this time, said that Thorne's XII Corps, within whose Kent command his 'model' Auxunit patrol was positioned, was thought by the Germans to be located in Wales. Revelations like this and the post-war Allied scrutiny of other captured OKW documents showed how poor German intelligence about British dispositions was. This, as Fleming himself wrote, 'may sound trivial,' but he reminded readers that a commander's task is not aided 'if he discovers that most of what he thought he knew about the enemy is seriously wide of the mark.' Fleming said he didn't really think the Auxunits would have made too much difference to the final outcome of the battle. Firstly, he pointed out that they were expected to operate in Britain, a tactical theatre that 'suffers from the fundamental disadvantage of being much too small. Many a would-be Lawrence, surveying the patchwork battlefield laced by ribbon development and encroached by suburbia, sighed for the torrid immensities of the Arabian Desert,' he wrote. Another handicap was the lack of sophisticated communications between the nucleus of twenty-odd Auxunit formations staffed by Army Regulars that Fleming called the 'striking force' and the far-flung Home Guard-developed Auxunit Patrols, or 'cells', as Fleming termed them. He also argued that only as long as 'the leaf was on the trees' – six or seven weeks after the first German landings in late September – would Auxunit OBs be inviolate. As winter approached and German intelligence improved, Auxunit hideouts would become increasingly obvious to Luftwaffe aerial reconnaissance.

The final nail in the British Resistance Organization's coffin would, he thought, be swift and violent. Nazi reprisals, 'from which, as we have seen, the Germans had no thought of shrinking' would soon loosen tongues and force citizens to betray any secrets about the whereabouts of fathers and sons who could not be readily accounted for. Nevertheless, he agreed with Churchill's assessment that Auxunits were 'a useful addition to the Regular forces'. It might have struck some effective blows against the invader before, as Fleming said, 'it melted away in the white heat of German ruthlessness.' Furthermore, within a bridgehead under vigorous British counter-attack (Fleming was scornful of the German assumption that the British wouldn't be able to strike back at the invasion beaches or landing grounds for at least four days), Fleming thought, 'its diversionary activities would have had a value wholly disproportionate to the number of guerrillas involved.'

Throughout the grimmest years of tension of the Cold War, perhaps the British authorities felt that the planning and organizational structure developed for Auxunits during the war might serve as a model for some kind of civil defence militia that could be deployed after a nuclear strike. However, it is more likely to have been decided that the Auxiliary Units would be best quietly forgotten. The many Operational Bases that survived the war's end would prove ideal hideouts for criminals and terrorists and might even entomb curious children. So they were best left secret. Above all I think that the reason the Auxiliary Unit story is largely unknown is because few if any records were ever kept. It is, I believe, for this reason alone that some OBs still survive. No one recorded the whereabouts of each of them in detail and consequently the Royal Engineers would have been unable to locate and demolish them. Some Auxunit volunteers weren't on any official list and couldn't be contacted and consequently many of their secret hideouts may remain untouched to this day.

Epilogue

This is Britain. This is the land which has withstood the tramp of invaders for 900 years. This is the soil we are fighting for. We are not fighting to snatch what belongs to someone else. We are fighting to protect what is ours.

Picture Post, 22 June 1940

In the early 1970s, in a rare interview with a newspaper journalist about the activities of the Auxunits, Sir Colin Gubbins confidently announced that, 'the Auxiliary Units would have been ready' should the Nazis have chosen to invade during the last critical fortnight of August during the Battle of Britain. He was keen to point out, however, that his secret soldiers were simply a supplement to Britain's armed forces and could not be relied on to defend Britain on their own:

> I think the point is that the Army had to fight to the last man. There could be no question of allowing the German military to establish themselves here ... they [the Auxunits] were something additional – don't forget, we hadn't taken men from Regular formations, but from depots. We were expendable. We were a bonus, that's all.

Too often today some commentators arrogantly argue that the German invasion of Britain, Operation Sea Lion, could never have been successful and probably wouldn't even have been attempted at all. It is worth reminding them and other sceptics that the Luftwaffe offensives during the Battle of Britain were nothing less than the opening moves of the German invasion strategy. The *landing* phase of the operation never came to fruition simply because the *aerial* phase proved to be a limited success from the Germans' point of view.

When *Picture Post* declared after a feature on 'THE EPIC OF DUNKIRK' that, 'At home the threat of invasion daily grows more real,' it was only recording what was, at the time, a widely acknowledged sentiment. Bearing in mind that the Ministry of Information was censoring defeatist articles, the *Picture Post* viewpoint was clearly considered by the authorities to be merely a statement of fact.

Despite having had more than half a year to consolidate their defences and work out every possible battle scenario, the Anglo-French armies on the Continent were overcome by the Nazi juggernaut in a matter of weeks. And, if the Germans had gone on to attempt an invasion by sea, I think it is likely that they would have achieved a measure of success. British stoicism, the courage and inspiration of the Royal Air Force pilots and those who guided them, the failings of the German High Command and the whims of the evil genius, Adolf Hitler himself, have since made the question academic.

However, in July 1940, with the Battle of Britain undecided, it was in an atmosphere of high tension and expectation that a programme was instituted for the selection and training of men who were to operate covertly behind enemy lines. As we have seen, these men were a special breed, inspired as much by the adventurous, imaginative flair of Peter Fleming and the exploits of T.E. Lawrence as by the down-to-earth gritty determination of Colin Gubbins. Like Peter Wilkinson and Norman Field, they were men who were readily identified by their superiors as having exceptional qualities and yet, like Geoffrey Bradford, Frank Penfold, Eric Johnson, Dick Body, Arthur Gabbitas, Bill Webber, Bob Millard, Tom Smith and all the rest, these qualities were hidden behind a veil of reserve and quiet self-confidence that, even today, tends towards downplaying the task they were expected to perform.

If the Luftwaffe had continued its onslaught on the RAF, daily depleting the numbers of operational pilots until there were not enough trained ones to replace them while they systematically smashed up Fighter Command's airfields, British aerial resistance would have been finished. As a consequence waves of battle-hardened German paratroopers and seaborne troops, protected from the air, would have made a landfall in England. If the Nazi Invader had set foot on Britain's shores who can say how the men of the Auxunits would have performed? When asked the question directly, the Auxunit members themselves have, characteristically, played down the impact they would have had.

Those who volunteered for service in Auxiliary Units endured the knowledge that if worse came to worse their closest friends and family might not know how they met their end. The secret was even kept from spouses, with some wives assuming their husbands were out all night having an affair. Little did they know that their menfolk were preparing for an evening closeted in a dark, damp underground lair, familiarizing themselves with their Operational Bases in preparation for active duty.

However, I think perhaps the greatest inequity suffered by those brave souls who gave up their time for service in Auxunits, was the lack of post-war recognition they received.

Many not only went to their deaths without receiving the British Defence Medal, let alone a specific award recognizing their top-secret status, but also, because they had signed the Official Secrets Act, without ever revealing that they actually served in a covert guerrilla army.

Fortunately, in the last twenty years, the story of Auxiliary Units has been more widely revealed than ever before and the efforts of informed friends and relatives has at least resulted in some Auxunit veterans receiving a Defence Medal before it was too late.

The MOD's own website says:

The Defence Medal (1939-45) was awarded for non-operational service. This type of service in the UK included those service personnel working in headquarters, on training bases and airfields and members of the Home Guard. Home Guard service counts between the dates of 14 May 1940 and 31 December 1944. The Defence Medal was also awarded for non-operational service overseas, for example in India or South Africa.

Whilst it is not surprising that members of the Home Guard, Royal Observer Corps, National Fire Brigade, Police and Coast Guard were deemed eligible for the award, it might come to a shock to some that, although Auxiliary Unit veterans were overlooked, those involved with ENSA (the Entertainments National Service Association), or the American Ambulance Service in Great Britain and, even though chemical warfare never happened, members of the Civil Defence Gas Identification Service, could apply for the medal.

At the time of writing, organizations such as the Coleshill Auxiliary Research Team (CART) are actively involved in trying to secure a specific award for those involved with Auxiliary Units. Perhaps they and others will succeed and settle the debt owed to this small band of heroes.

When in the Autumn of 1944 General Sir Harold Franklyn, Commander-in-Chief Home Forces, decided Auxiliary Units had served their purpose and were no longer required, Colonel Frank Douglas, the last commander of Auxunits, wrote to all those who had served in Britain's secret resistance, saying:

In view of the fact that your lives depended on secrecy no public recognition will be possible.

This was followed in April 1945 with a message of thanks published in *The Times* from General Franklyn to the men and women of the operational Auxiliary Units and the Special Duties Section:

I realize that every member of the organization from the first invasion days beginning in 1940 voluntarily undertook a hazardous role that required both skill and courage well knowing that the very nature of their work would allow of no public recognition. This organization, founded on the keenness and patriotism of selected civilians of all grades, has been in a position, through its constant and thorough training, to furnish accurate information of raids or invasion instantly to military headquarters throughout the country.

Auxiliary Units deserve a better epitaph.

Bibliography

ANGELL, STEWART, *The Secret Sussex Resistance*, Middleton Press
BECKER, CAJUS, *The Luftwaffe War Diaries*, Corgi
BRIGHT ASTLEY, JOAN, *The Inner Circle*, Hutchinson
BRYANT, ARTHUR (ed.), *The Alanbrooke War Diaries*, Collins
CARTON DE WIART, ADRIAN, *Happy Odyssey*, Jonathan Cape
CHURCHILL, WINSTON S., *The Second World War, Vol. II, Their Finest Hour*, Penguin
CLAYTON, ANTHONY, *Forearmed*, Brasseys
COCKS, A.E., *Churchill's Secret Armies 1939-45*, The Book Guild
DEIGHTON, LEN, *The Battle of Britain*, Jonathan Cape
FAIRBAIRN, W.E., *All-In Fighting*, Faber and Faber
FLEMING, PETER, *Invasion 1940*, Hamish Hamilton
FLEMING, PETER, *The Flying Visit*, Jonathan Cape
FLEMING, PETER, *Operation Sea Lion*, Simon & Schuster
FOOT, M.R.D., *SOE in France*, HMSO
FRASER, DAVID, *Alanbrooke*, Collins
GILBERT, ADRIAN, *Britain Invaded*, Century
GILBERT, MARTIN, *Finest Hour*, Heinemann
GUDGIN, PETER, *Military Intelligence*, Arms & Armour
HART DAVIS, DUFF, *Peter Fleming*, OUP
HINSLEY, F.H., *British Intelligence in the Second World War Vols I & IV*, HMSO
IRONSIDE, FIELD MARSHAL LORD, *The Ironside Diaries*, Constable
ISMAY, GENERAL SIR HASTINGS (BARON), *The Memoirs of Lord Ismay*, Heinemann
KESSELRING, FIELD MARSHAL, *The Memoirs of Field Marshal Kesselring*, William Kimber
KEEGAN, JOHN (ed.), *Churchill's Generals*, Warner
KUROWSKI, FRANZ, *The Brandengurgers – Global Mission*, J.J. Fedorowicz
LAMPE, DAVID, *The Last Ditch*, Cassell
LAWRENCE, T.E., *Seven Pillars of Wisdom*, Jonathan Cape/Penguin

LIDDELL HART, BASIL, *The Defence of Britain*, Faber & Faber

LONGMATE, NORMAN, *If Britain Had Fallen*, BBC/Hutchinson

MACKSEY, KENNETH, *Invasion! The German Invasion of England, July 1940*, Greenhill Books

MORRIS, ERIC, *Churchill's Private Armies*, Hutchinson

OXENDEN MC, MAJOR NV, *Auxiliary Units History and Achievement 1940-44*, BRO Museum

PARKINSON, ROGER, *The Auk*, Granada

PILE, GENERAL SIR FREDERICK, *Ack Ack*, Harrap

PIMLOTT, BEN, *Hugh Dalton*, Jonathan Cape

PONTING, CLIVE, *1940: Myth and Reality*, Cardinal

POWNALL, LIEUTENANT GENERAL SIR HENRY, *Chief of Staff*, Leo Cooper

RICH, NORMAN, *Hitler's War Aims*, Norton

SCARTH, RICHARD, *Mirrors by the Sea*, Hythe Civic Society

SCHENK, PETER, *Invasion of England 1940*, Conway

SPEARS, MAJOR GENERAL SIR EDWARD, *Assignment to Catastrophe*, Heinemann

The Defence of Britain Project, Handbook of, *20th Century Defences in Britain*

TREVOR-ROPER, HUGH, *Hitler's War Directives*, Pan

WARWICKER, JOHN, *With Britain in Mortal Danger*, Cerberus Publishing Ltd

WARWICKER, JOHN, *Churchill's Underground Army*, Frontline Books

WESTWELL, IAN, *Brandenburgers – The Third Reich's Special Forces*, Ian Allen

WILKINSON, PETER, and BRIGHT ASTLEY, JOAN, *Gubbins & SOE*, Leo Cooper

WILLIS, *Pillboxes*, Leo Cooper

Glossary

AA	Anti-aircraft
ADGB	Air Defence of Great Britain organization
AFS	Auxiliary Fire Service
ARP	Air Raid Precautions
AT	Anti-tank
ATS	Auxiliary Territorial Service
BEF	British Expeditionary Force
Blitzkrieg	lightning war
BRO	British Resistance Organization
CART	Coleshill Auxiliary Research Team
CD	Civil Defence
CH	Chain Home (Britain's early warning defence – later 'CH Low' and 'CH High')
Das Heers	German Army
DMI	Directorate of Military Intelligence
Fallschirmjäger	German paratroops – part of the Luftwaffe in WWII
Gebirgsjäger	German mountain troops – used to scale the cliffs along England's south coast
GHQ	General Headquarters
GHQ Line	the 'last ditch', a series of trenches, earth banks and anti-tank obstacles in Southern England
GS(R)	General Staff (Research)
HG	Home Guard
HSSPF	Höhere SS and Polizeiführer German High Command of the SS and Police
Kriegsmarine	German Navy
LDV	Local Defence Volunteers, the short-lived predecessor of the Home Guard
Luftwaffe	German Air Force
MI(R)	Military Intelligence (Research)
MOI	Ministry of Information

OB	Operational Base
OKH	Oberkommando des Heeres, German army high command
OKM	Oberkommando der Marine, Nazi Germany's Naval High Command
OP	Observation Post
OT	Organization Todt
RAF	Royal Air Force
RN	Royal Navy
ROC	Royal Observer Corps
RSHA	Reichssicherheitshauptamtor, Nazi Central Security Agency
SD	Sicherheitsdeitsdienst, Nazi SS security and counter espionage bureau
Seelöwe	Operation Sea Lion, the Nazi plan for an amphibious invasion of Britain in 1940
SIP	self-igniting phosphorous grenade
Staffel	a Luftwaffe squadron
Stuka	Junkers Ju 87, the Luftwaffe's principal dive-bomber ('Sturzkampfflugzeug')
WAAF	Women's Auxiliary Air Force
Waffen SS	the armed branch of the Schutzstaffel (the 'SS' initially the Nazi 'protection squadron')
Wehrmacht	German armed forces
WLA	Women's Land Army
WVS	Women's Voluntary Service

Index

Tracing Your Family History?

Read Your Family HISTORY

ESSENTIAL ADVICE FROM THE EXPERTS

FREE COPY!

Your Family History is the only magazine that is put together by expert genealogists. Our editorial team, led by Dr Nick Barratt, is passionate about family history, and our networks of specialists are here to give essential advice, helping readers to find their ancestors and solve those difficult questions.

In each issue we feature a **Beginner's Guide** covering the basics for those just getting started, a **How To** ... section to help you to dig deeper into your family tree and the opportunity to **Ask The Experts** about your tricky research problems. We also include a **Spotlight** on a different county each month and a **What's On** guide to the best family history courses and events, plus much more.

Receive a free copy of *Your Family History* magazine and gain essential advice and all the latest news. To request a free copy of a recent back issue, simply e-mail your name and address to marketing@your-familyhistory.com or call 01226 734302*.

Your Family History is in all good newsagents and also available on subscription for six or twelve issues. For more details on how to take out a subscription, call 01778 392013 or visit **www.your-familyhistory.co.uk**.

Alternatively read issue 31 online completely free using this QR code

*Free copy is restricted to one per household and available while stocks last.

www.your-familyhistory.com